continuing to build in the first part of the twenty-first century. But despite some similarity in effects, these theories arose from very different traditions. Transformational leadership is more leader-centric in terms of its emphasis on what a leader does or the impact of the leader's behaviour on followers. LMX is more firmly rooted in the quality of the relationship that is thought to be negotiated and developed between a leader and someone considered to be a follower (e.g., associate, subordinate). In this way, LMX theory adopts a wider theoretical lens by explicitly including the follower in the leadership process.

Much of the theoretical and empirical work in the area of consensus has focused on LMX given that it explicitly acknowledges differences in relationship quality between leader and member (e.g., Dansereau, Graen, & Haga, 1975). On the other hand, agreement between leader and follower in terms of leadership ratings has often been addressed in the context of 360-degree feedback (e.g., Atwater, Ostroff, Yammarino, & Fleenor, 1998). Yammarino and Atwater (1997) found that leaders' self-ratings of charismatic leadership are often higher than the ratings by their subordinates or supervisors. This can be problematic as overestimators may not be performing as well as other leaders (cf. Yammarino & Atwater, 1997). Although relatively less work on agreement and consensus has been done with regard to transformational leadership, that oversight is addressed with a couple of articles in this Special Issue.

This brief overview of prior research suggests that more research into consensus and agreement is needed. This includes research into agreement in LMX or consensus in transformational leadership as well as consensus and agreement in other leadership approaches. In addition, too little is known yet about antecedents of consensus and agreement. Thus, a purpose of this Special Issue is to attempt to address some of the gaps and shortfalls in the extant literature through theoretical and empirical examinations of core issues in leadership consensus and agreement, and to encourage future research in the area.

OVERVIEW OF THE SPECIAL ISSUE

There are four articles in the Special Issue that examine various antecedents of agreement and/or consensus, Spitzmuller and Illies study the role of leaders' authenticity on consensus in followers' perceptions of transformational leadership. They propose that leaders' authenticity influences followers' perception of transformational leadership both on an individual and a group level (consensus among followers). Specifically, they argued that relational authenticity would be relevant for different aspects of transformational leadership. Their results support this general framework.

Eckert, Ekelund, Gentry, and Dawson examine the role of culture in the context of 360-degree feedback. Their guiding theoretical assumption is that power distance influences agreement between self- and other-ratings such that there is less agreement in high relative to power-distance cultures. Results provide mixed or partial support for this proposition and suggest the possibility of additional moderators to consider in future research.

In an effort to explain the often-noted issue of overall low agreement between leader and member with respect to their mutual relationship quality (Gerstner & Day, 1997), van Gils, van Quaquebeke, and van Knippenberg theoretically examine the role of implicit leader and implicit follower theories in LMX agreement. They argue that these various forms of implicit theories shape expectations of the relationship partner and thereby influence relationship quality perceptions.

In another theoretical contribution, Schyns, Maslyn, and Weibler examine how span of control as a proxy for leader distance influences consensus regarding different dimensions of LMX. Consistent with prior research on leader distance, they suggest that span of control affects follower consensus across different dimensions of LMX in different ways.

The remaining two articles investigate the effects of consensus/agreement in transformational leadership. Korek, Felfe, and Zaepernick-Rothe examine the effects of consensus in transformational leadership on affective and normative commitment in the context of hypothesized mediating effects of meaningful task content and organizational climate. They argue that meaningful task content allows leaders to show transformational leadership (if the leader has the proper scope to influence the task) and gives followers the feeling that they should reciprocate. Their research also includes organizational climate as a mediator in the relationship between consensus in transformational leadership and commitment. Their results mainly support the moderating effects on affective commitment.

Finally, Felfe and Heinitz examined the effects of consensus among followers and agreement between leaders and their team members in transformational leadership on, among others, customer satisfaction. Specifically, they found that consensus and agreement moderate the relationships between leadership and commitment. They conclude that direct and indirect effects of consensus and agreement are clearly important for organizational outcomes.

CONCLUSIONS AND FUTURE RESEARCH

The importance of follower consensus and leader/follower agreement has been highlighted with regard to different leadership approaches. As the various articles in this Special Issue demonstrate, there continue to be many

EUROPEAN JOURNAL OF WORK AND
ORGANIZATIONAL PSYCHOLOGY
2010, 19 (3), 253–258

ΨP Psychology Press
Taylor & Francis Group

The importance of agreement and consensus in leadership research: Introduction to the Special Issue

David V. Day

University of Western Australia Business School, Crawley, Australia

Birgit Schyns

Portsmouth Business School, University of Portsmouth, Portsmouth, UK

Questions regarding the nature of leadership have persisted for decades. Specifically, is leadership best considered a behaviour that leaders convey or is it more phenomenological in nature such as based in the perceptions of followers? Complicating this already complex picture, what are the implications regarding the nature of leadership if leaders do not behave the same towards all their followers, or if followers do not perceive their leader the same way? And with regard to effective leadership, is it important that leaders and followers agree on their perception of leadership? These are some of the underlying questions guiding this Special Issue.

Leadership theory and research increasingly acknowledges that what leaders do is only part of what leadership is. Recent developments emphasize the role of the follower (e.g., Collinson, 2005; Uhl-Bien, 2006) and the context (Porter & McLaughlin, 2006) in the process called leadership. One could argue that the focus of modern leadership research is shifting towards more follower-centric approaches that include taking into account interactions between leaders and followers and interactions among followers within teams or workgroups. Researchers are more attuned to addressing not only the interactional nature and process of leadership but also the role that followers' interaction with each other has in shaping leaders and its results. Of course, leadership does not occur in a vacuum devoid of followers; rather, it is very much a group phenomenon where

Correspondence should be addressed to David V. Day, University of Western Australia Business School M261, 35 Stirling Highway, Crawley WA 6009, Australia. E-mail: david.day@uwa.edu.au

http://www.psypress.com/ejwop   DOI: 10.1080/13594320903448766

leader–follower dyads are often interdependent with each other. The different relationships a leader has with each follower can influence other relationships in the collective that affect the results of leadership in positive or negative ways.

Concepts such as consensus in follower ratings of their leaders (e.g., Henderson, Liden, Glibkowski, & Chaudhry, 2009; Nishii & Mayer, 2009; Zhou & Schriesheim, 2009) or the agreement between leader and follower regarding their shared relationship (e.g., Basik & Martinko, 2008; Cogliser, Schriesheim, Scandura, & Gardner, 2009) have gained recent interest. Continued methodological advancements in areas such as Within and Between Analysis (WABA; Yammarino, 1998) and Multilevel Analysis (e.g., Raudenbush & Bryk, 2002) have further spurred these developments.

Nonetheless, a primary question behind these developments has remained relatively constant over the years: How do leaders influence or otherwise work with followers in reaching shared organizational goals? Research into agreement and consensus tries to answer this question by investigating the pattern of connections within groups: How does the agreement between leader and follower with respect to the leader's type of leadership influence followers' attitudes and behaviours? And how does a consensus among followers about their leader's leadership style influence followers' attitudes and behaviours? Research in this area as has shown that, as expected, consensus and agreement are positively related to relevant and important organizational outcomes (Cogliser et al., 2009; Henderson et al., 2009). Recently, Schyns and Day (2010) argued that the most successful combination of agreement and consensus in achieving so-called Leader–Member Excellence would consist of a high-quality exchange relationship, agreement between a leader and a given follower on this relationship, and consensus among followers in a workgroup regarding their respective relationships with the leader. Following this line of thinking, it would appear that consensus and agreement in leadership relationships is something organizations should value and support.

This Special Issue addresses issues of consensus and agreement across two different and predominant leadership approaches. The six papers included in this Special Issue address consensus and agreement in transformational leadership (e.g., Bass, 1985; Bass & Riggio, 2006) as well as Leader-Member Exchange (LMX; Graen & Uhl-Bien, 1995). These approaches stem from quite different traditions; however, it has been argued that it is possible for LMX to be transformational at least under certain conditions (Gerstner & Day, 1997). Day (in press) recently characterized transformational leadership theory and LMX theory as examples of "bridging" theories in terms of linking leadership approaches that emerged in the last quarter of the twentieth century with those emerging and open questions with regard to the antecedents of consensus and agreement in leadership processes; however, their effects seem to becoming clearer. Contributions to this Special Issue (Korek et al.) as well as prior research (e.g., Liden, Erdogan, Wayne, & Sparrowe, 2006) demonstrate consistent positive effects of follower consensus on organizational outcomes. In addition, contributions to this Special Issue (Felfe & Heinitz) as well as previous research (Cogliser et al., 2009) show that leader–follower agreement on a high level is positively related to organizational outcomes. The knowledge of these positive outcomes of consensus and agreement suggest an important need to for additional work on their respective antecedents. In this Special Issue, culture (Ekert et al.), leader authenticity (Spitzmuller & Illies), implicit theories (van Gils et al.), as well as (low) span of control (Schyns et al.) are discussed. Further research into the development of consensus and agreement is needed in further understanding how agreement and consensus develop—and to identify obstacles to that development—so that leaders and their organizations can learn how to better use these important positive forces for enhancing leadership effects and associated work-related outcomes.

REFERENCES

Atwater, L. E., Ostroff, C., Yammarino, F. J., & Fleenor, J. W. (1998). Self-other agreement: Does it really matter? *Personnel Psychology*, *51*, 577–598.

Basik, K. J., & Martinko, M. J. (2008, August). *The relationship of LMX agreement combinations and key outcomes: Exploring a "mismatch penalty"*. Paper presented at the annual meeting of the Academy of Management, Anaheim, CA.

Bass, B. M. (1985). *Leadership and performance beyond expectations*. New York: Free Press.

Bass, B. M., & Riggio, R. E. (2006). *Transformational leadership* (2nd ed.). Mahwah, NJ: Lawrence Erlbaum Associates, Inc.

Cogliser, C. C., Schriesheim, C. A., Scandura, T. A., & Gardner, W. L. (2009). Balance in leader and follower perceptions of leader–member exchange: Relationships with performance and work attitudes. *Leadership Quarterly*, *20*, 452–465.

Collinson, D. (2005). Dialectics of leadership. *Human Relations*, *58*, 1419–1442.

Dansereau, F., Graen, G., & Haga, W. (1975). A vertical dyad linkage approach to leadership within formal organizations: A longitudinal investigation of the role making process. *Organizational Behavior and Human Performance*, *13*, 46–78.

Day, D. V. (in press). Leadership. In S. W. J. Kozlowski (Ed.), *The Oxford handbook of industrial and organizational psychology*. New York: Oxford University.

Gerstner, C. R., & Day, D. V. (1997). Meta-analytic review of leader-member exchange theory: Correlates and construct issues. *Journal of Applied Psychology*, *82*, 827–844.

Graen, G. B., & Uhl-Bien, M. (1995). Development of leader-member exchange (LMX) theory of leadership over 25 years: Applying a multi-level multi-domain perspective. *Leadership Quarterly*, *6*, 219–247.

Henderson, D. J., Liden, R. C., Glibkowski, B. G., & Chaudhry, A. (2009). Within-group LMX differentiation: A multilevel review and examination of its construct definition, antecedents and outcomes. *Leadership Quarterly*, *4*, 517–534.

Liden, R. C., Erdogan, B., Wayne, S. J., & Sparrowe, R. T. (2006). Leader-member exchange, differentiation, and task interdependence: Implications for individual and group performance. *Journal of Organizational Behavior, 27,* 723–746.

Nishii, L. H., & Mayer, D. M. (2009). Do inclusive leaders help the performance of diverse groups? The moderating role of leader-member exchange in the diversity to group performance relationship. *Journal of Applied Psychology, 94,* 1412–1426.

Porter, L. W., & McLaughlin, G. B. (2006). Leadership and organizational context: Like the weather? *Leadership Quarterly, 17,* 559–576.

Raudenbush, S. W., & Bryk, A. S. (2002). *Hierarchical linear models.* Thousand Oaks, CA: Sage.

Schyns, B., & Day, D. (2010). Critique and review of leader-member exchange theory: Issues of agreement, consensus, and excellence. *European Journal of Work and Organizational Psychology, 19,* 1–29.

Uhl-Bien, M. (2006). Relationship leadership theory: Exploring the social processes of leadership and organizing. *Leadership Quarterly, 17,* 654–676.

Yammarino, F. J. (1998). Multivariate aspects of the varient/WABA approach: A discussion and leadership illustration. *Leadership Quarterly, 9*(2), 203–227.

Yammarino, F. J., & Atwater, L. E. (1997). Do managers see themselves as other see them? Implications of self-other agreement for human resource management. *Organizational Dynamics, 25,* 35–44.

Zhou, X., & Schriesheim, C. A. (2009). Supervisor-subordinate convergence in descriptions of leader-member exchange (LMX) quality: Review and testable propositions. *Leadership Quarterly, 20,* 920–932.

EUROPEAN JOURNAL OF WORK AND
ORGANIZATIONAL PSYCHOLOGY
2010, 19 (3), 259–278

Ψ Psychology Press
Taylor & Francis Group

"I don't see me like you see me, but is that a problem?" Cultural influences on rating discrepancy in 360-degree feedback instruments

Regina Eckert

Center for Creative Leadership, Brussels, Belgium

Bjørn Z. Ekelund

Human Factors AS, Oslo, and Agder University, Agder, Norway

William A. Gentry

Center for Creative Leadership, Greensboro, NC, USA

Jeremy F. Dawson

Department of Work & Organisational Psychology, Aston University, Birmingham, UK

360-degree feedback from a variety of rater sources yields important information about leaders' styles, strengths and weaknesses for development. Results where observer ratings are discrepant (i.e., different) from self-ratings are often seen as indicators of problematic leadership relationships, skills, or lack of self-awareness. Yet research into the antecedents of such self–observer rating discrepancy suggests the presence of systematic influences, such as cultural values. The present study investigates the variation of rating discrepancies on three leadership skills (decision making, leading employees, and composure) in dependence of one exemplary culture dimension (power distance) on data from 31 countries using multilevel structural equation modelling. Results show that cultural values indeed predict self–observer rating discrepancies. Thus, systemic and contextual influences such as culture need to be taken into consideration when

Correspondence should be addressed to Regina Eckert, Research Associate, Center for Creative Leadership, Avenue de Tervueren 270, 1150 Bruxelles, Belgium.
E-mail: eckertr@ccl.org
The authors would like to thank Felix Brodbeck and Marcus Dickson for their helpful comments on an earlier version of this manuscript.

http://www.psypress.com/ejwop   DOI: 10.1080/13594320802678414

interpreting the importance and meaning of self–observer rating discrepancies in 360-degree instruments.

Keywords: 360-degree feedback; Self–observer discrepancy; Cultural differences.

Feedback is one of the most important elements for learning and development. In current leadership development initiatives, 360-degree feedback from a variety of rater sources (i.e., boss, peers, direct reports, customers) is a popular method for developmental feedback to managers. This type of feedback is an important mechanism to give managers a sense of how they are perceived by others around them. Feedback information from subordinates, bosses, peers, suppliers, vendors, and other groups highlights individual and organizational strengths and weaknesses (Dalessio, 1998; London & Smither, 1995; Morgeson, Mumford & Campion, 2005; Tornow, 1993; Yammarino, 2003).

Previous research has indicated that a gap or discrepancy exists (i.e., a difference, dissimilarity, disagreement, or incongruity) between self- and observer ratings on the same constructs or dimensions of 360-degree feedback instruments (Brutus, Fleenor & McCauley, 1999; Morgeson et al., 2005; Mount, Judge, Scullen, Sytsma & Hezlett, 1998; Ostroff, Atwater & Feinberg, 2004; Sala, 2003). It is generally argued that such discrepancies have a negative impact for the manager as they indicate inaccurate self-perceptions, low self-awareness, or deficiencies in other soft skills (Kulas & Finkelstein, 2007). However, recent studies (Atwater, Waldman, Ostroff, Robie & Johnson, 2005; Gentry, Hannum, Ekelund & de Jong, 2007) indicate that such interpretation of discrepancies might be too hasty, as discrepancies are also influenced by systematic variables other than managers themselves. In order to interpret discrepancies correctly, it is important to know what underlying factors may be antecedents to such discrepancies.

The current article addresses this issue by examining cultural influences on the self–observer rating discrepancies of leadership skills across a multitude of cultures.

REASONS FOR RATING DISCREPANCIES

The forms and consequences of rating discrepancies are well explored. Atwater and Yammarino's (1997) model distinguishes the cases of overrating (self > observer), underrating (self < observer), and agreement (self = observer, either in high or in low ratings). Higher disagreement between self- and observer ratings is related to lower performance (Ostroff et al., 2004) and a lower motivation to improve future behaviour, as well as less actual improvement (Atwater & Brett, 2005).

The background and reason for such rating discrepancies, however, has received less attention. The most widely held assumption is that rating discrepancies are an expression of low self-awareness, putting the "blame" for the discrepancy on the manager. However, the validity of interpreting rating discrepancies as low self-awareness is doubted. In their meta-analysis of rating discrepancies, Harris and Schaubroeck (1988) propose three other reasons for rating discrepancy.

First, a manager overrating him/herself could be the result of an inflated self-view or a self-enhancement bias. This explanation resonates with findings that overrating oneself compared to others has the most detrimental effect on performance ratings (Ostroff et al., 2004). Evidence indeed found that some individuals do systematically overrate themselves; however, this was not due to personality differences but to influences such as gender, race, and education (Ostroff et al., 2004). Second, organizational level influences rating discrepancies, because rater groups on different hierarchical levels might have different ideas of what good leadership actually is. Evidence shows that managers on higher levels have bigger rating discrepancies than managers in lower levels (Gentry et al., 2007; Sala, 2003). Third, different rater groups may have different observational opportunities for forming a perception of a target manager. Assuming that leadership behaviour differs according to whom the manager interacts with, the baseline information available to different rater groups is inconsistent. Interestingly, the reasons proposed by Harris and Schaubroek question the interpretation of rating discrepancies as expressing low self-awareness because they refer to influences only partly within the manager's control.

Another antecedent that needs attention may be culture of origin. The earlier mentioned research and theory focused on the individual and the organizational level as influence factors. However, as the use of 360-degree instruments increases globally, the level of societal culture becomes more and more important and it would be interesting to know whether cultural values affect such ratings (Brutus, Leslie & McDonald-Mann, 2001). Most recently, Gentry et al. (2007) examined 360-degree ratings of managerial derailment behaviours, and found a culture-level difference: The self–observer rating discrepancy was higher (i.e., bigger or wider) for US-American managers than for Europeans. This suggests that cultural-level determinants, such as values, norms, and beliefs, have an impact on self–observer rating discrepancies.

Taken together, past research shows that multiple reasons for self–observer rating discrepancies exist. In order to make sense of such discrepancies and identify useful avenues for development, managers need information to differentiate discrepancies that are indicative of low self-awareness from those that are due to influences outside their control, such as culture. To understand more about the influence of culture on the self–observer rating discrepancy, a multilevel approach to 360-degree research is needed that examines culture systematically. Therefore, we examine in the current study how the rating discrepancies between self- and observers on three core leadership skills in a 360-degree feedback instrument called BENCHMARKS®[1] (Lombardo, McCauley, McDonald-Mann & Leslie, 1999) are influenced by cultural values. Although a complete discussion of this issue would integrate all dimensions of cultural value orientations, sources of feedback, and an array of managerial leadership skills, such an effort would be beyond the scope of a single article. Thus, we focus on how power distance, as one exemplary cultural value dimension, might predict rating discrepancies in three leadership skills (decisiveness, leading employees, and composure).

CULTURAL INFLUENCES ON RATING DISCREPANCIES

In order to examine the influence of cultural values, it is necessary to take a closer look at the cognitive processes in leadership perception. Observers' perception of leaders is based two processes (Lord & Maher, 1991): On the one hand, leadership can be inferred from certain outcomes for which a leader is seen as responsible (inference-based perception); on the other hand, leaders are recognized by comparing their behaviour and characteristics with one's implicit theories about leadership in general (recognition-based perception). In both cases, culture can play a role: Cultural norms on workplace behaviour impact on the amount and type of interaction that various observers have with a leader, resulting in varying opportunities to observe leadership behaviour as well as leadership outcomes. This leads to cultural differences in leadership perception processes (see Ensari & Murphy, 2003, for a detailed study of these differences). Moreover, cultural values also play a role in that they determine observers' implicit theories of leadership (ILTs). As various studies have shown, ILTs vary widely across cultures and covary systematically with cultural values (Brodbeck et al., 2000; Gerstner & Day, 1994). Thus, the same leaders might be perceived as bad, average, or good leaders depending on the culturally determined ILTs of their observers (Schyns, 2006).

What do these cultural influences mean for the discrepancy between self- and observer ratings in 360-degree feedback? Broadly, it can be expected that the magnitude of this discrepancy differs between cultures in which social interaction with the leaders allows observers a very close look at their behaviour, and cultures where leadership is a more "distant" process and

---

[1]BENCHMARKS® is a registered trademark of the Center for Creative Leadership.

observers need to infer leaders' competence from their leadership outcomes, such as group performance. In cultures where observers have a more distant perspective on leaders, the discrepancy between self- and observer ratings will likely be larger.

Various dimensions of cultural values can be involved in this: Stark, Hanson, and Thomas (1998) suggested the dimensions of individualism/ collectivism, power distance, and gender egalitarianism as most likely to influence on the scores in 360-degree feedback, due to their impact on the broader social interactions in organizations. However, they did not proceed with empirical tests for these propositions. The current study fills this gap by examining the effects of power distance on rating discrepancy. We chose this culture dimension from the GLOBE study (House, Hanges, Javidan, Dorfman & Gupta, 2004), because it is directly related to the perception of leadership and has been shown to have a great influence on interpersonal interaction at work (e.g., Badjo & Dickson, 2001; Feldman & Bolino, 1999; van der Vegt, van de Vliert & Huang, 2005).

Power distance

The cultural value dimension of power distance refers to "the extent to which a community accepts and endorses authority, power differences, and status privileges" (Carl, Gupta & Javidan, 2004, p. 513). In high power distance cultures, more emphasis is given to managers' hierarchical status in the organization. Managerial behaviour in these cultures will differ widely depending on the relative status of their interaction partner—boss, peers, or subordinates. The impressions of bosses, peers, and subordinates about the manager's performance will be formed on the basis of very different information, resulting from different observation possibilities, and thus will likely differ from each other more widely than in low power distance cultures, where managerial behaviour will not depend as much on the status of the interaction partner. Specifically, we expect this discrepancy to be expressed in the perception of three leadership skills: decision making, leading employees, and managerial composure.

Decision making

Decision making is a core leadership task that varies in its style across cultures. As Hofstede (1984) described, one aspect of cultural power distance relates to the preferred style of managerial decision making: High power distance cultures prefer decision making styles that are autonomous or autocratic, and which rarely include others. Low power distance cultures, on the other hand, are characterized by more participative (consultative and democratic) decision-making styles. Managers in low power distance cultures are thus more likely to include others, such as their bosses, peers and subordinates, into their decision making, thereby giving them better opportunities to observe the manager in decision making situations. Observers are also more likely to have shared opportunities for observation, e.g., in round-table meetings. Based on this observational advantage, we expect that the discrepancy between bosses, peers, and subordinates compared to self-perception decision making in low power distance cultures will be smaller than in high power distance cultures.

Hypothesis 1:   In high power distance cultures, the self–subordinate, self–boss, and self–peer rating discrepancy on decisiveness is higher than in low power distance cultures.

Leading employees

We also expect that power distance should relate to the discrepancy between self and observers regarding the manager's skill in leading employees. According to Dansereau, Graen, and Haga (1975), the tasks of a manager can be divided into supervision and leadership. Supervision is more aligned with a cultural orientation towards high power distance (Carl et al., 2004). In environments where this style prevails, there is little rapport between managers and subordinates. The relationships between managers and their subordinates, as well as their bosses, are likely less intense in high power distance cultures than in low power distance cultures (Sullivan, Mitchell & Uhl-Bien, 2003). This should have a negative effect on the congruence of their perception about the manager's skills in leading employees.

Besides the strength of the leadership relationship, feedback behaviour is another factor that could ensure agreement between managers and observers in this area. In high power distance cultures, feedback is given along the vertical lines of hierarchy in organization and is largely unidirectional, top down (Sully de Luque & Sommer, 2000). In these cultures, feedback is given and sought less frequently bottom up, i.e., from subordinates to a manager, or from a manager to higher level manager (Schermerhorn & Bond, 1997). Thus, in low power distance cultures, managers and their bosses (or subordinates) have less bidirectional communication and thus are less likely to be in unison in their perception of a manager's skills of leading employees. Taken together, we hypothesize:

Hypothesis 2:   In high power distance cultures, the self–subordinate and self–boss rating discrepancy on leading employees is higher than in low power distance cultures.

Managerial composure

Managerial composure refers to a manager's skill to keep emotions under control, not blame or abuse others, and maintain calmness in times of crisis. As power distance is a cultural dimension that emphasizes behaviours to ensure and enhance power and social status, we also expect that it should influence the discrepancy between self and others in the perception of managerial composure. For a leadership style mostly characterized by supervisory (rather than leadership) behaviours, managers need to show high composure and ensure they maintain their social status, especially towards their subordinates. In their relationship with subordinates, for example, managers can be expected to show less affect, responsiveness, and equivalence in their social interactions (Sullivan et al., 2003). Moreover, their behavioural leeway is smaller, defined mostly by norms and expectations towards their social roles rather than them as individual persons. In low power distance cultures, however, managers focus less on supervisory tasks and engage more in direct leadership behaviours. In those leadership relationships, close leadership relationships are built and trust is established, which in turn enable managers and subordinates to be more personal, emotional, and approachable than in high power distance cultures. Thus, we expect that managers and subordinates in low power distance cultures are more aligned in their perception of managerial composure than those in high power distance cultures.

Hypothesis 3:   In high power distance cultures, the self–subordinate rating discrepancy on composure is higher than in low power distance cultures.

METHOD

Participants and procedure

Data were obtained via the use of the BENCHMARKS® assessment tool in leadership development feedback exercises. Managers who took part in a leadership development process between October 2000 and May 2006 provided self-ratings on this instrument and selected observers (one boss, a minimum of three subordinates, and minimum of three peers) to provide ratings on the same tool. Because culture (i.e., country) was an integral part of the analysis, we only selected cases where self and observers were native to and currently working in the same country. We also set a minimum of 15 self-raters from each country. The final sample totalled 4019 managers (self-raters) from 31 countries. The average age of these managers was 41.6 years, 71.8% were male, 83.3% had at least a Bachelor's level of education, 69.5% were middle or upper-middle level managers. Table 1 displays the number of managers from each country.

TABLE 1
Number of managers within countries studied

Country	n
Argentina	30
Australia	170
Brazil	60
Canada	815
Denmark	29
Finland	15
France	110
Germany	133
Hong Kong	21
India	100
Indonesia	36
Ireland	66
Italy	34
Japan	16
Malaysia	21
Mexico	128
Netherlands	190
New Zealand	77
Philippines	67
Poland	31
Portugal	25
Russia	18
Singapore	199
South Korea	31
Spain	177
Sweden	31
Switzerland	39
Thailand	23
Turkey	28
United Kingdom	484
United States*	815

*In order to keep sample size differences within proportions, the sample from the United States was a random sample of 815 managers selected from a much larger country data pool.

Measures

BENCHMARKS® is a multisource feedback instrument, accumulating ratings from the self, direct report, peer, and boss perspective (Lombardo & McCauley, 1994). It is a well-validated and reviewed 360-degree feedback instrument (Carty, 2003; Center for Creative Leadership, 2004; Douglas, 2003; McCauley, Lombardo & Usher, 1989; Spangler, 2003; Zedeck, 1995) and has also been used in prior research (e.g., Atwater, Ostroff, Yammarino

& Fleenor, 1998; Brutus, Fleenor & London, 1998; Brutus et al., 1999; Conway, 2000; Fleenor, McCauley & Brutus, 1996; Gentry et al., 2007). Raters used a 5-point Likert-type scale determining the extent to which a manager displays a leadership skill with 1 = "Not at all" to 5 = "To a very great extent". All items were identical for managers and their observers, only the item referent changed. We selected the three specific leadership dimensions of decisiveness, leading employees, and managerial composure, as the analyses of Braddy, Fleenor, and Campbell (2008) have shown that these scales showed good discriminative power on item and scale level, as well as sufficient scale reliabilities, to be considered separate leadership skills.

Decisiveness. This scale contains four items and refers to a preference for action rather than thinking, taking calculated risks, and being a quick decision maker when necessary ($\alpha = .78$).

Leading employees. This scale contains 11 items about delegating and broadening the skills of direct reports, being fair and patient, and setting clear performance goals ($\alpha = .90$).

Managerial composure. This scale contains four items that relate to tendencies of blaming and abusing others, not being arrogant, cynical or moody, and coping with situations beyond one's personal span of control ($\alpha = .74$).

Cultural values. We used the GLOBE values ("should be") scores to assess culture-level power distance (see House et al., 2004, for complete tables of these values). Similar value measures are available also from the Hofstede studies, but these measures have been critiqued for their low reliability (Spector, Cooper & Sparks, 2001) and questions of their validity, as they have shown shortcomings in replicating consistent patterns in later studies (Merritt, 2000). This scale measured power distance values with five items ($\alpha = .74$ across the GLOBE cultures).

Aggregation issues

An average of 4.14 direct reports and 3.92 peers rated each manager. To justify aggregation of ratings across observers, we computed ICC(1) and ICC(2) (Bliese, 2000), as well as $r^*_{WG(J)}$ (Lindell, Brandt & Whitney, 1999). These values are given in Table 2 and indicate suitable requirements to aggregate multisource feedback ratings (Greguras & Robie, 1998; James, 1988) and are similar to values reported in other multisource studies (Atwater et al., 1998; Fleenor et al., 1996; Ostroff et al., 2004), thus we

TABLE 2
Aggregation statistics, means, standard deviations, and intercorrelations of study variables

	ICC(1)	ICC(2)	$r^*_{WG(J)}$	Mean	SD	1	2	3	4	5	6	7	8	9	10	11	12
1. Power distance				2.70	0.30												
2. Decisiveness—self				3.83	0.57	-.39											
3. Leading employees—self				3.83	0.45	-.20	.56										
4. Composure—self				3.87	0.51	-.21	.41	.44									
5. Decisiveness—boss				3.93	0.60	-.23	.26	.16	.06								
6. Leading employees—boss				3.80	0.52	-.22	.15	.25	.10	.57							
7. Composure—boss				3.97	0.60	-.26	.01	.06	.18	.46	.51						
8. Decisiveness—peers	.25	.56	.78	3.86	0.43	-.26	.32	.19	.09	.41	.30	.15					
9. Leading employees—peers	.25	.57	.77	3.69	0.39	-.13	.18	.28	.15	.25	.41	.24	.64				
10. Composure—peers	.26	.57	.75	3.83	0.45	-.27	.01	.05	.25	.13	.23	.41	.44	.60			
11. Decisiveness—subordinates	.27	.60	.76	3.93	0.45	-.13	.29	.21	.08	.31	.25	.10	.45	.34	.16		
12. Leading employees—subordinates	.26	.59	.71	3.79	0.44	.11	.17	.30	.12	.19	.32	.14	.29	.43	.22	.68	
13. Composure—subordinates	.27	.61	.72	3.91	0.47	-.11	.03	.11	.24	.10	.22	.29	.18	.31	.42	.53	.64

$N = 4019$ for all variables except power distance, where statistics are shown at the country level, thus $N = 31$. Culture-level correlations with $|r| > .35$ are significant with $p < .05$; all individual-level correlations are significant with $p < .01$. All Fs for ICC(1) > 2.25.

proceeded the analysis with aggregated scores across direct reports and peers.

Analytic procedure

The effects predicted by the hypotheses are all cross-level effects, in that the predictor variables (culture) are all measured at a higher level (country), while the outcome variables (discrepancy between raters) are at the individual manager level. Therefore it was necessary to employ a multilevel modelling framework (e.g., Bliese, 2002). The predicted variables were modelled as a discrepancy between self and observer ratings rather than simple difference scores. The problems with using difference scores for this type of variable are many: Because difference scores combine two distinct pieces of information into one, they cannot be unambiguously interpreted, lead to decreased reliability, put what is supposed to be measured with a multivariate model into a univariate framework, and consequently, can provide misleading results (Edwards, 1994, 1995), particularly in cases where measures are positively related (Johns, 1981). Therefore we used Edwards' (1995) framework for studying discrepancy as an outcome variable, which involves studying the simultaneous effects on ratings from different sources and determining whether these effects differ significantly. This procedure is based on multiple regression with concurrent dependent variables (or **MANOVA**), and examines the extent to which the effect of predictors on outcomes is different—in our case, examining the differential effect of power distance on ratings of different observers. This method is described in detail in Edwards (1995). However, as we needed to do this within a multilevel framework, we used Mplus (Muthén & Muthén, 2006) to run multilevel structural equation models (with manifest variables) in analogy to polynomial regression, which allowed the testing of differences via the imposing of constraints on parameters. All forms of ratings (self, boss, peers, subordinates) were modelled simultaneously as outcome variables on the culture variable of power distance. We set constraints to test the equivalence of the effects of power distance on each rating. Due to the use of the maximum likelihood ratio (MLR) estimator, we used Satorra's (2000) test for adjusted chi-squared values.

RESULTS

Table 2 shows aggregation statistics, means, standard deviations and intercorrelations of all study variables. Intercorrelations are given at the individual (manager) level, except for those involving the culture variables, which are given at the country level.

Hypotheses 1–3 were tested using the analytic procedure described earlier. A summary of the results from these tests is shown in Table 3,

TABLE 3
Summary of results for Hypotheses 1 to 3

	Effect size for ...			
Power distance	*Self*	*Boss*	*Peers*	*Subordinates*
H1: Decisiveness	−.23	−.16	−.16	−.07*
H2: Leading employees	−.16	−.12	–	.00*
H3: Composure	−.08	–	–	–

Figures in table are unstandardized regression weights (paths) in the unconstrained model. *indicates a difference from the effects on "Self" with $p < .05$.

showing partial support for our hypotheses. However, to understand the effects fully, it was necessary to plot them: These plots are shown in Figures 1, 2, and 3. The values depicted for the high and low end of power distance resemble scores of $+/-$ 1 *SD* from the grand mean. For the sake of completeness, all four rater sources are shown in each figure.

Hypothesis 1 was only partially supported, as the only significant rating discrepancy in decisiveness emerged between self and subordinates, and in the hypothesized direction. Figure 1 shows that self-ratings of decisiveness decrease considerably in cultures of high power distance, and thus these

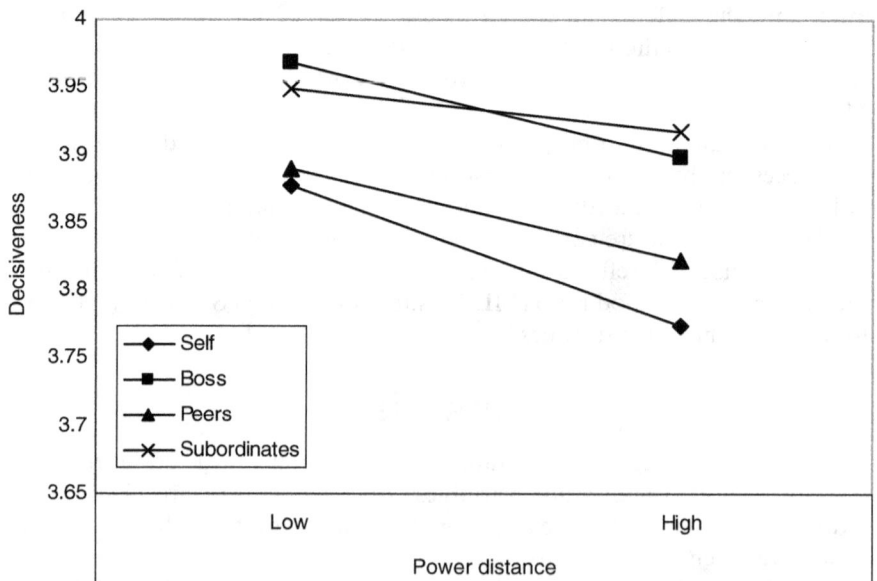

Figure 1. Differential effects of power distance on ratings of decisiveness.

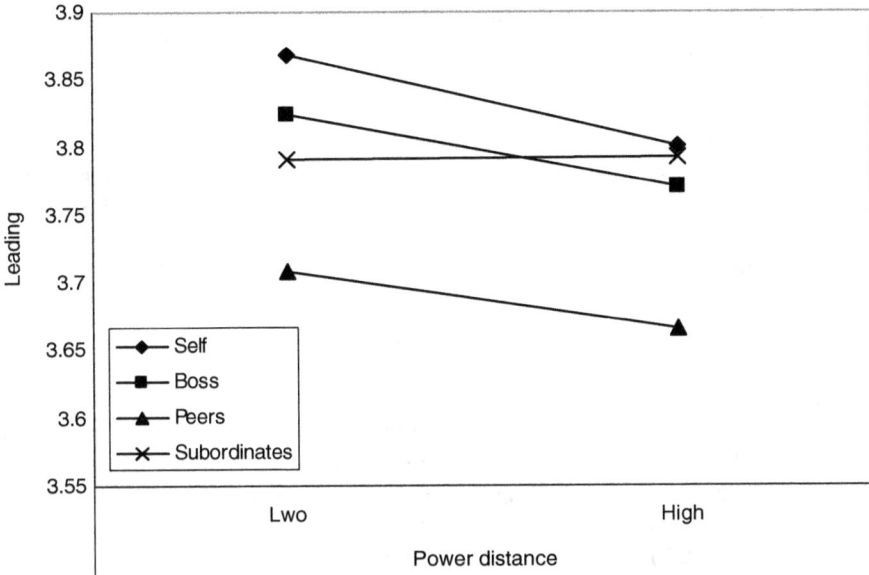

Figure 2. Differential effects of power distance on ratings of leading employees.

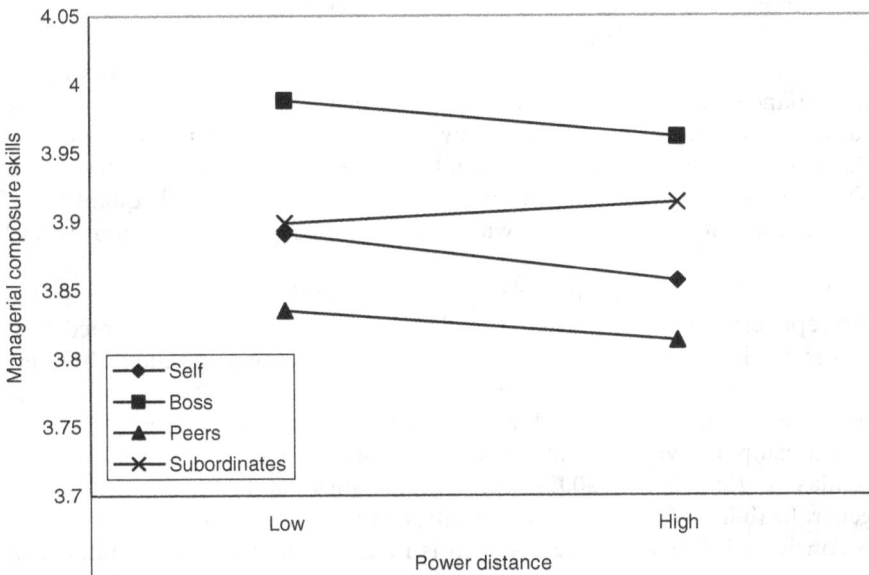

Figure 3. Differential effects of power distance on ratings of composure.

cultures show a higher discrepancy between self and observer ratings, most notably, subordinates. Hypothesis 2 regarding leading employees was not supported, as the only significant discrepancy, which again emerged between self- and subordinate ratings, widened with lower power distance scores, which was contrary to what we hypothesized (mostly because of a decrease in self-ratings, see Figure 2). Hypothesis 3 concerning managerial composure was supported as the discrepancy between self- and subordinate ratings widened with higher power distance (both due to increase in subordinate ratings and decrease in self ratings, see Figure 3).

DISCUSSION

In this study we examined the effect of power distance on perception discrepancy between managers, their bosses, peers, and subordinates, in three core leadership skills: Decisiveness, leading employees, and composure. Using multilevel modelling, we assessed the discrepancy of each kind of observer rating compared to self-ratings.

Our results did not support all our hypotheses, but in sum they strongly suggest that cultural values have a systematic effect on rating discrepancies between self and observers. As expected, we found that in high power distance cultures, the discrepancy between self and subordinate ratings about a manager's decisiveness and composure was higher than in low power distance cultures. We also found that the discrepancy between self- and subordinate ratings about a manager's skills in leading employees was lower in high-power distance culture, contrary to our hypothesis.

Overall, these results show that power distance indeed influences rating discrepancies between self and observers, especially between subordinate ratings, of leadership skills. How a manager's skills are perceived depends on the opportunities different observers have to observe the leader. These opportunities, in turn, depend on the quality and quantity of interaction with the manager, which is determined by cultural norms and values.

Although we examined the impact of cultural values only on selected discrepancies and three specific leadership skills, it can be assumed that cultural values also influence the perception of managers and their observers in other areas of leadership. Traditionally, a discrepancy between self- and observer ratings is regarded as a negative indication of the leadership relationship, or even as a lack of self-awareness with respect to the manager (Kulas & Finkelstein, 2007). Our results question the applicability and generalizability of such conceptualizations once a cross-cultural perspective is considered. Clearly, more research is necessary to examine the impact of rating agreement or discrepancy across cultures, ideally using theoretical frameworks such as dimensions of cultural values or practices.

Limitations

Our analyses were carried out with appropriate consideration to the multilevel nature of the effects in question. Limitations towards the external validity of our results, however, arise from the circumstance that most of the participants in this archival data study could be considered as having high leadership potential by their company, as they participated in 360-degree feedback for the purpose of their own development, rather than for assessment purposes. Such a sample of managers might not be representative of the population of managers at large.

Another limitation might stem from language: All participants received the 360-degree feedback tool in English, even if this was not their mother tongue. Thus, there is a certain risk that language might have influenced results, although it would be hard to understand how this might have led to the systematic differences that we found. Moreover, as reliabilities of the scales were high across all cultures, the impact of such a bias on our results should be rather small.

Finally, it should be noted that the country-level sample sizes differed and sometimes were rather small. This could have led to increased variability in the responses of managers within these countries, in turn leading to systematic underestimation of culture-level influences and overly conservative hypothesis tests.

Implications for research

Research should now consider culture, along with individual and organizational level variables in tandem, as well as the relationship between manager and observer, as influences for the pattern of self and observer ratings in 360-degree feedback. Examining the interactive effects of individual, organizational, and cultural variables as well as the relationship between managers and observers may give great insight into why rating discrepancies exist.

Specifically, we see three main directions for future research. First, it would be important to look not only at the magnitude of perception discrepancies, but also at their direction, examining whether there might be culturally determined patterns in the way managers systematically over- or underrate themselves compared to their observers.

Second, our study implies that the relationship of rating discrepancies with managerial outcomes, such as leadership performance, employee satisfaction, or promotion, will likely differ across cultures. If discrepancies are not based on shortcomings from the manager (e.g., a lack of self-awareness), then why should they have negative consequences? Although research in Western cultures shows that higher discrepancies are related to negative career outcomes, such a relationship cannot simply be assumed to hold true in other cultures. First evidence for this notion can be found in Atwater et al. (2005), showing less importance of rater agreement in European countries than in the US, as well as significant variation between European countries. Similar studies including systematic differences in values, development, or other country characteristics need to be conducted to help us judge the predictive value of rating agreement overall.

Third, cases of expatriate leadership or multicultural leadership, where managers and observers have different cultural backgrounds, should also be examined. In these cases, the cultural influence on rating discrepancies does not only stem from value differences but also from differences in culturally endorsed implicit leadership theories, which determine the course of leadership perception (Den Hartog et al., 1999). In order to really understand the role of culture in 360-degree feedback ratings globally, these results should then be integrated into a comprehensive model about the influence of leadership perception by multiple stakeholders in multiple cultures.

Implications for practice

When managers receive their 360-degree feedback and look at the discrepancies between self- and observer ratings, they are often confused. Managers may not only be at a loss about which information to trust (their own thoughts, or the perception of their observers), but also may not understand what the reasons for such discrepant information might be. Our study demonstrates that one reason for such discrepancy lies within cultural values rather than managers themselves. This insight is of high practical relevance as it can help prevent misinterpretation of rating discrepancies and is particularly relevant as many organizations are using 360-degree feedback around the world (Atwater et al., 2005; Brutus et al., 2001). It raises question to the traditional interpretation of rating discrepancies of low self-awareness and the implication of such discrepancies for future leadership development.

The interpretation of rating discrepancies is based on results about the negative impact of overrating and highly discrepant ratings on managerial performance and derailment for managers in the United States (e.g., Atwater et al., 1998; van Velsor & Leslie, 1991). Managers who do not achieve congruence between their self-perception and their impact on others are likely to face negative outcomes for their career (Wohlers & London, 1989; Yammarino & Atwater, 1993). If discrepancies are in fact driven by cultural values, such interpretations are not appropriate and managers will need to be counselled differently about what to do with their feedback. Indeed, we assume that managerial attempts to reduce discrepancies that are based on cultural issues will likely not be fruitful—nor necessarily appreciated. In order to create the conditions for lower rating discrepancy, managers could find themselves in a situation where they would have to behave contrary to the culturally endorsed expectations about good leadership. Such a violation of expectations would likely result in a negative reaction of others around them and not be conducive to their overall leadership effectiveness.

Our results also question whether high rating discrepancies should be continued to be regarded as something negative that needs to be improved or a deficiency that needs development. Attempts to reduce such discrepancies without questioning their origin is oversimplified and will not always lead to satisfying results. Shipper, Hoffman, and Rotondo (2007) have already found that US managers who engage in 360-degree feedback for their own development and take it repeatedly have a higher decrease in their perception discrepancy than managers from other countries. If, as we have shown, these discrepancies are due to contextual influences rather than individual leadership capabilities, such findings about cultural variations in the longitudinal development of discrepancies are not surprising.

Lastly, our findings have implications for coaches of cross-cultural managers: They can use our findings and purposefully include culture-level information and advice to cross-cultural managers when going through their 360-degree feedback with them.

To sum up, our study shows that cultural values systematically influence how managers and others around them perceive various leadership skills. This has wide-reaching implications of the interpretation of rating discrepancies in 360-degree feedback. In order to fully understand these discrepancies and their practical meaning, further systematic research into the unique and interactive effects of culture on leadership perception from the perspectives of self and observers is needed.

REFERENCES

Atwater, L. E., & Brett, J. F. (2005). Antecedents and consequences of reactions to developmental 360° feedback. *Journal of Vocational Behavior, 66*, 532–548.

Atwater, L. E., Ostroff, C., Yammarino, F. J., & Fleenor, J. W. (1998). Self-other agreement: Does it really matter? *Personnel Psychology, 51*(3), 577–598.

Atwater, L., Waldman, D., Ostroff, C., Robie, C., & Johnson, K. M. (2005). Self-other agreement: Comparing its relationship with performance in the US and Europe. *International Journal of Selection and Assessment, 13*, 25–40.

Atwater, L. E., & Yammarino, F. (1997). Self-other rating agreement: A review and model. *Research in Personnel and Human Resources Management, 15*, 141–164.

Badjo, L. M., & Dickson, M. W. (2001). Perception of organizational culture and women's advancement in organizations: A cross-cultural examination. *Sex Roles, 45*(5/6), 399–414.

Bliese, P. D. (2000). Within-group agreement, non-independence, and reliability: Implications for data aggregation and analyses. In K. J. Klein & S. W. J. Kozlowski (Eds.), *Multilevel theory, research, and methods in organizations: Foundations, extensions, and new directions* (pp. 349–381). San Francisco: Jossey-Bass.

Bliese, P. D. (2002). Multilevel random coefficient modeling in organizational research: Examples using SAS and S-PLUS. In F. Drasgow & N. Schmitt (Eds.), *Measuring and analyzing behavior in organizations: Advances in measurement and data analysis* (pp. 401–445). San Francisco: Jossey-Bass.

Braddy, P. W., Fleenor, J. W., & Campbell, M. (2008). *Methods for reducing the length of 360-degree instruments*. Paper presented at the 23rd annual conference of the Society for Industrial and Organizational Psychology, San Francisco.

Brodbeck, F. C. (2000). Cultural variation of leadership prototypes across 22 European countries. *Journal of Occupational and Organizational Psychology, 73*(1), 1–29.

Brutus, S., Fleenor, J. W., & London, M. (1998). Does 360-degree feedback work in different industries? A between-industry comparison of the reliability and validity of multi-source performance ratings. *Journal of Management Development, 17*, 177–190.

Brutus, S., Fleenor, J. W., & McCauley, C. D. (1999). Demographic and personality predictors of congruence in multi-source ratings. *Journal of Management Development, 18*, 417–435.

Brutus, S., Leslie, J. B., & McDonald-Mann, D. (2001). Cross-cultural issues in multisource feedback. In D. Bracken, C. Timmreck, & A. Church (Eds.), *Handbook of multisource feedback* (pp. 433–446). San Francisco: Jossey-Bass.

Carl, D., Gupta, V., & Javidan, M. (2004). Power distance. In R. J. House, P. J. Hanges, M. Javidan, P. W. Dorfman, & V. Gupta (Eds.), *Culture, leadership, and organizations: The GLOBE study of 62 societies* (pp. 513–563). Thousand Oaks, CA: Sage.

Carty, H. M. (2003). Review of BENCHMARKS® [revised]. In B. S. Plake, J. Impara, & R. A. Spies (Eds.), *The fifteenth mental measurements yearbook* (pp. 123–124). Lincoln, NE: Buros Institute of Mental Measurements.

Center for Creative Leadership. (2004). *BENCHMARKS® facilitator's manual*. Greensboro, NC: Center for Creative Leadership.

Conway, J. M. (2000). Managerial performance development constructs and personality correlates. *Human Performance, 13*, 23–46.

Dalessio, A. T. (1998). Using multi-source feedback for employee development and personnel decisions. In J. W. Smither (Ed.), *Performance appraisal: State-of-the-art in practice* (pp. 278–330). San Francisco: Jossey-Bass.

Dansereau, F., Graen, G., & Haga, W. J. (1975). A vertical dyad linkage approach to leadership within formal organizations: A longitudinal investigation of the role making process. *Organizational Behavior and Human Performance, 13*, 46–78.

Den Hartog, D. N., House, R. J., Hanges, P. J., Ruiz-Quintanilla, S. A., Dorfman, P. W., & GLOBE co-authors. (1999). Culture specific and cross-culturally generalizable implicit leadership theories: Are attributes of charismatic/transformational leadership universally endorsed? *Leadership Quarterly, 10*(2), 219–256.

Douglas, C. A. (2003). *Key events and lessons for managers in a diverse workforce: A report on research and findings*. Greensboro, NC: Center for Creative Leadership.

Edwards, J. R. (1994). The study of congruence in organizational behavior research: Critique and proposed alternative. *Organizational Behavior and Human Decision Processes, 58*, 51–100.

Edwards, J. R. (1995). Alternatives to difference scores as dependent variables in the study of congruence in organizational research. *Organizational Behavior and Human Decision Processes, 64*, 307–324.

Ensari, N., & Murphy, S. E. (2003). Cross-cultural variations in leadership perceptions and attribution of charisma to the leader. *Organizational Behavior and Human Decision Processes, 92*(1–2), 52–66.

Feldman, D. C., & Bolino, M. C. (1999). The impact of on-site mentoring on expatriate socialisation: A structural equation modelling approach. *International Journal of Human Resource Management, 10*(1), 54–71.

Fleenor, J. W., McCauley, C. D., & Brutus, S. (1996). Self-other rating agreement and leader effectiveness. *Leadership Quarterly, 7*, 487–506.

Gentry, W. A., Hannum, K. M., Ekelund, B. Z., & de Jong, A. (2007). A study of the discrepancy between self- and observer-ratings on managerial derailment characteristics of European managers. *European Journal of Work and Organizational Psychology, 16*, 295–325.

Gerstner, C. R., & Day, D. V. (1994). Cross-cultural comparison of leadership prototypes. *Leadership Quarterly, 5*(2), 121–134.

Greguras, G. J., & Robie, C. (1998). A new look at within-source interrater reliability of 360-degree feedback ratings. *Journal of Applied Psychology, 83*, 960–968.

Harris, M. M., & Schaubroeck, J. (1988). A meta-analysis of self-supervisor, self-peer, and peer-supervisor ratings. *Personnel Psychology, 41*, 43–61.

Hofstede, G. (1984). *Culture's consequences: International differences in work-related values, Vol. 2.* Newbury Park, CA: Sage.

House, R. J., Hanges, P. J., Javidan, M., Dorfman, P. W., & Gupta V. (Eds.). (2004). *Culture, leadership, and organizations: The GLOBE study of 62 societies.* Thousand Oaks, CA: Sage.

James, L. R. (1988). Organizational climate: Another look at a potentially important construct. In S. G. Cole & R. G. Demaree (Eds.), *Applications of interactionist psychology: Essays in honor of Saul B. Sells* (pp. 253–282). Hillsdale, NJ: Lawrence Erlbaum Associates, Inc.

Johns, G. (1981). Difference score measures of organizational behavior variables: A critique. *Organizational Behavior and Human Performance, 27*, 443–463.

Kulas, J. T., & Finkelstein, L. M. (2007). Content and reliability of discrepancy-defined self-awareness in multisource feedback. *Organizational Research Methods, 10*(3), 502–522.

Lindell, M. K., Brandt, C. J., & Whitney, D. J. (1999). A revised index of interrater agreement for multi-item ratings of a single target. *Applied Psychological Measurement, 23*, 127–135.

Lombardo, M. M., & McCauley, C. D. (1994). *BENCHMARKS®: A manual and trainer's guide.* Greensboro, NC: Center for Creative Leadership.

Lombardo, M. M., McCauley, C. D., McDonald-Mann, D., & Leslie, J. B. (1999). *BENCHMARKS® developmental reference points.* Greensboro, NC: Center for Creative Leadership.

London, M., & Smither, J. W. (1995). Can multi-source feedback change self-evaluations, skill development, and performance? Theory-based applications and directions for research. *Personnel Psychology, 48*, 375–390.

Lord, R. G., & Maher, K. J. (1991). *Leadership and information processing: Linking perceptions and performance.* London: Routledge.

McCauley, C., Lombardo, M., & Usher, C. (1989). Diagnosing management development needs: An instrument based on how managers develop. *Journal of Management, 15*, 389–403.

Merritt, A. C. (2000). Culture in the cockpit: Do Hofstede's dimensions replicate? *Journal of Cross-Cultural Psychology, 31*, 283–301.

Morgeson, F. P., Mumford, T. V., & Campion, C. A. (2005). Coming full circle: Using research and practice to address 27 questions about 360-degree feedback programs. *Consulting Psychology Journal: Practice and Research, 57*, 196–209.

Mount, M. K., Judge, T. A., Scullen, T. E., Sytsma, M. R., & Hezlett, S. A. (1998). Trait, rater, and level effects in 360-degree performance ratings. *Personnel Psychology, 51*, 557–576.

Muthén, L., & Muthén, B. (2006). *Mplus (Version 4.0)* [Computer software]. Los Angeles: Author.

Ostroff, C., Atwater, L. E., & Feinberg, B. J. (2004). Understanding self-other agreement: A look at rater and ratee characteristics, context, and outcomes. *Personnel Psychology, 57*, 333–375.

Sala, F. (2003). Executive blind spots: Discrepancies between self- and other-ratings. *Consulting Psychology Journal, 55*, 222–229.

Satorra, A. (2000). Scaled and adjusted restricted tests in multi-sample analysis of moment structures. In R. D. H. Heimans, D. S. G. Pollock, & A. Satorra (Eds.), *Innovations in multivariate statistical analysis* (pp. 233–247). London: Kluwer Academic Publishers.

Schermerhorn, J. R., & Bond, M. H. (1997). Cross-cultural leadership dynamics in collectivism and high power distance settings. *Leadership and Organization Development Journal, 18*(4), 187–193.

Schyns, B. (2006). The role of implicit leadership theories in the performance appraisals and promotion recommendations of leaders. *Equal Opportunities International, 25*(3), 188–199.

Shipper, F., Hoffman, R. C. I., & Rotondo, D. M. (2007). Does the 360 feedback process create actionable knowledge equally across cultures? *Academy of Management Learning and Education, 6*(1), 33–50.

Spangler, M. (2003). Review of BENCHMARKS® [revised]. In B. S. Plake, J. Impara, & R. A. Spies (Eds.), *The fifteenth mental measurements yearbook* (pp. 124–126). Lincoln, NE: Buros Institute of Mental Measurements.

Spector, P. E., Cooper, C. L., & Sparks, K. (2001). An international study of the psychometric properties of the Hofstede Values Survey Module 1994: A comparison of individual and country/province level results. *Applied Psychology: An International Review, 50*(2), 269–281.

Stark, E., Hansen, J., & Thomas, L. T. (1998). *A field study of accuracy, agreement, and outcomes of multi-source feedback: Implications across international boundaries.* Paper presented at the international conference of the Academy of Business and Administrative Sciences.

Sullivan, D. M., Mitchell, M., & Uhl-Bien, M. (2003). The new conduct of business: How LMX can help capitalize on cultural diversity. In G. Graen (Ed.), *Dealing with diversity* (pp. 183–218). Charlotte, NC: Information Age.

Sully de Luque, M. F., & Sommer, S. M. (2000). The impact of culture on feedback-seeking behavior: An integrated model and propositions. *Academy of Management Review, 25*, 829–849.

Tornow, W. W. (1993). Perceptions or reality: Is multi-perspective measurement a means or an end? *Human Resource Management, 32*, 246–264.

Van der Vegt, G. S., van de Vliert, E., & Huang, X. (2005). Location-level links between diversity and innovative climate depend on national power distance. *Academy of Management Journal, 48*(6), 1171.

Van Velsor, E., & Leslie, J. B. (1991). *Feedback to managers: Vol. 1. A guide to evaluating multi-rater feedback instruments.* Greensboro, NC: Center for Creative Leadership.

Wohlers, A., & London, M. (1989). Ratings of managerial characteristics: Evaluation difficulty, co-worker agreement and self-awareness. *Personnel Psychology, 42*, 235–261.

Yammarino, F. (2003). Modern data analytic techniques for multisource feedback. *Organizational Research Methods, 6*, 6–14.

Yammarino, F., & Atwater, L. (1993). Understanding self-perception accuracy: Implications for human resource management. *Human Resource Management, 32*(2/3), 231–247.

Zedeck, S. (1995). Review of BENCHMARKS®. In J. Conoley & J. Impara (Eds.), *The twelfth mental measurements yearbook* (Vol. 1, pp. 128–129). Lincoln, NE: Buros Institute of Mental Measurements.

EUROPEAN JOURNAL OF WORK AND
ORGANIZATIONAL PSYCHOLOGY
2010, 19 (3), 279–303

Ψ Psychology Press
Taylor & Francis Group

The impact of consensus and agreement of leadership perceptions on commitment, Organizational Citizenship Behaviour, and customer satisfaction

Jörg Felfe

Department of Psychology, University of Siegen, Siegen, Germany

Kathrin Heinitz

FU Berlin, Berlin, Germany

Based on a follower-centred approach to transformational leadership, the meaning of team consensus for relevant organizational outcome measures is examined. It is argued that high consensus among followers with regard to their respective leaders' behaviour is an indicator of consistent transformational leadership. It is also hypothesized that the team consensus concerning leadership moderates the relation between transformational leadership and outcome criteria. Furthermore we expect leader–team agreement in leadership evaluation between the leader and the group to be related to followers' and customers' reactions. Data was collected from 27 supervisors and 233 subordinates representing 36 service-oriented organizations. Independent measures were taken from 1463 customers. For data analysis a multilevel approach was employed. The results show that consensus is an important predictor for commitment, Organizational Citizenship Behaviour (OCB), and customer satisfaction, and moderates the relationship of transformational leadership with commitment and OCB. Agreement is related to commitment and customer satisfaction and moderates the relationship between leadership and commitment. The findings are discussed in a practical light with regard to the consequences of consensus about leadership within a group and of agreement between a group and the respective leader. Moreover, practical

Correspondence should be addressed to Jörg Felfe, Social and Organizational Psychology, University of Siegen, Adolf-Reichwein-Strabe 2, Siegen 57068, Germany. E-mail: j.felfe@zedat.fu-berlin.de

We are grateful to Anja Beck and Andrea Herz who collected the data when conducting their diploma thesis. We also thank the anonymous reviewers and the editor for their helpful comments.

http://www.psypress.com/ejwop   DOI: 10.1080/13594320802708070

implications are given for the improvement of commitment, OCB, and customer satisfaction.

Keywords: Commitment; Consensus and agreement; Customer satisfaction; Leadership perceptions; Multilevel analysis; Organizational Citizenship Behaviour.

Most empirical research in the field of charismatic leadership is based on the behaviour-oriented and pragmatic conceptualization introduced by Bass (1985), who distinguished between transformational and transactional leadership. Several meta-analyses underline the effectiveness of transformational leadership (Fuller, Patterson, Hester, & Stringer, 1996; Judge & Piccolo, 2004; Lowe, Kroeck, & Sivasubramaniam, 1996). Studies using European samples have shown similar results (Den Hartog, van Muijen, & Koopman, 1997; Felfe, Tartler, & Liepmann, 2004; Geyer & Steyrer, 1998). Due to considerable theoretical and empirical overlap between charismatic and transformational leadership we use both terms synonymously, as proposed by Hunt and Conger (1999). Following Bass and Avolio (1994), transformational leadership is defined as a set of behaviours including idealized influence, inspirational motivation, intellectual stimulation, and individualized consideration that transform followers' needs and expectations to a higher level. As a result, followers perform beyond expectations and show higher levels of satisfaction and commitment. Previous research has proven the benefit of transformational leadership for different outcomes of success. In fact, many studies showed substantial relationships to organizational commitment (Barling, Weber, & Kelloway, 1996; Bycio, Hackett, & Allen, 1995; Felfe et al., 2004; Rafferty & Griffin, 2004; Schmidt, Hollmann, & Sodenkamp, 1998), employee satisfaction (Felfe, 2005; Judge & Bono, 2000; Podsakoff, MacKenzie, & Bommer, 1996), and Organizational Citizenship Behaviour (OCB; Deluga, 1995; Felfe, 2006; Organ, Podsakoff, & MacKenzie, 2006).

Whereas most scholars agree that charismatic or transformational leadership is an interactive phenomenon (Gardner & Avolio, 1998; Klein & House, 1995; Shamir, House, & Arthur, 1993), most research questions concentrate on the leader's behaviour, which, most often, is measured by the followers' reactions. However, in the last decade research with a follower-centred perspective that emphasizes the role of the followers in an interactive, dyadic process has received increased attention (e.g., Awamleh & Gardner, 1999; Gardner & Avolio, 1998; Lord & Maher, 1993; Meindl, 1995; Nye, 2002, 2005; Schyns & Felfe, 2006). From this line of research there is evidence that the chance to emerge as and to remain an effective leader does not solely depend on the leaders' own behaviour but also on followers' information processing (Lord & Emrich, 2000). Perception and the preference for a certain type of leader are influenced by followers' self-conceptions (Keller, 1999), their personality (Felfe & Schyns, 2006), perceived similarity (Felfe & Heinitz, 2008; Felfe & Schyns, in press), implicit leadership theories (Schyns, Felfe, & Blank, 2007), and situational cues such as performance information (Lord, 1985; Rush, Phillips, & Lord, 1981). Similarly social identity theorists claim that the emergence of a leader is based on the leader fitting a prototype ("prototypicality") for the characteristics of a group in a specific situation (Haslam & Platow, 2001).

Extending this interactive perspective, it has to be noted that leadership also is a group phenomenon. Mumford, Dansereau, and Yammarino (2000) challenge the assumption that group members can operate independently. They assess their status and performance through peer comparison processes as well as leader support. Therefore, Mumford et al. conclude that the examination of relationships on the individual level should be extended to take into account cross-level interactions. This means that relationships on the individual level are influenced by group-level phenomena. Accordingly Meindl (1995, 1998) points out that leadership can be regarded as a social construction. The social construction of leadership is based on individual- and group-level processes. The individual-level processes consist of input variables that are connected to different constructs of leadership, including definitions, criteria for evaluation, etc. These individual processes are influenced by group-level processes that can be described by concepts such as social contagion and interaction networks. The social construction is a result of an intersubjective collaboration and negotiation on the basis of a shared system of leadership concepts. Emotional reactions also arise from social processes as Maslach and Leiter (1997) state: "[E]motions are not just private and personal but rather social experiences, both in their origin and effect" (p. 30). Also the Leader–Member Exchange (LMX) theory addresses group-level issues (Graen & Uhl-Bien, 1995). Following this line, leaders do not only exert influence on an individual level but also address their influence to the whole group by fostering cohesion, developing a positive team climate, etc. Leaders may treat their subordinates equally, and therefore perception may be homogeneous. On the other hand, they may treat the members of their group differently, which may result in ingroup and outgroup differentiation, as proposed by the LMX approach.

Coming back to the case of transformational leadership, it can be assumed that the impact of transformational leadership on a group level will be stronger if all members share a similar perception, as building and developing a collective identity, collective self-efficacy, and cohesion is a central issue of this leadership concept (Bass, 1985; Shamir et al., 1993). However, due to different expectations and values on the followers' side, differences in evaluation may also occur even though there is equal treatment from the group leader. Some followers may appreciate a specific style of behaviour, whereas others are reluctant when confronted with this kind of leadership.

Hence, to examine the meaning of the consensus in follower perceptions of their leader is an important issue. Team consensus may on the one hand lead to stronger group cohesion and on the other hand reflect higher levels of transformational leadership, which both may enhance performance. It may be an indicator of clear group goals, social support, and a positive climate. Different levels of the perception of leadership, i.e., low team consensus, on the other hand, may lower cohesion and social support within the group and reduce performance standards.

Comparable to the importance of team consensus for the development of positive work attitudes and performance, agreement between the group and the leader with regard to leadership evaluation may be meaningful as well. High leader–team agreement reflects an appropriate self evaluation, as well as similar expectations and categories between group and leader when assessing leadership behaviour. The aim of this study is to examine the role of homogeneity of leadership perceptions as in team consensus and leader–team agreement on organizational outcomes.

TEAM CONSENSUS

Classical leadership research often focuses on relationships between the level of leadership behaviour and certain outcomes. However, this view neglects important insights provided by Graen and his colleagues (e.g., Graen & Uhl-Bien, 1995) about the variability of subordinates' perceptions of their leaders' behaviour. Classical leadership studies treat variance in followers' ratings concerning a mutual leader as error variance and concentrate on the level of the leaders' behaviour, whereas, from a relationship-based point of view, that variance can be regarded as a meaningful true-score variance (Schyns & Day, 2010 this issue). Team consensus is usually simply used to justify the appropriateness of the aggregation of group member evaluations with regard to their leader and has only recently been accepted as an independent construct (Chan, 1998). Consensus can, however, provide additional information to the level of exhibited leadership behaviour when it comes to understanding the relation of leadership with organizational outcome criteria, this being commitment, satisfaction, or effectiveness. On the other hand, team consensus can also have a direct effect on the aforementioned criteria.

More generally, the level of team consensus reflects the degree of variation among group members' perceptions with regard to shared phenomena where high consensus means low variation. Lindell and Brandt (2000) suggest that in addition to focusing on the simple arithmetic mean of group members' climate perceptions, climate consensus may be of value in predicting workplace outcomes. On a group level, consensus about leadership means homogeneity with regard to members' shared social reality (Bliese & Halverson, 1998). From the perspective of the social influence theory, team consensus would indicate a well-functioning group. In contrast, low team consensus would imply negative performance outcomes as group members engage in behaviours to overcome dissent and to establish consensus (Cole & Bedeian, 2007).

Team consensus may lead to higher performance via several processes on the group level, e.g., fostering of group cohesion and a positive climate, the enhancement of social support within the group, as well as a generally consistent leadership behaviour that can be perceived as reliable and trustworthy by the followers. According to Graen and Uhl-Bien (1995), leaders should try to establish a good relationship with all of their subordinates. A high team consensus should be a desired and effective way of leading, also fostering the leaders' credibility. Furthermore, Feinberg, Ostroff, and Burke (2005) noted that developing team consensus among the subordinates has to be seen as one of the core attributes of transformational leadership, and therefore can also be interpreted as a parameter to assess a leader's transformational behaviour (Conger, Kanungo, & Menon, 2000). Having a look at transformational behaviour as described by Bass (1985), forming a collective identity is one central part as well as it being important that the leader projects a consistent image to his followers (Feinberg et al., 2005; Gardner & Avolio, 1998). Accordingly, Klein and House (1995) pointed out that the extent of effective transformational leadership may be lowered when the leader exhibits varying levels of charisma to individual followers.

Cole and Bedeian (2007) also suggest that leaders serve as "interpretive filters". They shape group members' climate perceptions and contribute to within-group consensus through their own behaviour. Therefore, it can be expected that the development of consensual perceptions among a leader's subordinates will foster a similarity and predictability in group–member behaviour and thereby enhance within-group relations. In turn, engagement and performance losses would be likely to occur as increased time and energy are required to resolve intragroup conflicts, as members struggle to gain congruence when team consensus is low.

Empirical support is provided by Bliese and Halverson (1998), who confirmed the contention that consensus on leadership is a meaningful indicator of the quality of the shared social environment and assesses a unique aspect of group functioning. Consensus about leadership climate accounted for unique variance in average group psychological well-being after controlling for level effects of leadership. In accordance with these findings, Sanders and Schyns (2006) showed that team consensus in the perception of transformational leadership is positively related to cohesiveness and to horizontal solidarity behaviour. In another study on LMX, Schyns (2006) found an effect of consensus on job satisfaction and commitment for the LMX dimension of contribution. Furthermore, recent research on leadership consensus amongst subordinates shows that there is a positive relationship between leaders' transformational behaviour and team consensus concerning this behaviour (Feinberg et al., 2005).

In addition to the direct effects of consensus on outcome variables, Cole and Bedeian (2007) found that consensus in leadership judgement also serves as a moderator. Their results showed that group consensus regarding transformational leadership moderated the relationship between followers' emotional exhaustion and individual-level work commitment. The results of Feinberg et al. (2005) also indicate that "the attribution of transformational leadership to an individual depends on both the leader exhibiting a set of positive leadership behaviours as well as also fostering consensus among subordinates in their perceptions of the leader" (p. 483). Furthermore, in a recent meta-analysis, DeGroot, Kiker, and Cross (2000) found stronger relationships between transformational leadership and outcomes on the group level than on the individual level. As an explanation they suggested that the effects of transformational leadership are "stronger when a leader has similar relationships with subordinates or uses a single style to relate to each group" (p. 363). Van Breukelen, Konst, and van der Vlist (2002) showed that the effect of LMX on commitment was higher when there was little differential treatment towards the subordinates in a work group than when there were high differences in the treatment of the subordinates.

All in all, the results point out the importance of team consensus for the effectiveness of a work group. Consensus in leadership perception indicates that group members share a common group reality. This may also reflect higher group cohesion and similarity with regard to followers' implicit leadership theories, values, and needs within a group.

LEADER–TEAM AGREEMENT

Self-ratings have been empirically investigated from different perspectives. Due to the self-serving bias in self-evaluations (e.g., Harris & Schaubroeck, 1988; Mabe & West, 1982; Moser, 1999), however, research on the agreement between leaders' self-rating and their followers' rating for leadership behaviour has shown only modest agreement (Sanders & Schyns, 2006). On the other hand, level of leader–follower agreement does seem to have an effect on organizational outcomes. Differences in the leader–follower agreement may result from different expectations and values on the followers' side in comparison to their leaders' values and expectations. They may be relevant to the leader's future behaviour and hence for team performance. The results of Tartler, Goihl, Kroeger, and Felfe (2003), for example, show clear correlations between differences in self- and other-ratings of transformational leadership and success criteria such as extra effort, satisfaction, effectiveness, as well as commitment and quality of communication on the individual level. Furthermore, small differences between self- and other-ratings were found to covary with the type of leadership that is perceived, so that transformational leadership was more likely to be found with small differences in leader–follower ratings (Felfe et al., 2004; Tartler et al., 2003). This indicates a clear and consistent communication of values and expectations. Overall agreement in the evaluation of leadership between leader and group on the group level may have a positive effect on outcomes, reflecting similar perceptions that are based on similar categories, standards, and expectations between leaders and followers. This is in line with the results of Atwater and Yammarino (1992), who found that the level of leader–follower agreement moderated the relationship between transformational leadership and performance. Leaders who were more aware of how they were perceived by their followers were rated as being more transformational. Furthermore, leader behaviour was most highly correlated with performance for teams with high leader–follower agreement.

In this study we are not considering the dyadic leader–follower agreement, but rather the agreement on the group level, hence the average agreement between a leader and his or her team. Although one could argue that this is only relevant if there is a high team consensus, a more differentiated view might be needed. In the case of high team consensus, leaders can (low agreement) or cannot (high agreement) differ from their follower's evaluation and therefore indicate a shared set of expectations (amongst other things) or not. The case of low team consensus indicates a differentiated behaviour towards followers or differing perceptions. A leader who is in agreement with the average follower perception of his behaviour still indicates a relatively shared set of perceptions with his team, although low team consensus may be a crucial point. However, in the case of low team consensus and low follower–team agreement, neither the team sees consistent leadership behaviour nor have team and leader mutual perceptions of the leadership behaviour, which reflects a high degree of ambiguity or lack of clarity. All in all, a team should be more effective if there is a common perception rather than if the leader "lives in a world of his or her own" and if there is a consensus among followers.

In order to examine consequences for performance we refer to organizational citizenship behaviour (OCB) as an internal self-rated performance measure and to customer satisfaction as an independent external measure of performance. Moreover, we address affective organizational commitment as an attitudinal outcome. Commitment, OCB, and customer satisfaction are relevant predictors for organizational success.

ORGANIZATIONAL COMMITMENT

As Meyer and Allen (1997) stated, most of the definitions consider commitment to be a stabilizing force that gives direction to behaviour and binds a person to a course of action. In this sense, commitment towards an organization is "a bond or linking of the individual to the organization" (Mathieu & Zajac, 1990, p. 171). An increasing number of current researchers refer to the three component model of Meyer and Allen, which consists of affective, continuance, and normative commitment. The varying forms include desire, perceived costs, as well as the obligation to continue with a course of action. Affective commitment describes the emotional attachment between an employee and the organization. This linkage is characterized by common values, fulfilment of needs, and identification with organizational goals, combined with feelings of pride and attachment. Employees with a high degree of affective commitment stay in their organization because they want to. In a current meta-analysis based on this multidimensional approach, Meyer, Stanley, Herscovitch, and Topolnytsky (2002) show that organizational commitment serves as an important predictor for several positive and negative outcome variables. The authors conclude that a specific behaviour (positive or negative) may more likely occur with primarily affective commitment, followed by normative commitment and—last of all—continuance commitment. Differences in commitment are also meaningful on the group level. Business units with higher levels of commitment are performing better in terms of quality and productivity (Harter, Hayes, & Schmidt, 2002; Schmidt, 2006).

Several studies give evidence of a consistent relationship between transformational leadership and commitment on the individual level (Bycio et al., 1995; Felfe, 2006; Meyer et al., 2002). However, studies that consider the multilevel structure of data are rare. As mentioned earlier, DeGroot et al. (2000) generally found stronger relationships between leadership and outcomes on the group level than on the individual level. Due to a lack of research this result could not yet be confirmed for commitment.

ORGANIZATIONAL CITIZENSHIP BEHAVIOUR

Organizational Citizenship Behaviour (OCB) is an important indicator of employee performance in the field of I/O psychology on the individual and on the group level (Podsakoff, MacKenzie, Paine, & Bachrach, 2000). Individuals as well as business units that display higher levels of OCB perform better than their counterparts. According to Organ (1988), OCB "represents individual behaviour that is discretionary, not directly or explicitly recognized by the formal reward system, and that in the aggregate promotes the effective functioning of the organization" (p. 4). OCB comprises different dimensions of extrarole behaviour that are favourable to the organization: altruism, conscientiousness, courtesy, sportsmanship, and civic virtue. These behaviours are not part of official working contracts (in role behaviour). It can be assumed that OCB depends considerably on employees' motivation. As LePine, Erez, and Johnson (2002) showed in their meta-analysis, theoretically postulated subdimensions are highly correlated.

Transformational leadership has been proven to positively influence followers' OCB (Felfe, 2006; Felfe, Yan, & Six, 2008; Podsakoff et al., 2000). Again, the focus of these studies was on the individual level, and the direct and indirect impact of team consensus and leader–follower agreement on the group level has not yet been examined.

CUSTOMER SATISFACTION

In today's competitive business environment, customer satisfaction is an increasingly important component of an effective organization (Berry & Parasuraman, 1992; Fornell, Mithas, Morgeson, & Krishnan, 2006). Particularly in service-oriented companies, customer satisfaction is essential for organizational success. The quality of the direct interaction with the customer, and hence the customers' level of satisfaction with the service, will determine customer commitment (Homburg, Fassnacht, & Werner, 2000; Nerdinger, 2003; Parasuraman, Zeithaml, & Berry, 1988; Stock, 2003). Thus, customer-oriented communication, building positive relationships with customers and striving for their satisfaction, is crucial for business success. An important reason is that in the service-oriented sector, services and products seem to be more and more interchangeable: price levels, product features, and quality standards are becoming increasingly similar. Thus, service and sales personnel do make the difference through the important role they play in the development of customer satisfaction by engaging in customer-oriented behaviour.

Customer satisfaction can be defined as the cognitive and affective evaluation of the entire experience with a certain company and its products (Homburg et al., 2000). A distinction has been suggested between overall customer satisfaction ("All in all, how satisfied are you with this company") and a more differentiated approach that considers separate facets of customer satisfaction (Parasuraman et al., 1988). Only a few empirical studies have examined the relationship between the characteristics of an organization and this important aspect of organizational effectiveness (e.g., Conrad, Brown, & Harmon, 1997). In particular, only a few studies have addressed the relationship between transformational leadership and customer satisfaction. One can, however, assume that the interaction with the employees is one important factor of customer satisfaction (Grund, 1998). Transformational leaders can influence a positive service climate by articulating the corresponding visions and values and by serving as a role model. Accordingly, Bettencourt and Brown (1997) and Goodwin, Wofford, and Whittington (2001) found relationships between transformational leadership and customer-oriented behaviour on an individual level. Furthermore, customer satisfaction seems to be related to team climate and cohesiveness (Gillepsie, Denison, Haaland, Smerek, & Neale, 2008). We do not know of any studies that examined the direct and indirect impact of team consensus and leader–team agreement with regard to transformational leadership on customer satisfaction.

HYPOTHESES

Derived from the theory on transformational leadership and leadership climate, we claim that high team consensus about the perception of transformational leadership indicates a shared quality with regard to leadership. Therefore we can expect a better team climate and lower levels of conflict which lead to higher levels of commitment and performance. If transformational leadership is considerably high, a homogeneous evaluation also indicates that a leader succeeds in building transformational relationships with all group members. It is a core characteristic of transformational leadership not only to address individuals but also to influence the group as a whole. The enhancement of group cohesion and the fostering of group spirit is an important precondition in order to improve team performance. Therefore, team consensus is supposed to produce a positive organizational climate, which is expected to have a positive influence on the level and homogeneity of organizational outcomes in terms of followers' and customers' reactions:

> **Hypothesis 1a**: The consensus in leaders' perceived behaviour within teams shows a positive direct relation to organizational commitment, OCB, and to customer satisfaction.

In addition to the direct effects of team consensus on several outcomes, empirical research also showed moderating effects of team consensus. When considered as accumulating effect, a higher relation of leadership and outcomes will result with high team consensus. On the other hand, one could also argue that there might be a compensating effect, in that way that especially in the case of low consensus the impact of leadership behaviour on several outcomes might be higher. We therefore will not assume a direction of the moderating effect, but:

> **Hypothesis 1b**: The consensus in leaders' perceived behaviour within teams moderates the relationship between transformational leadership and organizational commitment as well as OCB.

It is also assumed that high agreement between leaders and team with regard to leadership evaluation results from similar values, expectations, and needs. A common and similar basis of evaluation is an indicator of role clarity and an important precondition for successful improvement of the leader–group relationship. On the other hand, low leader–team agreement may explain misunderstanding and results from unrealistic self-perceptions. Feedback processes may be inappropriate. Therefore agreement is supposed to have a positive influence on the level of organizational outcomes in terms of followers' and customers' reactions:

Hypothesis 2a: Leader–team agreement with regard to the leaders' perceived leadership style is positively related to organizational commitment, OCB, and customer satisfaction.

As in the case of team consensus, agreement has also been shown to moderate the relationship between leadership and performance (Atwater & Yammarino, 1992). As empirical evidence for this effect is still scarce, we will also not hypothesize a direction of the moderating effect, but:

Hypothesis 2b: Leader–team agreement with regard to the leaders' perceived leadership style moderates the relationship between transformational leadership and organizational commitment as well as OCB.

METHODS

Participants, design, and procedure

To test the influence of consensus, data must be available on the group level. Data was collected from 27 supervisors and 233 subordinates from 36 organizational units. Independent measures were taken from 1463 customers. Organizations represent different branches (retail, health, tourism). All employees had frequent direct customer contact, as their duties also comprised consulting customers and selling products (e.g., clothes, pharmaceuticals, or flight tickets). With regard to their job characteristics, there were similar types of interaction with the customers and customer relationships were equally important for customer satisfaction. 74.1% of the supervisors, 83.3% of the employees, and 74.7% of the customers were women. Supervisors were $M = 41.2$ ($SD = 9.4$) years old, employees were $M = 33.8$ ($SD = 10.6$) years old, and customers were $M = 35.8$ ($SD = 16.3$) years old. Employees had been working in the organization for $M = 5.6$ ($SD = 5.6$) and supervisors for $M = 10$ ($SD = 5.5$) years. Supervisors mainly held full-time (96%) and unlimited working contracts (87.5%). Employees mainly had part-time contracts (64%), but most of them were unlimited (82.7%). 24.3% of the customers had been customers for more than 5 years, 41.1% for 1–4 years, and 31.5% were new customers (< 1 year). 35.5% answered that they were frequent customers (at least once a week). 24.2% came at least once a month, 17% came four times a year, and 23.2% visited twice a year. All participants were volunteers. First supervisors were asked to participate in the study. Depending on their agreement questionnaires were distributed to them as well as to their employees. Customers were approached when leaving the store or office and asked to fill in a short questionnaire. All participants were informed that they were taking part in a scientific study and that the data would be handled confidentially. Companies and employees were provided with a short report.

Measures

To assess followers' affective organizational commitment, we used Meyer and Allen's (1997) multidimensional concept, which was adapted for use in German samples (Felfe, 2006). The scale ranges from 1 = "not at all true" to 5 = "completely true". The internal consistency (Cronbach's alpha) of the 6-item measure was good ($\alpha = .86$).

To measure followers' perceptions of transformational leadership, a translated and modified version by Felfe (2006) according to the MLQ5X Short by Bass and Avolio (1995) was administered. Six transformational dimensions are distinguished: charisma, idealized influence attributed and behaviour, inspirational motivation, intellectual stimulation, and individualized consideration. The scales range from 1 = "never" to 5 = "almost always". As the correlations between the three subdimensions were rather high a combined measure was computed (on the individual level the range is $r = .63$–$.84$, and on the group level the range is $r = .74$–$.94$). Cronbach's alpha for the combined overall measure was $\alpha = .97$. Leaders' self-rated transformational leadership behaviour was assessed with a self-rating version of the same instrument. Cronbach's alpha for the combined overall measure was $\alpha = .91$.

Organizational citizenship behaviour (OCB) was assessed with a self-developed instrument based on the questionnaire used by Podsakoff, Ahearne, and MacKenzie (1997). In this study we used items from the three subscales: courtesy, conscientiousness, and altruism. As LePine et al. (2002) found in their meta-analysis, the subdimensions cannot be clearly separated. Therefore, it seems justified to use a combined measure. The answer format ranges from 1 = "not at all true" to 5 = "completely true". The internal consistency (Cronbach's alpha) of the measure was acceptable ($\alpha = .73$).

Customer satisfaction. Customers' satisfaction with the interaction with employees was measured with a single item—overall measure ("All in all, how satisfied are you with this company?").

Aggregation. The level of analysis in this study is the group level. Therefore considerable variance between groups is required in order to justify aggregation on the group level. As can be seen in Table 1, the values for ICC (1) indicate sufficient between-groups variance for our measures. The ICC (1) can be interpreted as a measure for nonindependence according to the context (Bliese, 2000). For transformational leadership ICC (1) values vary from .32 to .41, indicating high proportions of between-group variance. For commitment, OCB, and customer satisfaction ICC (1) values are .28, .25, and .19, respectively. Thus, group means vary enough for further analysis on the group level. Moreover, ICC (2) values above .70 indicate sufficient reliability for group means. ICC (1) and ICC (2) are related to each other as a function of group size (Bliese, 2000). The r_{wg} is an indicator of within-group agreement, and can be interpreted as the degree to which ratings from group members are interchangeable. Results show high within-group agreements for all measures.

Measures for consensus and agreement. Following Bliese and Halverson (1998), team consensus was computed from group variances on the transformational leadership evaluations. Group variances were calculated for the subscales of transformational leadership, and then averaged for a combined transformational leadership consensus score. This was done as the use of the variance of the overall scale score "tends to reduce the variability of the consensus measure and may result in restriction of range" (Bliese & Halverson, 1998, p. 568). As high values represent large variances, the values were multiplied by −1 so that high values represent high team consensus. Agreement measures were squared differences between leader and follower ratings of leadership behaviour (perceived and self-rated), averaged on the team level. Again, the values were multiplied by −1, so that high values indicate high leader–team agreement and vice versa.

RESULTS

Test of hypotheses

With H1a we postulated that team consensus about the perception of transformational leadership within a group is related to affective organizational commitment, OCB, and customer satisfaction. Before analysing multilevel models, simple zero-order correlations are examined. As can be seen in Table 1, the perception of transformational leadership is highly

TABLE 1
Means, standard deviations, and correlations of the scales

	M	SD	ICC (1)	ICC (2)	r_{wg}	1	2	3	4	5	6
1. Transformational leadership (F)	3.61	0.60	.41	.81	.86		_.61***_	_.20**_			
2. Commitment (F)	3.87	0.49	.28	.71	.62	.60***		_.30***_			
3. OCB (F)	3.52	0.36	.25	.68	.69	-.24	-.13				
4. Customer satisfaction (C)	4.41	0.32	.19			.35*	.42*	-.14			
5. Transformational leadership (L)	4.21	0.44				.37*	.11	-.34	-.03		
6. TL team consensus (F)	0.68	0.22				.49**	.46**	-.35*	.42*	.34	
7. TL leader–team agreement (F, L)	0.67	1.13				.68***	.43*	-.19	.23	.29	.29

TL = transformational leadership; source: (F) = follower, (C) = customer, (L) = leader; values below the diagonal represent group-level correlations (N = 36 groups; N = 27 leaders), correlations above the diagonal (italics) were computed on the individual level (N = 233). *p < .05, **p < .01, ***p < .001.

correlated with affective organizational commitment and OCB ($r = .61$ and .20) on the individual level. Commitment and OCB are also correlated. The analysis on the group level reveals a slightly different result. As expected, on the group level followers' perception of transformational leadership is positively correlated with commitment and customer satisfaction as well as leader self-rated transformational leadership, but there was no significant relationship with OCB. Moreover the level of transformational leadership is related to team consensus with regard to leadership. Though not significant, team consensus and leader–team agreement show a positive relationship ($r = .29$). As postulated in our hypothesis, team consensus is correlated with commitment ($r = .49$) and with customer satisfaction ($r = .42$). Unexpectedly the relation between team consensus and OCB is negative.

Due to the nested structure of the data we employed multilevel analysis using HLM 6. Followers' commitment and OCB as well as customers' satisfaction were outcome variables on Level 1 (see Table 2, Model A). In order to control for effects of levels of leadership the individual perception of leadership was added as a predictor on Level 1. Team consensus served as a predictor for direct effects (intercept: G01) and moderating effects (slope: G11) on Level 2. In the model that predicted customer satisfaction, perception of transformational leadership was modelled on the group level (intercept: G01) because customers' reactions were nested in groups but not in followers. For this reason we can only examine direct effects of team consensus on customer satisfaction (intercept: G02). As shown in Table 2, the results indicate that team consensus with regard to leadership perceptions directly influences followers' commitment, OCB, and customers' satisfaction. The coefficients are 3.1 ($p = .06$), 2.12 ($p = .05$), and .50 ($p = .05$), respectively. The effect of consensus only scarcely fails the 5% level when predicting commitment. Additionally we postulated with H1b that consensus (G11) moderates the relationship between perception of transformational leadership and outcomes on Level 1 in terms of a cross-level interaction. The results show significant cross-level interaction for commitment and OCB. The coefficients are $-.76$ ($p = .05$) and $-.71$ ($p = .01$). Thus, after controlling for levels of transformational leadership we found direct and moderating effects for consensus. H1a and b are mainly supported.

With H2a we postulated that agreement between group perception and the leader's self-rating are positively related to commitment, OCB, and customer satisfaction. As can be seen in Table 1, the level of transformational leadership is related to leader–team agreement with regard to leadership ($r = .68$). As postulated in our hypothesis, leader–team agreement is correlated with commitment ($r = .43$). The correlation between leader–team agreement and customer satisfaction, though not significant, is pointing in the expected direction. A lack of power is an important issue

TABLE 2
Multilevel random coefficient model predicting commitment, OCB, and customer satisfaction

	OCA				OCB				Customer satisfaction			
	Coefficient	SE	t-ratio	p-value	Coefficient	SE	t-ratio	p-value	Coefficient	SE	t-ratio	p-value
Model A												
Level 1												
G00 Intercept	3.66	1.16	3.15	.00	4.31	0.86	4.99	.00	4.41	0.54	8.11	.00
G10 T Leadership	0.12	0.27	0.44	.66	−0.29	0.19	−1.49	.15				
Level 2												
G01 Intercept consensus	3.06	1.59	1.92	.06	2.12	1.05	2.02	.05	G01 TS 0.09	0.11	0.80	.43
G11 Slope consensus	−0.76	0.37	−2.04	.05	−0.71	0.25	−2.90	.01	G02 Consensus 0.50	0.24	2.04	.05
G02												
Model B												
Level 1												
Intercept	1.41	0.46	3.08	.01	2.67	0.34	7.72	.00	4.54	0.07	62.46	.00
Transformational leadership	0.64	0.11	5.61	.00	0.19	0.10	2.00	.06				
Level 2												
Intercept agreement	0.57	0.25	2.24	.04	0.06	0.17	0.33	.74	0.09	0.03	2.83	.01
Slope agreement	−0.21	0.06	−2.97	.01	−0.07	0.06	−1.22	.23				

on the group level. Due to small sample size correlations, equal or even above $r = .35$ fail to become significant but should not be ignored. The smaller sample size for the analysis with the leader–team agreement variable is also the reason why we conducted separate multilevel analyses (Model B). The results show that leader–team agreement on the group level enhances followers' commitment but not OCB (Table 2). The coefficients are .57 ($p = .04$) and .06 ($p = .74$). Due to the high intercorrelation between leader–team agreement and level of transformational leadership, the effect of leader–team agreement on customers' satisfaction is only significant if we do not control for group-level differences (coefficient: .09, $p = .01$). With regard to H2b, a cross-level effect of leader–team agreement was found for commitment ($-.21$, $p = .01$) but not for OCB. Thus, H1a and b are clearly supported for commitment but not for OCB. H1a is also partly supported for customer satisfaction.

DISCUSSION

The aim of this study was to have a look at the impact of the level of homogeneity and congruence in leadership evaluations on several organizational outcomes. Therefore, the influence of team consensus, as the homogeneity amongst subordinates, and of leader–team agreement, as the congruence of leaders and subordinate evaluations of leadership, on affective organizational commitment, OCB, and customer satisfaction were examined. Hence, this study extends the research on the effect of leadership and its perception to organizational outcomes from the individual to the group level (Graen & Uhl-Bien, 1995; Mumford et al., 2000) and adds to the increasing line of follower-centred literature (Lord & Emrich, 2000). Team consensus is also a result of followers' collective information processing and can be seen as a social construction that is based on intersubjective collaboration, negotiation, social contagion, and mutual influence (Meindl, 1995, 1998). Team consensus can be seen as a core aim of transformational leadership and can hence be an important additional predictor for organizational criteria (Bliese & Halverson, 1998; Cole & Bedeian, 2007; Feinberg et al., 2005). Leader–team agreement, as an indicator of clear and transparent communication and expectations between leader and follower, especially in the case of transformational leadership, should also have an effect on climate and performance (Sanders & Schyns, 2006; Tartler et al., 2003). Following previous research, it was also assumed that team consensus and leader–team agreement do not only directly influence organizational outcomes but also moderate the relationships between leadership and outcomes (Atwater & Yammarino, 1992; Cole & Bedeian, 2007) in terms of cross-level interactions (Mumford et al., 2000).

Our hypotheses were mainly confirmed and our results provide empirical evidence for the meaning of team consensus and leader–team agreement for organizational outcomes. Specifically, team consensus among group members with regard to leader perception as a group variable was found to be related with followers' affective commitment, OCB, and customers' satisfaction. Leader–team agreement with regard to leader perception is also related to commitment and customer satisfaction. However, we did not find a relationship between leader–team agreement and OCB. Both, team consensus and leader–team agreement on the group level have significant relations with followers' commitment and customers' satisfaction. Additionally, the results reveal that even after controlling for the level of transformational leadership, both team consensus and in part leader–team agreement, explain unique variance in commitment, OCB, and customer satisfaction. This provides evidence that individual perceptions of leadership on the level of followers and variables that reside on the group level such as team consensus and leader–team agreement independently influence organizational outcomes. Our results extend the line of previous research that has addressed the meaning of consensus (Bliese & Halverson, 1998; Feinberg et al., 2005; Sanders & Schyns, 2006; van Breukelen et al., 2002) and agreement (Tartler et al., 2003).

We interpret the meaning of team consensus for outcomes on the basis of a shared quality with regard to leadership among followers. On the basis of a common view one can expect a better team climate, more social support, and lower levels of conflict, which lead to higher levels of commitment and performance (Cole & Bedeian, 2007). Moreover a homogeneous evaluation indicates that a leader succeeds in building transformational relationships to all group members and influences the group as a whole which is a core characteristic of transformational leadership (Conger et al., 2000; Feinberg et al., 2005). The enhancement of group cohesion and team spirit are important for the improvement of team performance. Individual engagement in OCB and customers satisfaction may be valid indicators of this effort.

With regard to the meaning of agreement, we argued that high leader–team agreement between the leader and the group resembles similar values, expectations, and needs. A similar basis of evaluation is also an indicator of role clarity and efficient feedback processes. Previous research has addressed this issue on an individual level (see Tartler et al., 2003) but not examined agreement as a group variable. As our findings show, agreement on a group level, however less consistent than for team consensus, positively influences organizational outcomes.

Moreover agreement and consensus have not yet been analysed in one study. Examining the zero-order correlations on the group level reveal that information about levels of leadership and information about consensus or agreement with regard to leadership are correlated but distinct phenomena. Thus, it seems to be justified to consider consensus and agreement as different and somewhat independent concepts. Their specific relationships with outcomes and the moderate correlation of $r = .29$ between team consensus and leader–team agreement indicate their independence.

Following the suggestions of Mumford et al. (2000), Feinberg et al. (2005), and Cole and Bedeian, (2007), we examined cross-level interaction effects. Actually we were able to show that, as expected, team consensus also moderates the relationship between transformational leadership and followers' commitment and OCB. For leader–team agreement a similar effect was found for the relationship between leadership and commitment but not with OCB. Due to our data structure we could not examine cross-level interaction effects with customer satisfaction. Interestingly we detected negative interaction effects. This means that the relationship between leadership and outcomes is lower when there is a high level of team consensus or leader–team agreement. Though one might intuitively expect an opposite mechanism, one might argue that there might be a compensating effect, in that way that especially in the case of low consensus or low agreement the impact of leadership behaviour on several outcomes might be higher: Low transformational leadership will lead to low commitment and low performance, whereas high transformational leadership will enable high performance. In the case of high agreement and/or high consensus higher cohesion, support and positive climate may enhance commitment and performance and the variation of leadership is not as influential. However, we have to state our results contradict previous findings (e.g., Cole & Bedeian, 2007). As only few studies have addressed cross-level interactions in this field, further research is needed to better understand the underlying mechanisms. Nevertheless the assumption of a simple accumulating effect is challenged.

To sum up, extending the body of previous research that mainly focused on the individual level, we found that group-level analyses do provide important additional information when looking at organizational outcomes.

Limitations and future research

Finally, several limitations of this approach should be mentioned. Although the number of participants was quite high, the number of observed units was relatively small. Due to the fact that not all supervisors participated in our study, the sample for the analysis with leader–team agreement was even smaller. We were also not able to realize a complete nested structure with consumers nested in employees who are nested in units. However, a complete three-level structure may only be considered appropriate if consumers are always served by the same employee. As soon as they are served by different employees our model, where customers are nested in units and not in employees, may be closer to reality. Another issue may be the lack of control of missing data. Systematic differences in participation quotes between units may have influenced our results. For future research it is recommended to control for this variable. Moreover, other variables that characterize the different groups might be taken into account more systematically (e.g., group size, tenure, age, and sex diversity). Furthermore, units of investigation in this study were solely so-called business-to-customer organizations, as these ensure a continuous customer–follower contact. In order to generalize our results, it would be interesting to also examine organizations that belong to the business-to-business area. Hence, the results could be prone to sample effects. Additionally, this research would also benefit from a longitudinal or experimental design that could vary the extent of consistency in the leaders' behaviour. This would allow for a more rigorous text of the impact of consistency on team consensus and the outcomes. Furthermore, our study only used a single item measure for customer satisfaction. This results in a lack of reliability information. Also, as multifaceted approaches to satisfaction exist, a use of these measures might also provide a more differentiated view on the importance of team consensus and leader–team agreement on these subfacets.

It is also likely that the relations we found are influenced by other variables. Especially on the side of the follower, variables such as self-esteem, self-concept, or role clarity could be of importance. Hence, future research would benefit from the examination of personality or other group variables such as team climate, tenure, diversity, support, or variables that reside on the organizational level, e.g., perceived organizational fairness, psychological contract, etc. Some of these variables may mediate the relationships between leadership and outcomes. We proposed that team consensus and leader–team agreement influence outcomes by enhancing cohesiveness, positive climate, mutual understanding, role clarity, etc. However, we did not empirically test these variables in our study. Future research should deepen the understanding why consensus and agreement positively influence outcomes by including the aforementioned variables. It is a matter of fact that our cross-level interaction effects challenge previous findings. It remains an open question if our results can be replicated and what factors lead to positive or negative interaction effects.

Implications

The results hold different implications for the organizational practice. Our study confirms the results of many earlier studies, that transformational leadership is related to organizational outcomes. However, the results also put emphasis on the importance of the group-oriented facets of transformational leadership. Although transformational leadership is a multifaceted concept, certain facets need special attention. Developing consensus among the followers, forming a collective identity, fostering group cohesiveness, or projecting consistent images turn out to be important for effectiveness criteria. A consistent behaviour on the side of the leader seems to be important for a positive team climate with committed team members. Furthermore, this consistency will also result in a positive public image, being reflected in high customer satisfaction. Team consensus may also be fostered by systematic feedback processes where group members develop a common view on the basis of leadership appraisal by exchanging their subjective perspectives and thereby reflecting and modifying their standards and categories towards a common value system.

Leader–team agreement also showed a clear relation to followers' and customers' attitudes. Hence, there is a clear recommendation for leaders to pay attention to an unmistakable and understandable communication of values, needs, and visions. This will lead to a shared frame of expectations and values, which is important for a good team climate. This is in turn reflected by highly committed followers. Again, the role of open and systematic communication and feedback has to be emphasized. On an individual level, useful and regular feedback will also lead to enhanced agreement; on the team level it can foster consensus as team goals and accomplishments will be evaluated in a consistent way. However, this effect will very much depend on the manner in which feedback is provided.

Nonetheless, the present study illustrates the need to further consider the respective roles of team consensus and agreement in studying the effects of leadership on work-related outcomes.

REFERENCES

Atwater, L. E., & Yammarino, F. J. (1992). Does self-other agreement on leadership perceptions moderate the validity of leadership and performance predictions? *Personnel Psychology, 45,* 141–164.

Awamleh, R., & Gardner, W. L. (1999). Perceptions of leader charisma and effectiveness: The effects of vision content, delivery, and organizational performance. *Leadership Quarterly, 10,* 345–373.

Barling, J., Weber, T., & Kelloway, E. K. (1996). Effects of transformational leadership training on attitudinal and financial outcomes: A field experiment. *Journal of Applied Psychology, 81,* 827–832.

Bass, B. M. (1985). *Leadership and performance beyond expectations.* New York: The Free Press.

Bass, B. M., & Avolio, B. J. (1994). *Improving organizational effectiveness through transformational leadership.* Thousand Oaks, CA: Sage.

Bass, B. M., & Avolio, B. J. (1995). *MLQ Multifactor Leadership Questionnaire: Technical report.* Redwood City, CA: Mind Garden.

Berry, L. L., & Parasuraman, A. (1992). Prescriptions for a service quality revolution in America. *Organizational Dynamics, 20,* 5–15.

Bettencourt, L., & Brown, S. (1997). Contact employees: Relationships among workplace fairness, job satisfaction and pro-social service behaviors. *Journal of Retailing, 73,* 39–61.

Bliese, P. D. (2000). Within-group agreement, non-independence, and reliability: Implications for data aggregation and analysis. In K. Klein & S. W. J. Kozlowski (Eds.), *Multilevel theory, research, and methods in organizations: Foundations, extensions, and new directions* (pp. 349–381). San Francisco: Jossey-Bass.

Bliese, P. D., & Halverson, R. R. (1998). Group consensus and psychological well being: A large field study. *Journal of Applied Social Psychology, 28,* 563–580.

Bycio, P., Hackett, D. H., & Allen, J. S. (1995). Further assessments of Bass's (1985) conceptualization of transactional and transformational leadership. *Journal of Applied Psychology, 80,* 486–478.

Chan, D. (1998). Functional relations among constructs in the same content domain at different levels of analysis: A typology of composition models. *Journal of Applied Psychology, 83,* 234–483.

Cole, M. S., & Bedeian, A. G. (2007). Leadership consensus as a cross-level contextual moderator of the emotional exhaustion–work commitment relationship. *Leadership Quarterly, 18,* 447–462.

Conger, J. A., Kanungo, R. N., & Menon, S. T. (2000). Charismatic leadership and follower effects. *Journal of Organizational Behaviour, 21,* 747–767.

Conrad, C. A., Brown, G., & Harmon, H. A. (1997). Customer satisfaction and corporate culture: A profile deviation analysis of a relationship marketing outcome. *Psychology and Marketing, 14,* 663–674.

DeGroot, T., Kiker, D. S., & Cross, T. C. (2000). A meta-analysis to review organizational outcomes related to charismatic leadership. *Canadian Journal of Administrative Sciences, 17,* 356–371.

Deluga, R. J. (1995). The relationship between attributional charismatic leadership and organizational citizenship behaviour. *Journal of Applied Psychology, 25,* 1652–1669.

Den Hartog, D. N., van Muijen, J. J., & Koopmann, P. L. (1997). Transactional versus transformational leadership: An analysis of the MLQ. *Journal of Occupational and Organizational Psychology, 70,* 19–34.

Feinberg, B. J., Ostroff, C., & Burke, W. W. (2005). The role of within-group agreement in understanding transformational leadership. *Journal of Occupational and Organizational Psychology, 78,* 471–488.

Felfe, J. (2005). *Charisma, transformationale Führung und Commitment.* Köln, Germany: Kölner Studienverlag.

Felfe, J. (2006). Validierung einer deutschen Version des "Multifactor Leadership Questionnaire" (MLQ 5 X Short) von Bass und Avolio (1995) [Validation of a German version of the "Multifactor Leadership Questionnaire" (MLQ 5 X Short) by Bass and Avolio (1995)]. *Zeitschrift für Arbeits- und Organisationspsychologie, 50,* 61–78.

Felfe, J., & Heinitz, K. (2008). The impact of followers' and leaders' personality and perceived similarity on followers' perceptions of transformational leadership and leader acceptance. In J. Deller (Ed.), *Personality and work* (pp. 197–217). München, Germany: Rainer Hampp Verlag.

Felfe, J., & Schyns, B. (2006). Personality and the perception of transformational leadership: The impact of extraversion, neuroticism, personal need for structure, and occupational self-efficacy. *Journal of Applied Social Psychology, 36,* 708–741.

Felfe, J., & Schyns, B. (in press). Followers' personality and the perception of transformational leadership: Further evidence for the similarity hypothesis. *British Journal of Management.*

Felfe, J., Tartler, K., & Liepmann, D. (2004). Advanced research in the field of transformational leadership. *Zeitschrift für Personalforschung—German Journal of Human Resource Research. Special Research Forum, 18,* 262–288.

Felfe, J., Yan, W., & Six, B. (2008). The impact of individual collectivism on commitment and its influence on OCB, turnover, and strain in three countries. *International Journal of Cross-Cultural Management, 8,* 211–237.

Fornell, C., Mithas, S., Morgeson, F. V., & Krishnan, M. S. (2006). Customer satisfaction and stock prices: High returns, low risk. *Journal of Marketing, 70,* 3–14.

Fuller, J. B., Patterson, C. E. P., Hester, K., & Stringer, D. Y. (1996). A quantitative review of research on charismatic leadership. *Psychological Reports, 78,* 271–287.

Gardner, W. L., & Avolio, B. J. (1998). The charismatic relationship: A dramaturgical perspective. *Academy of Management Review, 23,* 32–58.

Geyer, A., & Steyrer, J. (1998). Messung und Erfolgswirksamkeit transformationaler Führung. *Zeitschrift für Personalforschung, 4,* 377–401.

Gillespie, M. A., Denison, D. R., Haaland, S., Smerek, R., & Neale, W. S. (2008). Linking organizational culture and customer satisfaction: Results from two companies in different industries. *European Journal of Work and Organizational Psychology, 17,* 112–132.

Goodwin, V. L., Wofford, J. C., & Whittington, J. L. (2001). A theoretical and empirical extension to the transformational leadership construct. *Journal of Organisational Behaviour, 22,* 759–774.

Graen, G. B., & Uhl-Bien, M. (1995). Development of leader-member exchange (LMX) theory of leadership over 25 years: Applying a multi-level multi-domain perspective. *Leadership Quarterly, 6,* 219–247.

Grund, M. (1998). *Interaktionsbeziehungen im Dienstleistungsmarketing: Zusammenhänge zwischen Zufriedenheit und Bindung von Kunden und Mitarbeitern [Interaction relations in services marketing: Relations of satisfaction and commitment of customers and staff].* Wiesbaden, Germany: Gabler.

Harris, M. M., & Schaubroeck, J. (1988). A meta-analysis of self-superior, self-peer, and peer-supervisor ratings. *Personnel Psychology, 41,* 43–62.

Harter, J. K., Hayes, T. L., & Schmidt, F .L. (2002). Business-unit-level relationship between employee satisfaction, employee engagement, and business outcomes: A meta-analysis. *Journal of Applied Psychology, 87,* 268–279.

Haslam, S. A., & Platow, M. J. (2001). The link between leadership and followership: How affirming social identity translates vision into action. *Personality and Social Psychology Bulletin, 27,* 1469–1479.

Homburg, C., Fassnacht, M., & Werner, H. (2000). Operationalisierung von Kundenzufriedenheit und Kundenbindung. In M. Bruhn & C. Homburg (Eds.), *Handbuch Kundenbindungsmanagement: Grundlagen-Konzepte-Erfahrungen* (pp. 553–575). Wiesbaden, Germany: Gabler.

Hunt, J. G., & Conger, J. A. (1999). From where we sit: An assessment of transformational and charismatic leadership research. *Leadership Quarterly, 10,* 335–343.

Judge, T. A., & Bono, J. E. (2000). Five-factor model of personality and transformational leadership. *Journal of Applied Psychology, 85,* 751–765.

Judge, T. A. & Piccolo, R. F. (2004). Transformational and transactional leadership: A meta-analytic test of their relative validity. *Journal of Applied Psychology, 89,* 755–768.

Keller, T. (1999). Images of the familiar: Individual differences and implicit leadership theories. *Leadership Quarterly, 10,* 589–607.

Klein, K. J., & House, R. (1995). On fire: Charismatic leadership and levels of analysis. *Leadership Quarterly, 6,* 183–198.

LePine, J. A., Erez, A., & Johnson, D. E. (2002). The nature and dimensionality of organizational citizenship behaviour: A critical review and meta-analysis. *Journal of Applied Psychology, 87,* 52–65.

Lindell, M. K., & Brandt, C. J. (2000). Climate quality and climate consensus as mediators of the relationship between organizational antecedents and outcomes. *Journal of Applied Psychology, 85,* 331–348.

Lord, R. G. (1985). An information processing approach to social perceptions, leadership and behavioral measurement in organizations. *Research in Organizational Behaviour, 7,* 87–128.

Lord, R. G., & Emrich, C. G. (2000). Thinking outside the box by looking inside the box: Extending the cognitive revolution in leadership research. *Leadership Quarterly, 11,* 551–579.

Lord, R. G., & Maher, K. J. (1993). *Leadership and information processing: Linking perceptions and performance.* London: Routledge.

Lowe, K. B., Kroeck, K. G., & Sivasubramaniam, N. (1996). Effectiveness correlates of transformational and transactional leadership: A meta-analytic review of the MLQ literature. *Leadership Quarterly, 7,* 385–425.

Mabe, P. A., III, & West, S. G. (1982). Validity of self-evaluation of ability: A review and meta-analysis. *Journal of Applied Psychology, 62,* 280–296.

Maslach, C., & Leiter, M. P. (1997). *The truth about burnout: How organizations cause personal stress and what to do about it.* San Francisco: Jossey-Bass.

Mathieu, J. E., & Zajac, D. M. (1990). A review and meta-analysis of the antecedents, correlates, and consequences of organizational commitment. *Psychological Bulletin, 108,* 171–194.

Meindl, J. R. (1995). The romance of leadership as a follower-centric theory: A social constructionist approach. *Leadership Quarterly, 6,* 329–341.

Meindl, J. R. (1998). Appendix: Measures and assessments for the romance of leadership approach. In F. Dansereau & F. J. Yammarino (Eds.), *Leadership: The multiple-level approaches, Part B: Contemporary and alternative* (pp. 199–302). Stamford, CT: JAI Press.

Meyer, J. P., & Allen, N. J. (1997). *Commitment in the workplace: Theory, research, and application.* Thousand Oaks, CA: Sage.

Meyer, J. P., Stanley, D. J., Herscovitch, L., & Topolnytsky, L. (2002). Affective, continuance, and normative commitment to the organization: A meta-analysis of antecedents, correlates, and consequences. *Journal of Vocational Behaviour, 61,* 20–52.

Moser, K. (1999). Selbstbeurteilung beruflicher Leistung: Überblick und offene Fragen [Self-evaluation of vocational performance: Overview and pending questions]. *Psychologische Rundschau, 50,* 14–25.

Mumford, D. M., Dansereau, F., & Yammarino, F. J. (2000). Followers, motivations, and levels of analysis: The case of individualized leadership. *Leadership Quarterly, 11,* 313–340.

Nerdinger, F. W. (2003). *Kundenorientierung.* Göttingen, Germany: Hogrefe.

Nye, J. L. (2002). The eye of the follower: Information processing effects on attribution regarding leaders of small groups. *Small Group Research, 33,* 337–360.

Nye, J. L. (2005). Implicit theories and leadership perceptions in the thick of it: The effects of prototype matching, group setbacks, and group outcomes. In B. Schyns & J. R. Meindl (Eds.), *The leadership horizon series* (Vol. 3, pp. 3–14). Greenwich, CT: Information Age Publishing.

Organ, D. W. (1988). *Organizational citizenship behaviour.* Lexington, MA: Lexington Press.

Organ, D. W., Podsakoff, P. M., & MacKenzie, S. B. (2006). *Organizational citizenship behaviour: Its nature, antecedents, and consequences.* Thousands Oaks, CA: Sage.

Parasuraman, A., Zeithaml, V. A., & Berry, L. L. (1988). SERVQUAL: A multiple item scale for measuring consumer perceptions of service quality. *Journal of Retailing, 64,* 12–40.

Podsakoff, P. M., MacKenzie, S. B., & Bommer, W. H. (1996). Transformational leader behaviors and substitutes for leadership as determinants of employee satisfaction, commitment, trust and organizational citizenship behaviors. *Journal of Management, 22,* 259–298.

Podsakoff, P. M., Ahearne, M., & MacKenzie, S. B. (1997). Organizational citizenship behavior and the quantity and quality of work group performance. *Journal of Applied Psychology, 82,* 262–270.

Podsakoff, P. M., MacKenzie, S. B., Paine, J. B., & Bachrach, D.G. (2000). Organizational citizenship behaviors: A critical review of the theoretical and empirical literature and suggestions for future research. *Journal of Management*, *26*, 513–563.

Rafferty, A. E., & Griffin, M. A. (2004). Dimensions of transformational leadership: Conceptual and empirical extensions. *Leadership Quarterly*, *15*, 329–354.

Rush, M. C., Phillips, J. S., & Lord, R. G. (1981). Effects of a temporal delay in rating on leader behaviour descriptions: A laboratory investigation. *Journal of Applied Psychology*, *66*, 442–450.

Sanders, K., & Schyns, B. (2006). Leadership and solidarity behaviour: Consensus in perception of employees within teams. *Personnel Review*, *5*, 538–556.

Schmidt, K.-H. (2006). Haupt- und Moderatoreffekte der affektiven Organisationsbindung in der Belastungs-Beanspruchungs-Beziehung. *Zeitschrift für Personalpsychologie*, *5*, 121–130.

Schmidt, K.-H., Hollmann, S., & Sodenkamp, D. (1998). Psychometrische Eigenschaften und Validität einer deutschen Fassung des Commitment-Fragebogens von Allen und Meyer (1990). *Zeitschrift für Differentielle und Diagnostische Psychologie*, *19*, 93–106.

Schyns, B. (2006). Are group consensus in LMX and shared work values related to organizational outcomes? *Small Group Research*, *37*, 20–35.

Schyns, B., & Day, D. V. (2010). Critique and review of leader-member exchange theory: Issues of agreement, consensus, and excellence. *European Journal of Work and Organizational Psychology*, *19*(1), 1–29.

Schyns, B., & Felfe, J. (2006). The personality of followers and its effect on the perception of leadership: An overview, a study and a research agenda. *Small Group Research*, *37*, 522–539.

Schyns, B., Felfe, J., & Blank, H. (2007). The relationship between romance of leadership and the perception of transformational/charismatic leadership: A meta-analysis. *Applied Psychology: An International Review*, *56*, 505–527.

Shamir, B., House, R. J., & Arthur, M. B. (1993). The motivational effects of charismatic leadership: A self-concept based theory. *Organization Science*, *4*, 577–594.

Stock, R. (2003). *Der Zusammenhang zwischen Mitarbeiter- und Kundenzufriedenheit: Direkte, indirekte und moderierende Effekte*. Wiesbaden, Germany: Deutscher Universitäts-Verlag.

Tartler, K., Goihl, K., Kroeger, M., & Felfe, J. (2003). Zum Nutzen zusätzlicher Selbsteinschätzung bei der Beurteilung des Führungsverhaltens. *Zeitschrift für Personalpsychologie*, *2*, 13–21.

Van Breukelen, W., Konst, D., & van der Vlist, R. (2002). Effects of LMX and differential treatment on work unit commitment. *Psychological Reports*, *91*, 220–230.

EUROPEAN JOURNAL OF WORK AND
ORGANIZATIONAL PSYCHOLOGY
2010, 19 (3), 304–332

Ψ Psychology Press
Taylor & Francis Group

Do they [all] see my true self? Leader's relational authenticity and followers' assessments of transformational leadership

Matthias Spitzmuller and Remus Ilies

The Eli Broad Graduate School of Management, Michigan State University, East Lansing, MI, USA

Responding to calls for a more positive and holistic perspective on leadership, Gardner, Avolio, Luthans, May, and Walumbwa (2005), Ilies, Morgeson, and Nahrgang (2005), and Luthans and Avolio (2003) have discussed the concept of authentic leadership. However, up to this point, little is known on how leader authenticity influences leader relationships with followers. Consistent with the overall theme of this special issue, we seek to fill this gap by investigating empirically how leader authenticity predicts transformational leadership behaviours. Specifically, we focus on relational authenticity as a component of authenticity because it has been argued to be particularly salient for interpersonal relationships (Ilies et al., 2005). We further propose that leader authenticity is associated with a greater convergence of followers' perceptions of transformational leadership behaviours. Finally, we predict that not all group members will be influenced by leader authenticity to the same extent. Instead, we hypothesize and find that more critical group members are especially likely to be positively influenced by leader authenticity.

Keywords: Authentic leadership; Leader-follower relationships; Transformational leadership.

Correspondence should be addressed to Matthias Spitzmuller, The Eli Broad Graduate School of Management, Michigan State University, N475 North Business Complex, East Lansing, Michigan 48824-1122, USA. E-mail: spitzmuller@bus.msu.edu

http://www.psypress.com/ejwop   DOI: 10.1080/13594320902754040

Then wear the gold hat, if that will move her;
If you can bounce high, bounce for her too,
Till she cry "Lover, gold-hatted, high-bouncing lover,
I must have you!" (F. Scott Fitzgerald, *The Great Gatsby*, 1925)

Scott Fitzgerald's famous quote illustrates both the temptations and risks associated with inauthentic behaviour, illustrated by the tragic life and death of Jack Gatsby, the protagonist in Fitzgerald's most well-known novel. Gatsby's desperate wish to turn himself into a well-respected member of the elite East Coast society results in the corruption of his character and preludes his tragic death at the end of the novel.

Moral issues such as those illustrated in Fitzgerald's novel have never been more relevant than today: One of the most severe economic crisis is unravelling in front of us, and a series of corporate scandals over the past decade in firms such as Enron, WorldCom, Siemens, and Samsung have shocked societies around the globe and have lead to a renewed interest in incorruptible behaviour and leadership. Put differently, recent societal developments have called for leaders capable of producing sustainable economic performance, that is, ethical corporate behaviour which reflects the interests of all stakeholders of corporations: employees, the general public, shareholders, suppliers, and customers. At the forefront of this development has been a revived interest in research on authentic leadership where leaders express their true selves in order to build enduring, value-based relationships.

In order to understand the importance of authenticity for ethically responsible leadership, it is instructive to review factors which explain why people engage in unethical behaviour. Previous research indicates that there are two primary factors that induce unethical behaviour. First, individuals have a general disposition towards morally responsible/irresponsible behaviour, also referred to as moral identity (Aquino & Reed, 2002). Second, other evidence suggests that some individuals can also be overwhelmed by the power of situations (Bandura, 1986) such that even individuals with high moral standards can be corrupted by prevailing corporate norms, reward mechanisms, or simply by the fear of losing their jobs in the future. For managers in organizations, situational factors exert a considerable pressure to maximize profitability: Managers are largely compensated by the performance of the organizational unit or division which they lead, creating a strong incentive to reach performance goals, even in adverse conditions. This pressure is amplified by the fact that managers' actions have important consequences for the job securities, salaries, and careers of all their subordinates. Hence, there are strong situational forces which promote potentially unethical behaviours. To summarize, unethical behaviour is generally a function of individual differences, situational factors, or a combination of both. The pressure to engage in potentially unethical behaviour is higher for managerial positions than for other employees.

We contend in this article that authentic leadership[1] assumes a key role in defining leaders' ethical behaviour in the workplace. For authentic leaders, excellence of character or virtue takes centre stage (Ilies et al., 2005). Since authentic leaders are deeply aware of their values, virtues, and belief systems, it is unlikely that situational forces will undermine the integrity of authentic leaders. Authentic leaders continuously reflect on whether their actions are consistent with their selves, ensuring that their virtues take precedence over external influence processes, and not vice versa. Restated, the introspective nature of authentic leadership ensures moral integrity and reduces individual corruptibility, both of which have important consequences for the well-being of leaders and their followers in organizations, as well as for sustainable corporate behaviour.

The increased interest in authentic leadership is part of a larger shift in psychology and in the organization sciences to focus on positive organizational phenomena leading to enhanced human well-being. Research in psychology has been criticized for overly focusing on the pathological nature of the human enterprise (Seligman, 1999). In order to counter this often-maligned tendency, a group of scholars in psychology and organization sciences has shifted its focus away from human malfunctioning towards investigations into "the best of the human condition" (Cameron, Dutton, & Quinn, 2003, p. 4). Consistent with this general idea, Frederickson challenged individuals in organizations to cultivate "positive emotions in themselves and others, not as end-states in themselves, but as a means to achieving individual and organizational transformation and optimal functioning over time" (2003, p. 164). Interestingly, this idea had already been reflected in research on leadership from its early beginnings, starting with the work of Weber (1946), Barnard (1968), and Selznick (1984). Unfortunately, however, subsequent research on leadership largely ignored this positive focus, conceptualizing performance-enhancing effects of leadership as a sine qua non (cf. Judge & Piccolo, 2004). Calling for a reorientation of leadership research, Podolny, Khurana, and Hill-Popper

---

[1]We emphasize at this point that our article discusses the effect of leader authenticity on transformational leadership, and not the effect of authentic leadership on transformational leadership. We further note, however, that authentic individuals can be expected to be more authentic in their leadership style, which is why we discuss our study in the context of authentic leadership theory. Extant research has rarely measured authentic leadership as a social influence process between leaders and followers. Instead, most of the previous articles on this topic were either conceptual, or used the existing measure on authenticity developed by Kernis (2003). The study conducted by Walumbwa, Avolio, Gardner, Wernsing, and Peterson (2008) is a noteworthy exception, but also falls short of capturing the social influence processes of leadership occurring at different levels in groups and organizations.

(2005) argued that this focus had been unduly narrow. They contended that "we need to assess the importance of leadership in terms of its ability to infuse purpose and meaning into the organizational experience" (p. 5).

Responding to calls for a more positive and holistic perspective on leadership (e.g., Podolny et al., 2005), Gardner, Avolio, Luthans, May, and Walumbwa (2005), Ilies, Morgeson, and Nahrgang (2005), and Luthans and Avolio (2003) have discussed the concept of authentic leadership, which has been conceptualized as the essence of all positive approaches to leadership (Luthans & Avolio, 2003; May, Chan, Hodges, & Avolio, 2003) and as a root concept for other positive leadership behaviours, such as charismatic or transformational leadership (see Avolio & Gardner, 2005; Luthans & Avolio, 2003). The notion of a root concept implies that authenticity is a necessary, but not sufficient condition for other positive leadership approaches, such as transformational leadership or servant leadership.

Given the recent introduction of the construct into the research domain, it is not surprising that research on authenticity and leader relationships is still in its nascent stages. As such, it is imperative for the research domain to reach consensus on definitional issues and to identify the nomological network of authentic leadership in order to lay the foundation for subsequent research. Avolio and Gardner (2005) and Cooper, Scandura, and Schriesheim (2005) called for additional research investigating the convergent and discriminant validities of authentic leadership, relative to other leadership constructs. Specifically, Avolio and Gardner suggested that research should clarify potential overlaps with transformational leadership, ethical leadership, spiritual leadership, or servant leadership theory. In a similar vein, Cooper et al. suggested that the multidimensionality of the authentic leadership construct necessitates a closer investigation of relationships of subscales of authentic leadership with relevant criteria. Conceptually, Gardner et al. (2005) posited positive relationships between authentic leadership and follower trust in the leader, engagement, and well-being. To date, however, the positive influence of authentic leadership on leadership relationships has not been documented empirically.

Consistent with the overall theme of this special issue, we seek to fill these gaps by investigating empirically how leader authenticity predicts followers' perceptions reflective of their relationship with the leader. Specifically, we focus on relational authenticity as a subdimension of authenticity because it has been argued to be particularly salient for interpersonal relationships (Ilies et al., 2005). Goldman and Kernis (2002) described relational authenticity as "involving valuing and achieving openness and truthfulness in one's close relationships ... and the development of mutual intimacy and trust" (p. 19). Based on this definition, Ilies et al. (2005) proposed that leaders with a relational authenticity orientation will strive for open and truthful relationships with their followers and such orientation will have a number of positive outcomes. As such, relationally authentic leaders can be expected to create higher levels of follower confidence in their values, which will eventually also result in higher levels of unconditional trust between authentic leaders and their followers. Moreover, Ilies et al. proposed that leader authenticity will lead to higher levels of identification with leaders. Consistent with these predictions and responding to Cooper et al.'s (2005) call for additional research investigating the nomological network of (subcomponents of) leader authenticity, we hypothesize that relational authenticity is associated with more favourable assessments of leader's transformational leadership behaviour. More specifically, we predict that relational authenticity will be most strongly associated with individualized consideration, one of four frequently used subcomponents of the transformational leadership construct (Bass & Avolio, 1995). We expect this because, compared to the other three subscales measuring transformational leadership, individualized consideration has a clear relational aspect and specifically focuses on the relationship between leader and follower (i.e., "this leader treats me as an individual rather than just as a member of a group").

Moreover, we will develop predictions on how leader authenticity will influence levels of agreement in and the distribution of followers' perceptions of transformational leadership. We argue that the genuine and value-based behaviour of authentic leaders will lead to a consistent leadership style across situations and time. This will in turn be reflected in followers' ratings of transformational leadership behaviours which will converge to a greater extent, compared to follower ratings of less authentic leaders. We further predict that leader authenticity does not influence all followers to the same extent. We argue that the most critical followers— followers who are especially sensitive to inconsistencies in leader behaviours—will be influenced more strongly than less critical followers. Put differently, leader authenticity will lead to a particularly strong increase in how critical followers rate transformational leadership behaviours of their supervisors, compared to how less critical followers rate their supervisors on transformational leadership behaviours.

HYPOTHESIS DEVELOPMENT

Authentic leadership—an emerging field of research

Psychological research has recognized the importance of authenticity for individual well-being and for enduring social relationships for a long time (Erickson, 1995; Rogers, 1959), conceptualizing authenticity as the "development of fully functioning or self actualized persons" (Avolio & Gardner, 2005, p. 319). Taking a humanistic psychological approach, Maslow (1968) suggested that satisfying higher order needs is a precondition to develop authenticity. Conversely, Seeman (1960) argued that a lack of authenticity constitutes excessive plasticity, that is, individuals' tendencies to give in to social expectations surrounding them. By drawing on the work of Erickson (1995), Avolio and Gardner (2005) and Ilies et al. (2005) both emphasized the introspective, self-referential nature of authenticity, describing the core of authentic behaviour as "existing wholly by the laws of its own being" (Erickson, 1995, p. 320).

The transfer of humanistic writings on authenticity to leadership research has occurred only very recently: Although early writings on organizational leadership conceptualized leadership as a social influence process which creates meaning for individuals in an organizational context (Barnard, 1968; Weber, 1946), it is only very recently that researchers have started to rediscover this holistic approach to leadership research (Podolny et al., 2005). For a long time, leadership has merely been considered a vehicle to maximizing economic performance in groups and organizations. Despite mixed findings on the relationship of leadership to economic performance, there has been a widespread belief among both practitioners and scholars in the salvationary power of leaders in organizations (Hackman & Wageman, 2005). However, an unprecedented hike in corporate scandals coupled with disappointing and often unethical performances of top executives has lead to a shift in our perspective on leadership, emphasizing the creation of long-lasting, value-based relationships among employees and their supervisors. Consistent with this general idea, Luthans and Avolio (2003) described authentic leadership as a process in which positive leader capacities and a highly developed organizational context combine to positively influence self-awareness and personal development for both leader and followers. Specifically, they defined authentic leaders as follows:

> The authentic leader is confident, hopeful, optimistic, resilient, moral/ethical, future-oriented, and gives priority to developing associates to be leaders. The authentic leader is true to him/herself and the exhibited behaviour positively transforms or develops associates into leaders themselves. (p. 243).

Avolio, Luthans, and Walumbwa (2004) offered a similar definition, emphasizing high degrees of self-awareness, optimism and self-efficacy as integral components of authentic leadership. In addition, Avolio et al. emphasized that authentic leaders have high moral standards and that they are generally perceived as being true to themselves in their values, strengths, social interactions, and relationships. In an effort to summarize these definitions, Cooper et al. (2005) viewed authentic leadership as multifaceted, containing elements from "diverse domains—traits, states, behaviours, contexts, or attributions" (p. 478).

Multicomponent models of authentic leadership

In order to lay the ground for our subsequent discussion of how authenticity in leaders predicts transformational leadership, we next discuss what the two definitions mentioned earlier imply about authentic leaders in organizations. In doing so, we draw on conceptual work by Avolio and Gardner (2005), Cooper et al. (2005), Gardner et al. (2005), and Ilies et al. (2005), whose contributions to a special issue in *Leadership Quarterly* in 2005 have helped advance our understanding of authentic leadership. In the subsequent discussion, it will become clear that the introspective nature of authentic leadership is an important prerequisite for the positive, enduring, and mutually empowering social relationships which transformational leaders share with their followers.

Providing the introduction to the aforementioned special issue in *Leadership Quarterly*, Avolio and Gardner (2005) described components of authentic leadership on a general level, that is, in relation to other leadership processes and perspectives, whereas Gardner et al. (2005) and Ilies et al. (2005) took a conceptually driven approach by building on the four components of authenticity developed by Goldman and Kernis (2002) and Kernis (2003). We integrate these approaches to authentic leadership in the following section of this article, emphasizing their commonalities.

Gardner et al. (2005) and Ilies et al. (2005) proposed a conceptually driven four-component model of authentic leadership that includes self-awareness, unbiased processing, authentic behaviour/acting, and authentic relational orientation. They posited that *self-awareness* refers to leader's awareness of and trust in his/her personal characteristics, values, motives, feelings, and cognitions. Similarly, according to Avolio and Gardner (2005), authentic leaders are highly aware of their strengths and weaknesses, values and beliefs; they are confident, optimistic, hopeful, and resilient. Taken together, these characteristics provide valuable psychological capital authentic leaders can draw on to develop themselves and associates in organizations.

Unbiased processing (Ilies et al., 2005), or balanced processing (Gardner et al., 2005) refers to how authentic leaders process self-relevant information, which involves "not denying, distorting, exaggerating, or ignoring private knowledge, internal experiences, and externally based information" (Kernis, 2003, p. 14). Consistent with this idea, Avolio and Gardner (2005) proposed that authentic leaders can be expected to have a positive moral perspective, arguing that the introspective nature of authentic individuals ensures a constant reflection on the rightness of their doings.

According to Ilies et al. (2005) and Gardner et al. (2005), *authentic behaviour* refers to the tendency of authentic leaders to act based on values, personal preferences, and needs. Avolio and Gardner (2005) argued that authentic leaders engage in self-regulating behaviours in which they use internally developed standards to align values with their intentions and actions. By ensuring this consistency in values, intentions, and actions, authentic leaders' behaviour becomes more predictable. At the same time, they can be expected to pursue long-term goals consistent with their values. By aligning personal resources with long-term goals that have been articulated based on deeply rooted personal values, authentic leaders create a compelling vision for themselves and their social environment. This long-term focus provides a strong and reliable orientation for associates in organizations where short-term goals often take precedence over long-term goals. Put differently, authentic behaviour refers to the immunity of personal actions to social and environmental demands and expectations.

Finally, *authentic relational orientation* refers to the desire of authentic leaders to strive for open and truthful relationships (Ilies et al., 2005). A prerequisite for such relationships is the disclosure of both positive and negative aspects of the self to other individuals in the organization. This will in turn facilitate the development of enduring and value-based relationships among authentic leaders and associates in an organization as self- and other-perspectives on authentic leaders are more likely to converge (Avolio & Gardner, 2005). As such, interpersonal relationships between authentic leaders and their associates will be characterized by less conflict. Also, relationships can be expected to be more stable as authentic leaders demonstrate consistent behaviours across situations and contexts. In general, associates are more likely to identify with authentic leaders: Authentic leaders' transparent decision making, confidence, and optimism will increase the identification of associates with authentic leaders as well as with the organization as a whole. Moreover, by providing transparent, value-driven leadership processes, followers themselves are stimulated to reflect on their values, intentions, and actions. As such, authentic leadership has a strong developmental component for both leaders and followers.

From a construct validation perspective, the four-component model suggested by Gardner et al. (2005) and Ilies et al. (2005) offers the noteworthy advantage that it builds on a validated measure of authenticity suggested by Goldman and Kernis (2002) and Kernis (2003). As such, the approaches by Gardner et al. and Ilies et al. established clear construct boundaries, which are important for our discussion of the relationship between authentic leadership and transformational leadership, two related yet distinct leadership processes. Also, the four-component model suggested by Gardner et al. and Ilies et al. points to the multidimensional character of authentic leadership. In fact, the multidimensional character of authentic leadership has also been emphasized by other researchers: For example, Cooper et al. (2005) pointed out that authentic leadership includes diverse elements such as traits, states, behaviours, contexts, and attributes. Also, Eagly (2005) discussed how authentic behaviour does not always have to lead to relational authenticity with followers. Consequently, for our discussion of the relationship of authentic leadership and perceptions of transformational leadership, besides predicting a link between general authenticity and transformational leadership behaviours, we will make component-specific predictions, focusing on relational authenticity as the component of authentic leadership that has the strongest relevance for interpersonal relationships and, as such, for perceptions of transformational leadership.

Transformational leadership

Based on his examination of political leaders, Burns (1978) introduced the concepts of transformational leadership and transactional leadership as two contrasting leadership styles. Burns posited that the main difference in the two leadership approaches lies in what leaders and followers have to offer to each other: leaders relying on a transformational leadership style focus on higher order needs by offering a purpose that transcends short-term goals (Conger & Kanungo, 1998; Judge & Piccolo, 2004). Transactional leaders, on the other hand, motivate followers by offering resources for follower contributions in a simple exchange. Following the introduction of transformational leadership into research on leadership, the concept has been revised several times. For example, Bass (1985) emphasized that transactional and transformational leadership are not opposite ends of one continuum, but rather two separate leadership processes which can reside within one leader. The most recent versions of transformational leadership theory include four dimensions: inspirational motivation, idealized influence, individual consideration, and intellectual stimulation (Bass & Avolio, 1995; Judge & Piccolo, 2004). According to Bass (1997), the facet inspirational motivation refers to the tendency of transformational leaders to articulate an appealing vision of the future and to provide encouragement and meaning for followers. Idealized influence reflects the tendency of transformational leaders to present their most important values and to emphasize a strong, common purpose. As a consequence, such leaders are admired as role models who generate pride in their group or organization. Inspirational motivation has been found to be strongly correlated with idealized influence. Due to their high intercorrelations, Bass (1998) suggested combining the two dimensions idealized influence and inspirational motivation into one measure of charisma. The facet individualized consideration refers to the tendency of transformational leaders to treat followers as unique individuals, with distinct needs, values, abilities, and aspirations (Bass, 1997). Finally, intellectual stimulation refers to the tendency of transformational leaders to question old assumptions and to simulate in others new perspectives and ways of doing things (Bass, 1997).

Transformational leadership and authentic leadership—two different yet related leadership processes

Avolio and Gardner (2005) have provided a useful discussion of the commonalities and differences between the two leadership processes. They note that both authentic leaders and transformational leaders are optimistic and hopeful. They have a strong developmental orientation both for themselves and for their followers. Both of them motivate followers with a long-term vision that provides a meaningful purpose beyond short-term goals. Their developmental orientation and focus on a motivating vision which casts a positive light on the future facilitate the development of enduring interpersonal relationships in which followers identify strongly with the personality of the leader.

However, Avolio and Gardner (2005) also discussed noteworthy differences between the two leadership processes: Most importantly, authentic leadership does not have to be charismatic. As mentioned previously, authentic leadership also engenders high standards of moral conduct and a strong vision for the future, but authentic leaders do not necessarily rely on the same means with which they convey their belief in their values and vision of the future to followers. Transformational leaders have been found to stimulate enthusiasm among followers by using symbolic actions and persuasive language (Bass, 1998; Bono & Judge, 2004), whereas authentic leaders are more inclined to use a level-headed leadership style with a strong focus on the actual content of the message, and a lesser focus on the means with which this message is conveyed to followers. They are "anchored by their own deep sense of self" (Avolio & Gardner, 2005, p. 329). As such, authentic leaders rely less on rhetoric in their interactions with followers. Overall, authentic leadership can be viewed as a more generic leadership process which functions as a "root construct" for other positive leadership processes such as transformational leadership (Avolio & Gardner, 2005). Authentic leadership theory assumes that, over time, leaders can only be truly transformational if they act in accord with their inner selves, that is, if they have a high degree of self-awareness of what they stand for as leaders and an authentic relational orientation. If this was not the case, then followers will eventually perceive leader behaviour as manipulative. Accordingly, we can view authentic leadership and transformational leadership as related, yet conceptually distinct constructs.

The influence of leader authenticity on perceptions of transformational leadership

In their meta-analysis on personality and transactional and transformational leadership, Bono and Judge (2004) suggested that future research should also investigate nondispositional antecedents of transformational leadership due to rather weak associations between personality traits and transformational leadership. Even though authenticity has a dispositional component, research on leader authenticity suggests that it is also socially defined. For example, Maslow (1968) emphasized the dynamic nature of authenticity by proposing that the satisfaction of higher order needs is a prerequisite for the discovery of one's true inner nature. In a similar vein, Avolio and Gardner (2005) emphasized the malleable nature of authentic leadership in their introductory article to a special issue on authentic leadership in *Leadership Quarterly*. In the same *Leadership Quarterly* special issue, Shamir and Eilam (2005) and Sparrowe (2005) further discussed the process in which leader authenticity can develop and unfold.

We first present arguments supporting a positive relationship between leader authenticity (as a composite construct) and transformational leadership. Next, we develop component-specific arguments and hypotheses relating the four components of authenticity to perceptions of transformational leadership. Even though the four facets of transformational leadership have been found to be strongly correlated, it is important to note that they represent related, yet distinct aspects of leadership processes (Bass, 1998). Accordingly, we map our predictions to individual facets of transformational leadership. For component specific predictions for leader authenticity, we rely on the multicomponent model of authentic leadership suggested by Ilies et al. (2005). Consistent with the overall topic of this special issue, we continue with a discussion of how leader authenticity influences the agreement of follower ratings of leaders' transformational leadership behaviour, arguing that authenticity makes leader behaviour more predictable, which will in turn lead to more consistent follower ratings of leadership behaviours. In a similar vein, we also predict that the most critical group members are especially likely to be positively influenced by leader authenticity.

We consider three of the four facets of transformational leadership to be particularly responsive to leader authenticity: inspirational motivation, idealized influence, and individualized consideration. These three facets all reflect transformational leaders' capacity to establish enduring and empowering relationships with their followers, which is why we expect these facets to be particularly relevant to leader authenticity. Intellectual stimulation, on the other hand, seeks to stimulate creativity in followers (Judge & Piccolo, 2004) in a promotive, task-focused manner. Bass (1995) noted that "the knowledge, skills, and abilities that may help one become more intellectually stimulating may be unconnected to one's individualized consideration" (p. 473). As a consequence, intellectual stimulation focuses less on the development of a strong relationship between leader and follower when compared to the other three facets of transformational leadership. Moreover, leader authenticity does not primarily target innovative behaviour or creativity. Instead, it emphasizes the consistent, value-based enactment of one's true inner self. As such, leader authenticity seeks to establish behavioural consistency, whereas intellectual stimulation seeks to provide behavioural variation. Overall, we see intellectual stimulation conceptually as only remotely connected to leader authenticity, which is why we do not formulate hypotheses for these relationships.

As authentic leaders seek to establish truthful relationships with followers, they can be expected to develop unique relationships with each follower, which will in turn influence follower perceptions of individualized consideration. Similarly, authentic leaders' strong belief in their values coupled with their high self-esteem will exert a strong motivating influence on followers, which we expect to lead to higher ratings of inspirational motivation. Finally, we expect that the high levels of integrity of authentic leaders as well as the developmental character of relationships between authentic leaders and their followers will be positively associated with perceptions of idealized influence.

H1: Leader authenticity will positively influence follower perceptions of individualized consideration, inspirational motivation, and idealized influence.

Consistent with the overall theme of this special issue, we chose to narrow our focus on relational authenticity as the one component of leader authenticity which is most relevant to our understanding of leader–follower relationships. In fact, all three other components of authenticity are self-directed: Self-awareness has the strongest introspective focus, referring to the degree to which individuals are aware of their values, beliefs, and virtues. Unbiased processing refers to the processing of self-relevant information, implying the absence of biased judgement in evaluating self-relevant information. As a cognitive process, the focus of unbiased processing is, by definition, introspective. Authentic behaviour has a stronger action orientation than the two previously discussed facets of authenticity, referring to whether "people act in accord with their true selves" (Kernis, 2003, p. 14). Despite its strong behavioural orientation, however, authentic behaviour also has a strong introspective focus: Ilies et al. (2005) pointed out that authentic behaviour is associated with the experience of greater flow and intrinsic motivation at work, which constitute introspective processes. Conversely, authentic relational orientation can be viewed as the facet of authenticity which translates the introspective character of self-awareness, unbiased processing, and authentic behaviour into positive relationships with followers which are characterized by high levels of trust (Ilies et al., 2005). For example, Ilies et al. proposed that leaders with an authentic relational orientation have more positive, trusting relationships with followers. Restated, we chose to focus on relational authenticity as this is the facet of authenticity that has the strongest relational orientation. Given the strong relational focus of three of the four facets of transformational leadership, we hypothesize a particularly strong relationship between relational authenticity in leaders and transformational leadership. As Ilies et al. have pointed out, relational authenticity is not independent of the other three components of authenticity. Hence, we investigate the relationship of the other three components of leader authenticity (self-awareness, unbiased processing, and authentic behaviour/actions) with transformational leadership on an exploratory basis.

Avolio and Gardner (2005) and Ilies et al. (2005) proposed that authentic leaders strive for open and truthful relationships in which they are willing to disclose both positive and negative aspects of their selves. As authentic leaders act based on their convictions and beliefs, their interpersonal behaviour is characterized by high levels of integrity and truthfulness, which will in turn reflect on their relationship with followers such that they will have more open and genuine relationships with their followers, compared to less authentic leaders. Also, Avolio and Gardner (2005) made a compelling case for the self-referential nature of authenticity. Hence, we expect that the belief system of authentic leaders will be largely unaffected by changes in corporate policies or environmental changes. In fact, authentic leaders' norms, beliefs, and values will not have to be (re-)negotiated with followers in different social situations and environments, which will function as a strong stabilizer for the interpersonal relationships of authentic leaders and their followers. Consistent with this idea, we expect that the nature of the relationship between authentic leaders and their followers will be of a stable, enduring nature. We further expect that followers will perceive the self-disclosure of both positive and negative information about their leader as a genuine attempt to develop an open, trusting relationship, which will give followers the feeling to have a unique, mutually empowering relationship with their leader. Therefore, we predict that an authentic relational orientation will be associated with higher follower ratings of individualized consideration.

H2:   Leader authenticity–relational orientation will positively influence follower perceptions of individualized consideration.

Due to the self-referential nature of authenticity, authentic leaders derive any legitimization for their actions from within themselves (Erickson, 1995). Avolio and Gardner (2005) pointed out that this self-referential nature of authenticity allows authentic leaders to "operate as a social force in its own right that is actively involved in the social construction of reality" (p. 320).

As such, authentic leaders will have a strong influence on their social environment: Their values and objectives do not merely reflect the current status quo in the organization, but rather a strong and well-reflected belief system that fosters constructive thinking, personal development, and learning (Ilies et al., 2005). It is important to note that these developmental consequences do not only occur for authentic leaders. Based on the modelling of their leader, followers of authentic leaders will also be challenged to discover their true inner selves and to create positive and enduring social relationships at work. We propose that the mutual learning opportunities which authentic leadership creates for both the leader himself/ herself and his/her followers will lead to positive leader follower relationships with a strong motivational appeal.

Ilies et al. summarized the motivating influence of authentic leaders on followers, positing that authentic leaders enhance "followers' organizational-derived self-concept by influencing followers' personal identification with the leaders" (p. 383). Consistent with our arguments and Ilies et al., we predict that leader authenticity–relational orientation will be positively related to follower perceptions of inspirational motivation.

H3: Leader authenticity–relational orientation will positively influence follower perceptions of inspirational motivation.

Consistent with our previous arguments, authentic leaders display their conviction and emphasize trust in interpersonal relationships. Authentic leaders have high standards of integrity, which will manifest themselves in interpersonal relationships through openness and truthfulness. Interestingly, all of these elements of relational authenticity are consistent with common definitions of idealized influence. For example, Bass (1997, p. 132) noted that idealized influence implies that leaders "display conviction; emphasize trust; take stands on difficult issues; present their most important values; and emphasize the importance of purpose, commitment, and the ethical consequences of decisions". We view all of these behaviours as consistent with relational leader authenticity as described previously.

H4: Leader authenticity–relational orientation will positively influence follower perceptions of idealized influence.

Traditionally, transformational leadership has been discussed as a universal approach to leadership, suggesting that transformational leaders use the same leadership principles irrespective of the context in which they operate. For example, Bass (1997) argued that the transformational leadership paradigm transcends organizational and national boundaries. Other researchers, however, emphasized that transformational leadership should best be viewed as a leadership approach according to which leaders are sensitive to the specific needs, values, abilities, and backgrounds of different followers in different social situations and environments. This idea portrays transformational leadership as an integrated leadership approach, reflecting the unique demands of the situation and followers. Consistent with this perspective, Deluga (1992) suggested that the positive performance consequences of transformational leadership can be explained by an improved quality in the individualized dyadic relationship between a subordinate and leader. A similar finding has been reported by Wang, Law, Hackett, Wang, and Chen (2005).

Among the four facets of transformational leadership commonly discussed in the literature (idealized influence, inspirational motivation, individualized consideration, and intellectual stimulation), the facet individualized consideration best reflects this view of transformational leadership as an integrated approach to leadership. For example, Bass (1997) noted that, in individualized consideration, "leaders deal with others as individuals; consider their individual needs, abilities, and aspirations; listen attentively; further their development; advise; teach; and coach" (p. 133). Similarly, Bass (1995) contended that "while charisma (or idealized influence) is the largest component in transformational leadership, other components are important theoretically and practically as they deal with different behaviours, attributions, and effects such as individualized consideration and intellectual stimulation. The abusive, abrasive, charismatic leader does not exhibit the same amount of individualized consideration as does the warm, socially concerned charismatic" (p. 473).

These two statements portray individualized consideration as related to relational authenticity, both of which emphasize open, truthful relationships among leader and followers characterized by high levels of interpersonal trust. Restated, it is the relationally authentic character of leaders which results into warm, socially charismatic leaders. This aspect of individualized consideration also becomes apparent when studying the individual items of the construct, such as "my manager provides advice to those who need it", reflecting a desire to consider followers individually based on their strengths, abilities, and backgrounds. Consistent with these arguments, we expect that the relationship between authentic relational orientation and individualized consideration will be stronger than with the other two relevant facets of transformational leadership (idealized influence and inspirational motivation).

H5: Leader authenticity—relational orientation will be more strongly associated with individualized consideration than with the other two interpersonal facets of transformational leadership (idealized influence and inspirational motivation).

A long tradition of research in psychology in general and in interactional psychology in particular has discussed the extent to which individual behaviour is a function of personality or the respective situation in which the individual is acting (Lewin, 1936; Schneider, 1983). In fact, Schneider (1983, p. 5) argued that the major question facing interactional psychologists is "whether behaviour is the result of proactivity or passivity on the part of the behaver". At this point, it is important to reiterate that authentic leaders operate as a social force in its own right. Hence, they are relatively immune against situational, environmental influences on their behaviours. They are influenced more strongly by internal forces originating in their personality and belief system, whereas less authentic leaders can be expected to be more strongly influenced by strong situations, such as reward mechanisms, organizational norms, task characteristics, or their social environments (Tett & Burnett, 2003). Authentic leaders have well-reflected norms, values, and beliefs, which guide their behaviour in interpersonal relationships. Put differently, the introspective nature of authenticity ensures consistent behaviour over time and across situations. An important effect of this behavioural stability is that once followers are aware of leaders' values and beliefs, leader behaviour becomes more predictable and understandable. Authentic leaders are consistently reliable, trustworthy, and genuine, which is why we expect that followers' assessment of individualized consideration will converge to a larger extent when compared with less authentic leaders. Even though we do not predict a similar association between leader relational authenticity and the other facets of transformational leadership, we investigate these relationships on an exploratory basis, expecting smaller, but positive bivariate correlations.

H6: Followers will demonstrate less discrepancy in their assessments of individualized consideration of relationally authentic leaders than in their assessments of individualized consideration of relationally inauthentic leaders.

We expect that not all group members are equally responsive to the positive effect of leader authenticity. Instead, we predict that followers who rate their leaders as least effective in their transformational leadership behaviour are most likely to be influenced by leader authenticity. Consistent with our previous arguments, we focus again on specific aspects of authenticity and transformational leadership, that is, we focus on the relationship of leader relational authenticity and individualized consideration, as rated by the group member who rated his/her leader lowest on this facet.

Before presenting arguments in support of this prediction, however, we discuss reasons which explain why ratings of transformational leadership behaviours diverge across followers. It is important to note that divergent ratings across followers cannot necessarily be explained by the same variables that are generally associated with higher ratings in transformational leadership behaviour, such as dispositional variables (Bono & Judge, 2004), demographics (Eagly, Johannesen-Schmidt, & Engen, 2003), or contextual variables (Bommer, Rubin, & Baldwin, 2004). For example, even though extraverted leaders are generally viewed as more transformational in their leadership behaviour by followers, their extraversion cannot explain who among their followers will view them as above average or below average in their transformational leadership behaviours, when compared to the average rating in the respective work group. Instead, in order to explain the variance in transformational leadership ratings across subordinates, we have to investigate how different subordinates form their judgements of their leaders' transformational leadership behaviours.

We propose that two judgemental biases can explain why some followers rate their leaders' transformational leadership behaviour lower than other subordinates. First, some individuals are generally critical of their environment and individuals with whom they interact. This general tendency of individuals to give consistently low ratings has been termed severity bias (Bass, 1956; Bernardin & Beatty, 1984). Even though it is unclear what actually causes severity bias in individuals, it is likely that such individuals pay special attention to negative characteristics of an object or a person who they are supposed to rate, assigning them larger weight than they do to positive characteristics of the object or person. For example, critical individuals can be expected to be particularly attentive to unjust and inconsistent leader behaviours. We assert, however, that relationally authentic leaders are relatively immune against severity bias: Relationally authentic leaders are "transparent in linking inner desires, expectations, and values to the way [they] behave every day, in each and every interaction" (May et al., 2003, p. 248). As such, their actions are internally consistent and guided by transparent values. Less critical followers can be expected to excuse occasional inconsistencies in leader behaviours by focusing on the positive attributes and behaviours of their leader, whereas more critical followers will react particularly sensitive to such deviations from their expectations. Consistent with these arguments, relationally authentic leaders can also be expected to approach social situations with high levels of integrity. As such, it is less likely that they take decisions that could be viewed as giving an unfair advantage to some group members. Instead, relationally authentic leaders adopt different angles before taking decisions in order to take into consideration different stakeholder needs (May et al., 2003). Once a decision is taken, relationally authentic leaders will communicate this decision openly to their subordinates, ensuring a high degree of acceptance of this decision among group members, particularly among the most critical group members.

A second potential reason for low ratings of transformational leadership may be a general disapproval of the leader. Restated, followers categorize their leader as "bad", as "unfair", or as "incompetent". Categorization processes are a well-known decision-making bias (Ilgen & Feldman, 1983; Rosch, 1978)—they have the interesting consequence that subsequent judgements which include a more fine-grained description of the object or person are biased towards the general characteristic of that category. For example, if followers have categorized their leader as "bad", it is likely that their judgements of their leader's transformational leadership will be biased towards this negative overall impression. Again, we posit that relationally authentic leaders should be relatively immune against this judgemental bias. By adopting different angles in their thinking and by establishing open and truthful relationships with their followers, relationally authentic leaders challenge their followers to engage in critical thinking and to reconsider stereotypical assessments of their leadership capabilities. Consistent with this rationale, we predict that relational authenticity will be associated with a particularly strong increase in the lowest ratings of individualized consideration, across leaders.

H7: Relational authenticity will be associated with an increase in the lowest ratings (among a number of followers) of individualized consideration, across leaders, but not with an increase in the maximum ratings.

METHODS

We tested these hypotheses in a sample of 91 mid-level managers enrolled at a large Midwestern university in the United States. These managers were first asked to complete an authenticity survey and were then instructed to select some of their direct reports who would then complete a follower assessment of the transformational leadership behaviour of their respective supervisors. In order to ensure that respondents would still describe the transformational leadership behaviours of their respective supervisors accurately, we added a section to the introduction to the study in which we emphasized that the supervisor would only receive aggregate feedback on his/her ratings, that is, the supervisor is only going to get feedback on his/her leadership behaviour which does not allow any conclusions on how individual study participants rated him/her. Observer ratings were provided approximately 2 weeks after the self-ratings had been obtained. On average, we obtained 4.17 subordinate ratings for each leader. Leader authenticity was measured with a 45-item version of the authenticity inventory (Goldman & Kernis, 2001). The inventory has four subscales.

Self-awareness was measured with 12 items ($\alpha = .77$). A sample item is "For better or for worse I am aware of who I am". Unbiased processing was measured with 10 items ($\alpha = .73$). A sample item is "I am very uncomfortable considering my limitations and shortcomings" (reverse scored item). Authentic behaviour was measured with 11 items ($\alpha = .79$). A sample item is "I frequently pretend to enjoy something when in actuality I really don't" (reverse scored item). Authentic relational orientation was measured with 12 items ($\alpha = .72$). A sample item was "I want people who are close to me to understand my strengths." We also aggregated all individual items into one composite score for authenticity ($\alpha = .93$). A 5-point scale was used on which respondents indicated the extent to which they agreed with a given statement (1 = "strongly disagree", 2 = "disagree", 3 = "neither disagree or agree", 4 = "agree", and 5 = "strongly agree"). At this point, it is important to reiterate that we did not measure authentic leadership as a process. Instead, we used Goldman and Kernis's measure of psychological authenticity to assess leader authenticity.

The relevant transformational leadership were measured with 16 items taken from the MLQ (Avolio, Bass, & Jung, 1995). Idealized influence was measured with 8 items ($\alpha = .73$). Inspirational motivation was measured with 4 items ($\alpha = .73$). Individualized consideration was measured with 4 items ($\alpha = .72$). For completeness, we also measured intellectual stimulation; however, the scores on this facet had low reliability ($\alpha = .52$) and did not relate to authenticity. The MLQ-facets were measured on a 5-point frequency scale on which respondents indicated the frequency with which they engage in these activities (1 = "not at all", 2 = "once in a while", 3 = "sometimes", 4 = "fairly often", 5 = "frequently, if not always").

RESULTS

Table 1 contains descriptive statistics and correlations for all study measures. The correlations among the components of authenticity are moderately strong to strong, ranging from .41 to .80. The correlations among the (mean ratings of the) four facets of transformational leadership are large in magnitude, ranging from .61 to .82.

Hypothesis tests

Hypothesis 1 predicted that a composite score of leader authenticity (consisting of the four components self-awareness, unbiased processing, authentic behaviour, and authentic relational orientation) would positively predict follower perceptions of three facets of transformational leadership behaviours: individualized consideration, inspirational motivation, and

TABLE 1
Means, standard deviations, and intercorrelations among study variables

Variable	M	SD	1	2	3	4	5	6	7	8	9	10	11	12	13	14	15	16	17	18	19	20
1. Leader Authenticity–Composite	3.79	0.40	—																			
2. Leader Authenticity–Self-Awareness	4.00	0.46	.84	—																		
3. Leader Authenticity–Unbiased Processing	3.58	0.55	.80	.63	—																	
4. Leader Authenticity–Behaviour	3.67	0.52	.79	.53	.41	—																
5. Leader Authenticity–Relational Orientation	3.95	0.44	.80	.55	.48	.58	—															
6. Transformational Leadership–Inspirational Motivation (Mean)	4.12	0.41	.27	.23	.28	.09	.26	—														
7. Transformational Leadership–Idealized Influence (Mean)	4.02	0.41	.22	.16	.16	.11	.30	.82	—													
8. Transformational Leadership–Individualized Consideration (Mean)	3.90	0.51	.21	.21	.11	.06	.31	.69	.79	—												
9. Transformational Leadership–Intellectual Stimulation (Mean)	3.97	0.43	.20	.20	.20	.10	.16	.61	.71	.68	—											
10. Transformational Leadership–Inspirational Motivation (Min)	3.65	0.67	.29	.22	.30	.10	.24	.89	.73	.61	.46	—										
11. Transformational Leadership–Idealized Influence (Min)	3.52	0.62	.29	.21	.23	.18	.32	.71	.86	.70	.59	.76	—									
12. Transformational Leadership–Individualized Consideration (Min)	3.31	0.72	.28	.23	.20	.13	.35	.60	.67	.86	.53	.60	.72	—								
13. Transformational Leadership–Intellectual Stimulation (Min)	3.38	0.66	.19	.16	.20	.11	.16	.51	.59	.57	.81	.49	.68	.66	—							
14. Transformational Leadership–Inspirational Motivation (SD)	0.48	0.30	-.21	-.11	-.23	-.06	-.10	-.39	-.30	-.24	-.05	-.69	-.45	-.28	-.14	—						
15. Transformational Leadership–Idealized Influence (SD)	0.46	0.28	-.21	-.18	-.17	-.13	-.19	-.38	-.43	-.36	-.26	-.54	-.75	-.41	-.40	.59	—					

(continued)

TABLE 1
(Continued)

Variable	M	SD	1	2	3	4	5	6	7	8	9	10	11	12	13	14	15	16	17	18	19	20
16. Transformational Leadership–Individualized Consideration (SD)	0.56	0.27	-.24	-.21	-.20	-.09	-.30	-.24	-.21	-.34	-.09	-.30	-.32	-.65	-.26	.28	.33	—				
17. Transformational Leadership–Intellectual Stimulation (SD)	0.55	0.26	-.09	-.07	-.14	.04	-.14	-.14	-.22	-.18	-.32	-.24	-.40	-.34	-.66	.31	.48	.35	—			
18. Transformational Leadership–Inspirational Motivation (Max)	4.62	0.44	.20	.22	.15	.08	.19	.75	.62	.51	.56	.44	.35	.29	.29	.18	-.00	.00	.11	—		
19. Transformational Leadership–Idealized Influence (Max)	4.50	0.39	.12	.14	.07	.03	.17	.51	.68	.54	.53	.28	.28	.27	.20	.10	.22	.05	.11	.72	—	
20. Transformational Leadership–Individualized Consideration (Max)	4.48	0.49	.03	.08	-.03	-.03	.11	.52	.61	.77	.61	.35	.39	.41	.30	-.05	-.12	.21	.08	.61	.65	—
21. Transformational Leadership–Intellectual Stimulation (Max)	4.54	0.46	.13	.17	.08	.12	.05	.47	.54	.53	.75	.23	.27	.23	.33	.12	.02	.14	.25	.68	.67	.72

$*p < .05$, $**p < .01$. Values greater than .20 are statistically significant, $p < .05$. Values greater than .26 are statistically significant, $p < .01$. Mean values (Mean) represent averaged observer ratings for leaders; minimum values (Min) represent lowest observer ratings for leaders; standard deviation (SD) represent standard deviation of observations for leaders.

idealized influence. Hypothesis 1 was supported, as all bivariate correlations between the composite score of leader authenticity and the three relevant facets of transformational leadership were positive and statistically significant ($p < .05$), with correlations of .21 for individualized consideration, .22 for idealized influence, and .27 for inspirational motivation.

Hypothesis 2 predicted that leader relational authenticity would positively predict individualized consideration, which was again supported, $r = .31$, $p < .01$. Hypothesis 3 predicted that leader relational authenticity would positively predict inspirational motivation, which was supported, $r = .26$, $p < .05$. Hypothesis 4 predicted that leader relational authenticity would positively predict idealized influence, which was again supported, $r = .30$, $p < .01$.

Hypothesis 5 predicted that the correlation between leader relational authenticity and individualized consideration would be larger than the correlation between leader relational authenticity and the other two relevant facets of transformational leadership behaviour. Even though the nominal bivariate correlation between leader relational authenticity and individualized consideration was largest (.31, compared to .30 and .26 for idealized influence and inspirational motivation, respectively), the differences were smaller than expected and not significant with the given sample size such that Hypothesis 5 was not supported.

Hypothesis 6 predicted that followers will demonstrate less discrepancy in their assessments of individualized consideration of relationally authentic leaders than in their assessments of individualized consideration of relationally inauthentic leaders. In support of Hypothesis 6, we found a negative association between leader self-ratings of relational authenticity and the standard deviation of followers' ratings on individualized consideration, $r = -.30$, $p < .01$, and the negative association was maintained when controlling for the mean individualized consideration score in regression analysis (see Table 2). However, contrary to our expectation,

TABLE 2

Summary of hierarchical regression analysis for leader authenticity–relational orientation predicting the standard deviation of follower perceptions of individualized consideration

Variable	B	SE B	β
Step 1			
Mean Individualized Consideration	−.177	.052	−.34**
Step 2			
Mean Individualized Consideration	−.142	.053	−.274**
Leader Authenticity–Relational Orientation	−.129	.062	−.213*

$R^2 = .12$ for Step 1; $\Delta R^2 = .041$ for Step 2. *$p < .05$, **$p < .01$.

leader relational authenticity did not predict the levels of agreement for the other facets of transformational leadership behaviour.

Hypothesis 7 predicted that relational authenticity will be associated with a particularly strong increase in the lowest ratings (among a number of followers) of individualized consideration, across leaders. As hypothesized, we found a significant correlation between minimum ratings of relational authenticity and individualized consideration, $r = .35$, $p < .01$. However, our results indicated that self-rated authenticity was not associated with maximum ratings of individualized consideration as we did not find significant correlations between the authenticity subscales and individualized consideration. Consistent with our expectations, we also find a positive association between leader relational authenticity and minimum ratings for the other two relevant facets of transformational leadership: $r = .24$, $p < .05$ for inspirational motivation; $r = .32$, $p < .01$ for idealized influence.

DISCUSSION

In the current study we sought to explore how leader authenticity predicts perceptions of transformational leadership behaviours, focusing on the relationship between relational authenticity and three facets of transformational leadership: individualized consideration, inspirational motivation, and idealized influence. Overall, we found support for the hypothesized relationships: Relationally authentic leaders were perceived to be more transformational in their leadership style than less relationally authentic leaders. This is consistent with the conceptual work of Ilies and colleagues (2005), who proposed that relationally authentic leaders would develop more positive relationships with their followers by generating greater intrinsic motivation, self-esteem, and creativity. Yet we found that other facets of leader authenticity, such as behavioural authenticity, did not exhibit a significant effect on perceptions of transformational leadership, supporting a multidimensional conceptualization of leader authenticity.

In addition, we found that relational authenticity in leaders was associated with a stronger convergence in followers' perceptions of transformational leadership behaviour. This supports the notion that authenticity is associated with more consistent behaviour in leaders, which is in turn reflected in followers' perceptions of leaders. Interestingly, however, even though followers converge to a greater extent in their perceptions of authentic leaders, our results also demonstrate that not all followers are equally influenced by leader authenticity. Instead, we find that the more critical followers who rated leaders' transformational behaviours lower than all other followers were most strongly influenced by leader authenticity. This represents one of the first empirical studies that have empirically investigated consequences of (facets of) leader authenticity on perceptions of leader behaviours, such as transformational leader behaviours (cf. Walumbwa et al., 2008, for a related study).

Implications for research and practice

The current research has at least three implications for research and practice. First, our finding that leader authenticity is associated with higher ratings of transformational leadership behaviours raises important questions about the underlying mechanisms through which the two constructs are related. Avolio and Gardner (2005) suggested that authentic leadership and transformational leadership should exhibit both discriminant and convergent validity. This raises the question whether the significant correlation between the two constructs in our study is due to overlapping construct definitions, or whether leader authenticity actually influences performance of transformational leadership behaviours. Even though our study uses ratings of leader authenticity and transformational leadership provided by different raters at different times, our results do not allow an unequivocal answer to this question. There are, however, at least two conceptual reasons that do support a causal relationship between leader authenticity and transformational leadership. First, Avolio and Gardner characterized authentic leadership as a root concept for other positive leadership approaches. The notion of a root concept implies causation between the two constructs, suggesting that leader authenticity is a necessary but not sufficient condition for performance of other positive leadership behaviours, such as transformational leadership. Second, Ilies et al. (2005) characterized leader authenticity as self-referential, leading to consistency in how leaders view themselves and how they perceive their environments across different situations. This self-referential nature will influence how authentic leaders define interpersonal relationships with their followers. Restated, the introspective nature of leader authenticity will affect the leadership style which authentic leaders use. This would in turn imply that authentic leadership is an antecedent of transformational leadership.

Second, we have extended research on leader–follower relationships by demonstrating that leader authenticity is associated with converging follower ratings of transformational leadership behaviour, evidenced by the lower standard deviation in these ratings. We suggest that a more consistent and predictable leadership style can create much needed orientation for employees in today's business world in which organizations operate in an increasingly complex environment which creates high and fast-changing demands for employees (Podolny et al., 2005; Sennett, 1998).

It is important to note, however, that behavioural consistency in leadership can also be a double-edged sword. For example, one reviewer of this manuscript noted that consistent and predictable leadership could also lead to ideological rigidity, which can in turn interfere with the ability of authentic leaders to consider the unique needs and backgrounds of followers, as predicted in Hypothesis 6 of this article. We acknowledge that leader authenticity can in extreme cases lead to reduced behavioural flexibility, which can in turn strain leader–follower relationships. Drawing on the work of Kernis (2003) and Ilies et al. (2005), however, we suggest that authenticity itself incorporates a defence mechanism against ideological rigidity. Kernis noted that authentic leaders engage in *unbiased processing*, which involves "not denying, distorting, exaggerating, or ignoring private knowledge, internal experiences, and externally based evaluative information" (p. 14). Hence, authentic leaders are very open to external information and different viewpoints, even if they appear to run counter to personal convictions. We view this aspect of authenticity as fundamentally opposed to ideological rigidity, which would imply the negation or distortion of information that runs counter to personal convictions.

Often times, authentic leaders will be able to reconcile external information with their well-reflected belief system, further strengthening the norms and values authentic leaders have chosen to endorse. Since authentic leaders process external information in an unbiased manner, it is likely that they will reexamine assumptions of their belief system if reconciliation is not an option. But even in times in which authentic leaders reexamine their assumptions and values, followers can expect a minimum of consistency in leader behaviour: Authentic leaders will apply the same principles and standards in such situations as they had in similar situations before. As such, even periods of change become predictable for followers.

Third, the current findings demonstrate that the consequences of leader authenticity do not materialize uniformly. Instead, we find that the most critical followers of authentic leaders are particularly receptive to leader authenticity. This suggests the value of investigating follower-specific consequences of leadership behaviour. Consistent with integrated leadership theories, our findings suggest that the effectiveness of leadership depends on the person of the leader (leader authenticity), the situational context in which leadership takes place (a well-developed organizational context; cf. Avolio & Gardner, 2005), and followers (with different inclinations to respond to different leadership behaviours).

Limitations and future research

Despite these positive features, the current research also has several limitations. First, it is important to reiterate that our study measured the authenticity of leaders with the measure developed by Kernis (2003), and not the process of authentic leadership. As such, our study does not operationalize authenticity specifically with respect to the leader–follower relationship. Instead, our study captures the authenticity of leaders in general, applying this measure to the context of leadership. This approach assumes that authenticity in leaders will also translate into authentic leadership. In support of this approach, May et al. (2003) noted that: "Authentic people are at the center of authentic leadership" (p. 249). Unfortunately, however, such an approach neglects the social dynamics of work (so does the measure of authentic leadership proposed by Walumbwa et al., 2008). Walumbwa et al. (2008) noted that "followers are nested within leaders, and because organizations are typically comprised of multiple levels of leaders, a multilevel approach to investigating leadership is certainly a plausible strategy that should be pursued" (p. 119). To our best knowledge, there is no available measure that captures these dynamics adequately. Clearly, more research and more refined measures are needed to investigate the multilevel implications of leadership processes at work, particularly with respect to authentic leadership development.

Second, although we found support for our hypotheses, it remains an open question as to whether leader authenticity actually accounts for the higher ratings of transformational leadership behaviour, or if alternative explanations can account for the findings. Future research should investigate the underlying mechanisms through which leader authenticity affects perceptions of transformational leadership behaviour. As discussed before, we suggest that there are strong conceptual reasons which support a causal link between leader authenticity and follower perceptions of transformational leadership behaviour, most importantly the notion of authentic leadership as a root concept for other positive leadership processes. But ultimately, despite the conceptually appealing nature of this relationship, future research should document this causal relationship empirically.

Third, although our findings show a positive association between leader authenticity and perceptions of transformational leadership, our research cannot provide answers to the question whether and how leaders can become more authentic over time. Several authors suggested that authentic leadership is "ultimately something one can develop in leaders" (Walumbwa et al., 2008, p. 93; also cf. Luthans & Avolio, 2003). We encourage future research to investigate the conditions under which leaders can become more authentic. Specifically, future research should investigate the extent to which a developed organizational context (Avolio & Gardner, 2005) or positive relational experiences with followers can further enhance the authentic leadership capabilities of leaders. By identifying conditions which help develop authentic leadership, researchers also get a step closer to identifying the causal mechanisms through which leader authenticity ultimately affects follower perceptions of transformational leadership.

Fourth, our study has focused on only one of several consequences of leader authenticity for the process of leadership as seen by followers. We believe that examining transformational leadership is an important first step, as suggested by other researchers (Avolio & Gardner, 2005; Walumbwa et al., 2008), but there are other leadership processes which should be investigated by future research. For example, we expect positive consequences of leader authenticity on the quality of leader member relationships and perceptions of leader effectiveness. Similarly, future research should investigate positive consequences of leader authenticity for team cohesiveness, team viability, team satisfaction, and team performance.

CONCLUSION

Research on leader authenticity presents an emerging research domain. Our current study adds to this body of research by exploring the positive effects of leader authenticity on follower perceptions of transformational leadership. Examining how leaders construe and enact their social work environment represents a fundamental question that has occupied organizational scholars for a long time (Barnard, 1968; Katz & Kahn, 1966). Although the current study adds to this research, clearly much more needs to be done.

REFERENCES

Aquino, K., & Reed, A. I. (2002). The self-importance of moral identity. *Journal of Personality and Social Psychology, 83,* 1423–1440.

Avolio, B. J., Bass, B. M., & Jung, D. I. (1995). *Multifactor leadership questionnaire technical report.* Redwood City, CA: Mind Garden.

Avolio, B. J., & Gardner, W. L. (2005). Authentic leadership development: Getting to the root of positive forms of leadership. *Leadership Quarterly, 16,* 315–338.

Avolio, B. J., Luthans, F., & Walumba, F. O. (2004). *Authentic leadership: Theory building for veritable sustained performance* (Working paper). Gallup Leadership Institute, University of Nebraska-Lincoln.

Bandura, A. (1986). *Social foundations of thought and action: A social cognitive theory.* Englewood Cliffs, NJ: Prentice Hall.

Barnard, C. (1968). *The functions of the executive.* Cambridge, MA: Harvard University Press.

Bass, B. M. (1956). Reducing leniency in merit ratings. *Personnel Psychology, 38,* 335–345.

Bass, B. M. (1985). *Leadership and performance beyond expectations.* New York: Free Press.

Bass, B. M. (1995). Theory of transformational leadership redux. *Leadership Quarterly, 6,* 463–478.

Bass, B. M. (1997). Does the transactional–transformational leadership paradigm transcend organizational and national boundaries? *The American Psychologist, 52,* 130–139.

Bass, B. M. (1998). *Transformational leadership: Industrial, military, and educational impact.* Mahwah, NJ: Lawrence Erlbaum Associates, Inc.

Bass, B. M., & Avolio, B. J. (1995). *Multifactor Leadership Questionnaire for Research.* Palo Alto, CA: Mind Garden.

Bernardin, H. J., & Beatty, R. W. (1984). *Performance appraisal: Assessing human behavior at work*. Boston: Kent.

Bommer, W. H., Rubin, R. S., & Baldwin, T. T. (2004). Setting the stage for effective leadership: Antecedents of transformational leadership behavior. *Leadership Quarterly, 15*, 195–210.

Bono, J. E., & Judge, T. A. (2004). Personality and transformational and transactional leadership: A meta-analysis. *Journal of Applied Psychology, 89*, 901–910.

Burns, J. M. (1978). *Leadership*. New York: Harper & Row.

Cameron, K. S., Dutton, J. E., & Quinn, R. E. (2003). Foundations of positive organizational scholarship. In K. S. Cameron, J. E. Dutton, & R. E. Quinn (Eds.), *Positive organizational scholarship: Foundations of a new discipline* (pp. 3–12). San Francisco, CA: Berrett-Koehler.

Conger, J. A., & Kanungo, R. N. (1998). *Charismatic leadership in organizations*. Thousand Oaks, CA: Sage.

Cooper, C. D., Scandura, T. A., & Schriesheim, C. A. (2005). Looking forward but learning from our past: Potential challenges to developing authentic leadership theory and authentic leaders. *Leadership Quarterly, 16*, 475–493.

Deluga, R. J. (1992). The relationship of leader–member exchange with laissez-faire, transactional, transformational leadership in naval environments. In K. E. Clark, M. B. Clark, & D. P. Campbell (Eds.), *Impact of leadership* (pp. 237–247). Greensboro, NC: Center for Creative Leadership.

Eagly, A. H. (2005). Achieving relational authenticity in leadership: Does gender matter? *Leadership Quarterly, 16*, 459–474.

Eagly, A. H., Johannesen-Schmidt, M. C., & van Engen, M. L. (2003). Transformational, transactional, and laissez-faire leadership styles. A meta-analysis comparing women and men. *Psychological Bulletin, 129*, 569–591.

Erickson, R. J. (1995). The importance of authenticity for self and society. *Symbolic Interaction, 18*(2), 121–144.

Fitzgerald, F. S. (1925). *The Great Gatsby*. New York: Charles Scribner's Sons.

Fredrickson, B. E. (2003). Positive emotions and upward spirals in organizations. In K. S. Cameron, J. E. Dutton, & R. E. Quinn (Eds.), *Positive organizational scholarship: Foundations of a new discipline* (pp. 163–175). San Francisco, CA: Berrett-Koehler.

Gardner, W. L., Avolio, B. J., Luthans, F., May, D. R., & Walumbwa, F. O. (2005). Can you see the real me? A self-based model of authentic leader and follower development. *Leadership Quarterly, 16*, 343–372.

Goldman, B. M., & Kernis, M. H. (2001). *Development of the Authenticity Inventory* [unpublished data]. University of Georgia, Athens, GA, USA.

Goldman, B. M., & Kernis, M. (2002). The role of authenticity in healthy psychological functioning and subjective well-being. *Annals of the American Psychotherapy Association, 5*, 18–20.

Hackman, J. R., & Wageman, R. (2005). When and how team leaders matter. *Research in Organizational Behavior, 26*, 39–76.

Ilgen, D. R., & Feldman, J. M. (1983). Performance appraisal: A process focus. In B. M. Staw & L. L. Cummings (Eds.), *Research in organizational behavior* (Vol. 5, pp. 141–197). Greenwich, CT: JAI Press.

Ilies, R., Morgeson, F. P., & Nahrgang, J. D. (2005). Authentic leadership and eudaemonic well-being: Understanding leader–follower outcomes. *Leadership Quarterly, 16*, 373–394.

Judge, T. A., & Piccolo, R. F. (2004). Transformational leadership and transactional leadership: A meta-analytic test of their relative validity. *Journal of Applied Psychology, 89*, 755–768.

Katz, D., & Kahn, R. L. (1966). *The social psychology of organizations*. New York: Wiley.

Kernis, M. H. (2003). Toward a conceptualization of optimal self-esteem. *Psychological Inquiry, 14*, 1–26.

Lewin, K. (1936). *Principles of topological psychology*. New York: McGraw-Hill.

332 SPITZMULLER AND ILIES

Luthans, F., & Avolio, B. J. (2003). Authentic leadership: A positive developmental approach. In K. S. Cameron, J. E. Dutton, & R. E. Quinn (Eds.), *Positive organizational scholarship: Foundations of a new discipline* (pp. 241–261). San Francisco, CA: Berrett-Koehler.

Maslow, A. (1968). *Motivation and personality* (3rd ed.). New York: Harper.

May, D. R., Chan, A. Y. L., Hodges, T. D., & Avolio, B. J. (2003). Developing the moral component of authentic leadership. *Organizational Dynamics, 32*, 247–260.

Podolny, J. M., Khurana, R., & Hill-Popper, M. (2005). Revisiting the meaning of leadership. *Research in Organizational Behavior, 26*, 1–37.

Rogers, C. (1959). A theory of therapy, personality, and interpersonal relationships as developed in the client-centered framework. In S. Koch (Ed.), *Psychology: A study of a science: Vol. 3. Formulations of the person and the social context* (pp. 184–256). New York: McGraw-Hill.

Rosch, E. (1978). Principles of human categorization. In E. Rosch & B. B. Lloyd (Eds.), *Cognition and categorization* (pp. 27–48). Hillsdale, NJ: Lawrence Erlbaum Associates, Inc.

Schneider, B. (1983). Interactional psychology and organizational behavior. *Research in Organizational Behavior, 5*, 1–31.

Seeman, M. (1960). *Social status and leadership: The case of the school executive.* Columbus, OH: Ohio State University Press.

Seligman, M. E. P. (1999). The President's address. *The American Psychologist, 54*, 559–562.

Selznick (1984). *Leadership in administration: A sociological interpretation.* Berkeley, CA: University of California Press.

Sennett, R. (1998). *The corrosion of character: The personal consequences of work in the new capitalism.* New York: W. W. Norton & Company.

Shamir, B., & Eilam, G. (2005). "What's your story?" A life-stories approach to authentic leadership development. *Leadership Quarterly, 16*, 395–417.

Sparrowe, R. T. (2005). Authentic leadership and the narrative self. *Leadership Quarterly, 16*, 419–439.

Tett, R. P., & Burnett, D. (2003). A personality-trait based approach interactionist model of job performance. *Journal of Applied Psychology, 88*, 500–517.

Walumbwa, F. O., Avolio, B. J., Gardner, W. L., Wernsing, T. S., & Peterson, S. J. (2008). Authentic leadership: Development and validation of a theory-based measure. *Journal of Management, 34*, 89–126.

Wang, H., Law, K. S., Hackett, R. D., Wang, D., & Chen, Z. X. (2005). Leader–member exchange as a mediator of the relationship between transformational leadership and followers' performance and organizational citizenship behavior. *Academy of Management Journal, 48*, 420–432.

Weber, M. (1946). *From Max Weber: Essay in sociology* (H. H. Gerth & C. Wright Mills, Trans. & Eds.). New York: Oxford University Press.

EUROPEAN JOURNAL OF WORK AND
ORGANIZATIONAL PSYCHOLOGY
2010, 19 (3), 333–363

Ψ Psychology Press
Taylor & Francis Group

The X-factor: On the relevance of implicit leadership and followership theories for leader–member exchange agreement

Suzanne van Gils*, Niels van Quaquebeke*, and
Daan van Knippenberg

*Rotterdam School of Management, Erasmus University Rotterdam,
Rotterdam, The Netherlands*

Although leader–member exchange (LMX) research shows that leaders engage in different kinds of relationships with different followers, it remains somewhat of an enigma why one and the same relationship is often rated differently by a leader and the respective follower. We seek to fill that conceptual void by explaining when and why such LMX disagreement is likely to occur. To do so, we reconsider antecedents of LMX quality perceptions and outline how each party's LMX quality perception is primarily dependent on the perceived contributions of the other party, moderated by perceived own contributions. We then integrate the notion of Implicit Leadership and Followership Theories (ILTs and IFTs) to argue that the currencies of contributions differ between leaders and followers. This dyadic model sets the stage to explain that LMX disagreement can stem from (1) differences in both parties' ILTs as well as both parties' IFTs, but also from (2) differences in perceptions of own and other's behaviour. We conclude by discussing communication as a means of overcoming LMX disagreement and propose an array of potential studies along the lines of our conceptualization.

Keywords: Leader; Follower; Leader–member exchange; Implicit theory; Agreement.

For the last few decades, leader–member exchange (LMX) research has successfully advanced its case that leadership effectiveness should be regarded as the result of the quality of the dyadic relationship between

Correspondence should be addressed to Suzanne van Gils, Room T08-52, Organization and Personnel Management, Rotterdam School of Management, Erasmus University Rotterdam, Burgemeester Oudlaan 50, 3062 PA Rotterdam, The Netherlands. E-mail: sgils@rsm.nl

*The first two authors were equal contributors to this manuscript. The order of their listing was determined alphabetically.

http://www.psypress.com/ejwop   DOI: 10.1080/13594320902978458

leader and follower. In a nutshell, the reasoning is that leaders engage with their followers in dyadic relationships of differing quality, where the quality of each leader–follower relationship depends on the reciprocation of contributions to that relationship. The experienced quality of the relationship motivates outcomes such as follower performance and satisfaction that are seen as indicative of leadership effectiveness (Graen, Novak, & Sommerkamp, 1982; Graen & Uhl-Bien, 1995; Liden, Wayne, & Stillwell, 1993; Mayfield & Mayfield, 1998; van Breukelen, Schyns, & LeBlanc, 2006).

However, whereas extant LMX research is predominantly built on the idea that relationships are experienced in a similar way by both members of the leadership dyad, meta-analytical findings show that the relationship is often rated differently by leaders and followers (i.e., Gerstner & Day, 1997, report a sample-weighted correlation between a leader's and a follower's LMX quality perception of .29, and Sin, Nahrgang, & Morgeson, 2009, report a true score correlation of .37). In other words, LMX agreement, that is, the similarity of leader and follower perceptions of their LMX relationship quality, is often very low despite the fact that both parties are part of and rate one and the same relationship.

Previous attempts set out to investigate correlates of LMX disagreement (e.g., Minsky, 2002; Paglis & Green, 2002; Sin et al., 2009), but their disjointed results by and large exemplify how little is known about antecedents of LMX agreement and how much variance is left unexplained even if individual aspects have been found to correlate. Evidence from further research suggests that LMX quality is likely to translate best into performance when the relationship is experienced similarly, that is, when LMX agreement is high (Atwater & Yammarino, 1992; Bass & Yammarino, 1991; Cogliser, Schriesheim, Scandura, & Gardner, 2009; Wexley, Alexander, Greenawalt, & Couch, 1980). Given these findings, the observation that LMX agreement is often lower than one would expect, despite both parties rating the same relationship, raises an important challenge for LMX theory and research.

In the present study, we present a conceptual analysis of LMX agreement to address this issue. To do so, we revisit different lines of LMX and information processing research, which we extend and combine into a fully dyadic model to explain leaders' and followers' LMX quality ratings. This model then sets the stage to outline when and why LMX disagreement may arise. As a final point, we discuss what can be done about LMX disagreement in practice, as well as what research can do to capture the complex processes involved.

LEADER–MEMBER EXCHANGE THEORY

Unlike leadership theories that contend that leaders have a predominant leadership style and tend to treat all their followers in a similar fashion, leader–member exchange (LMX) theory (originally introduced as the Vertical Dyad Linkage model; Dansereau, Graen, & Haga, 1975) asserts that leaders form unique exchange relationships of different quality with each of their followers. The role of the follower and the quality of the relationship itself are informally negotiated between followers and their leaders over time (Dienesch & Liden, 1986; Gerstner & Day, 1997; Graen & Scandura, 1987; Graen & Uhl-Bien, 1995). Whereas some followers develop a high quality exchange relationship with the leader which is characterized by mutual trust, respect, and liking (Dansereau et al., 1975), others are not only not considered to be part of that "inner circle" but also do not consider themselves to be part of it (Graen & Uhl-Bien, 1995). To explain how these differences in leader–follower relationships develop and ultimately form stable units, as well as how the relationship is experienced by the involved parties, LMX research uses a social exchange perspective (Blau, 1964; Graen & Scandura, 1987).

Regarding the development of the relationship, leader–follower relationships are thought to be initiated through an initial "offer" from the leader, which then is potentially reciprocated by the follower (Dienesch & Liden, 1986; Gerstner & Day, 1997; Graen, 2003; Graen & Scandura, 1987; Graen & Schiemann, 1978; Graen & Uhl-Bien, 1995). After this initial phase, in which the follower can "prove" him- or herself, the relationship continues with a reciprocation of contributions, that is, a reciprocation of positive actions that foster the relationship by fulfilling the other party's needs. Put differently, depending on the leader's perception of the follower's contribution, the leader will feel more or less indebted to reciprocate with an own contribution until he or she perceives an equilibrium of contributions. At this stage, the follower perceives the contribution of the leader and has to decide whether he or she needs to adjust his or her own contribution, etc. As long as either of the parties still perceives that an equilibrium of contributions is not reached, the relationship is still dynamic, that is, it can either deteriorate (when a party perceives the other to contribute less than him- or herself and thus also lowers his or her own contributions), or it can thrive (when a party perceives the other to contribute more than him- or herself and thus also increases his or her own contributions). Indeed, relationships are found to be more satisfying and thus stable when a party perceives the contributions to be almost equal or the other party to contribute more (Buunk, Doosje, Jans, & Hopstaken, 1993). Contrary, a lack of reciprocation by the other party will lead people to experience negative feelings, especially when they feel that they themselves have contributed a lot to the relationship (Walster, Walster, & Berscheid, 1978). Summarizing, the stability of a relationship depends on perceived reciprocation of one's own contributions by the other (Blau, 1964; Burgess & Huston, 1979) and the relationship can be considered stable when both parties perceive each other as contributing an approximately equal amount.

Related to the issue of relationship development, LMX theory further postulates that the main driver of the experienced relationship quality is the perceived contribution of the other party (e.g., Kim & Organ, 1982; Liden et al., 1993; Maslyn & Uhl-Bien, 2001; and similar results in other domains of leadership research such as self-sacrificial leadership, e.g., Choi & Mai-Dalton, 1999; de Cremer & van Knippenberg, 2004). The more the other party is perceived to contribute, the more satisfied people are with the relationship (even though, as outlined above, from a dyadic perspective, it might not be stable). This direct relationship is furthermore moderated by people's perceptions of own contributions. In other words, the more people perceive themselves to contribute to the relationship, the more their experienced relationship quality will depend on the other party's contribution—for better or worse. Put more concretely, individuals who perceive themselves as contributing a lot to a relationship will be more dissatisfied with the relationship when they perceive the other party to contribute little than individuals who perceive themselves as contributing little to the relationship. This interactive relationship is nicely illustrated in research by Maslyn and Uhl-Bien (2001), which demonstrates that, although perceptions of contributions by the follower directly influence a leader's rating of LMX quality, there is also a moderating effect of the leader's own contribution, such that leaders who perceive themselves as investing a lot into the relationship evaluate the relationship more negatively when they perceive subordinate effort to be low in comparison to those leaders who perceive themselves as investing less. In short, each party's LMX quality rating is primarily dependent on the perceived other party's contributions, and this holds more strongly when the perceived own contribution to the relationship is higher.

In general, the quality of a leader–follower relationship will determine how both parties, leaders and followers, experience their work and engage in it—with perceived relationship quality consequently being positively related to organizationally relevant and desirable outcomes (Gerstner & Day, 1997; Ilies, Nahrgang, & Morgeson, 2007). Research has, for instance, shown that followers in high quality LMX relationships work harder (Basu & Green, 1997; Duchon, Green, & Taber, 1986), perform better (Graen et al., 1982; Liden & Graen, 1980; Liden et al., 1993; Mayfield & Mayfield, 1998; Vecchio & Norris, 1996), experience more satisfaction with the leader (Duchon et al., 1986; Lagace, 1990; Schriesheim & Gardiner, 1992), experience more job satisfaction (Graen & Cashman, 1975; Graen et al., 1982; Scandura & Graen, 1984), and are less motivated to leave the team or organization (Scandura & Graen, 1984; Vecchio, 1995; Vecchio & Norris, 1996). Moreover, such results have been repeatedly obtained in different countries and cultures (e.g., Anseel & Lievens, 2007; Erdogan, Liden, & Kraimer, 2006; Schyns, Paul, Mohr, & Blank, 2005), thus suggesting that the effects of LMX are very robust.

THE PROBLEM OF LMX DISAGREEMENT

Despite early findings that suggest that own and other perceptions in work contexts are likely to differ (cf. Harris & Schaubroeck, 1988), extant LMX research is predominantly built upon the idea that relationships are experienced in a similar way by both members of the leadership dyad. Graen and Uhl-Bien (1995, p. 237) even write that "expected agreement between leader and member reports is positive and strong and used as an index of quality of data". Because studies commonly only survey one party of the dyad, predominately the follower, such assumptions have long been left unchallenged (e.g., Gerstner & Day, 1997, found only 24 studies which surveyed both perspectives in a total of 84 studies on LMX).

More recent studies, however, explicitly focus upon the issue of LMX agreement. Paglis and Green (2002) find, for instance, a correlation of only .19 between both parties' assessment of LMX quality (across 127 leader–follower dyads). A meta-analysis by Gerstner and Day (1997) across 24 independent samples with a combined sample size of 3460 dyads corroborates such findings in that they also find a mean sample-weighted correlation of only .29, and .37 when corrected for unreliability. The most recent meta-analysis by Sin et al. (2009) raises similar concerns, finding that overall LMX agreement across 64 samples with a combined sample size of 10,884 dyads was only moderate with $\rho = .37$.

Although some researchers argued that disagreement in ratings of LMX does not warrant conceptual analysis because it merely reflects measurement error (Graen & Uhl-Bien, 1995), a plethora of studies suggests otherwise, that is, despite heterogeneity in LMX assessments from various angles and with various scales, the finding that leaders and followers provide disagreeing accounts of LMX quality still persists (cf. Bernerth, Armenakis, Feild, Giles, & Walker, 2007; Schriesheim, Castro, & Cogliser, 1999). Measurement error is notoriously difficult to rule out as an explanation, but there are further conceptual reasons to believe that LMX disagreement is not solely attributable to it. Indeed, Gerstner and Day (1997) argue that disagreement on ratings of LMX quality is a complex issue that is an interesting outcome variable in its own right.

In line with Gerstner and Day's (1997) call, previous studies set out to explain LMX disagreement. However, they by and large failed to coherently explain the driving force behind it. In her dissertation, Minsky (2002), for instance, only found feedback to be moderately related to LMX agreement (an issue we revisit later). Paglis and Green (2002), on the other hand, only found a correlation of agreement with lower levels of conflicts. Due to the correlational nature of both studies, these authors are, however, unable to ascertain whether feedback or lower levels of conflict are antecedents or merely consequences of LMX agreement. The same holds true for the most recent meta-analysis on LMX agreement (Sin et al., 2009). Although the amount of considered studies in this meta-analysis is impressive, the authors also only report correlational patterns without being able to confirm the implied causality. Nevertheless, their results are noteworthy because they, for instance, address some sampling issues (ad hoc vs. a priori) that explain a small degree of variance in LMX disagreement. Further, although their results are not unambiguous when dissected along different dimensions of perceived LMX quality, they show that dyadic tenure as well as intensity of dyadic interaction significantly moderate the relationship between followers' and leaders' perception of overall LMX quality. Despite such first promising results, their analyses also suggest that only little variance in LMX agreement is explained by these factors.

For the present theoretical consideration, we build upon these first endeavours; however, we also think that the largely disjointed picture with little variance explained can be illuminated by revisiting the specific aspect of social exchange in LMX, and in particular, by reconsidering what it is that leaders and follower exchange and how they do it. In contrast to empirical studies, our conceptualizations are not limited by data opportunity or feasibility of research designs which potentially unnecessarily restrain the conceptualization. However, to illustrate the testability of our model, we will describe concrete research designs at the end of this article.

CURRENCIES OF EXCHANGE IN LMX

Despite the fact that social exchange theory suggests that LMX relationships are governed by a reciprocity norm (cf. Cialdini, 1984; Gouldner, 1960; Uhl-Bien & Maslyn, 2003) that should motivate both parties to contribute evenly and thus to ultimately judge the quality of the relationship in the same way, empirical research has demonstrated that dyadic partners often have different perceptions of the relationship quality (Gerstner & Day, 1997) and different grounds for their ratings (Huang, Wright, Chiu, & Wang, 2008; Tekleab & Taylor, 2003). Such existence and persistence of disagreement about one and the same relationship cannot be explained within the basic rationale of social exchange theory. Rather, we argue that we have to revisit the notion of contributions to fully grasp the issues at stake here.

There has been some debate in the literature regarding the way in which leaders and followers should contribute to the relationship in order for both persons to benefit equally. Some have argued that equal benefits can only be reached when leaders and followers contribute in the same way (Dienesch & Liden, 1986; Liden & Maslyn, 1998); others have argued that equal benefits can be reached when leaders and followers contribute to the relationship with different behaviours that are similar in perceived value (Coyle-Shapiro & Kessler, 2002; Tekleab & Taylor, 2003). In line with the latter, and with research that argues that leaders and followers contribute to the relationship based on their unique roles (Blau, 1964; Dansereau et al., 1995; Day & Crain, 1992; Dockery & Steiner, 1990; Yammarino & Dansereau, 2002), we suggest that leaders and followers contribute to the relationship in different "currencies of exchange".[1]

To understand the issue of different currencies in LMX in more depth and specifically how different currencies relate to LMX (dis)agreement, we use the next sections to elaborate on the notion of expectations, or so called implicit theories, for leaders and followers. The basic rationale is similar for both kinds of implicit theories: First of all, an individual behaves in a certain way. This behaviour is perceived by the individual him- or herself as well as by the other party of the dyad. For both, the perceptual process is governed by implicit expectations about how this person should act within his or her leader or follower role. Behaviour within the range of the expectations will be far more likely to be perceived as a contribution and thus it will be considered when judging relationship quality.

Leaders' currency of exchange: Matching behaviour to Implicit Leadership Theories

We propose that both dyadic partners are likely to perceive the contribution each person makes to the relationship based on their expectations for the particular role of the person (i.e., leader or follower). In the case of the leader, both dyadic partners will compare the leader's behaviour to the expectations they have for a person in a leadership role. Such expectations for the leader role are captured by the concept of Implicit Leadership Theories (ILTs; Lord, 1985; Lord, Foti, & de Vader, 1984; Lord & Maher, 1991; Schyns & Meindl, 2005). ILTs represent cognitive schemas which specify the traits and behaviours that followers expect of leaders (Kenney,

---

[1]Note that we follow a broader understanding of *currencies* and *contributions* in the present article (cf. Schriesheim et al., 1999) compared to some previous works (e.g., Dienesch & Liden, 1986; Liden & Maslyn, 1998). Specifically, we understand a contribution as something that is perceived as a valuable addition to the relationship and the reaching of mutual goals. Our understanding of contributions thus subsumes aspects that have previously been called currencies next to contributions, such as loyalty, affect, or respect. In that sense, we also have a less restricted understanding of currency in that contributions can be made along the lines of Implicit Leadership Theories and Implicit Followership Theories—which we will elaborate in the coming sections.

Schwartz-Kenney, & Blascovich, 1996; Lord & Maher, 1991; Weick, 1995). Research in ILTs suggests that people hold such implicit assumptions because most people have been brought up and socialized in groups where leadership is a natural phenomenon (Lord & Brown, 2001; Lord & Maher, 1991). Abstracted from experienced leader exemplars, people eventually develop more elaborate knowledge structures on how a leader is (to be) like. Importantly in the context of leadership, these knowledge structures serve as an interpretational background which subordinates use as a basis for their evaluations of actual leaders, for instance, when judging a leader's qualification for the job. ILTs can thus be regarded as a means by which people make sense of and respond to the organizational world around them (cf. Weick, 1995).

When adopting this perspective, a leader's quality and his or her effectiveness are to a great extent determined by followers' perceptions and interpretations (i.e., "leadership is in the eye of the beholder", cf. Nye, 2002). Indeed, the follower-centric approach to leadership emphasizes the information-processing aspect in leadership dyads (Lord & Maher, 1991; cf. Meindl, 1995; Shamir, Pillai, Bligh, & Uhl-Bien, 2007). Through the follower-centric lens of ILT theory, leadership is not seen as directly related to a "true reality" (i.e., as a result of a leader's actual personality and behaviour), but rather to the perceiver's socially constructed reality—a mental representation of leadership that is as much informed by "objective" input from the environment (e.g., leader behaviour and characteristics) as by the cognitive frame of reference through which leadership is understood (i.e., ILTs; cf. Gioia, Thomas, Clark, & Chittipeddi, 1994).

Work by Lord (e.g., 1985) on developing leader categorization theory in particular has been instrumental in developing this perspective that can be roughly summarized as saying that ILTs are benchmarks that followers use to categorize the leader and eventually determine an adequate response towards the leader (Engle & Lord, 1997; Lord & Brown, 2004; Lord & Hall, 2003; Ritter & Lord, 2007). According to the theory's assumptions, followers compare their actual leader to their ILTs and any discrepancies that are derived from that comparison are assumed to affect the follower's impression of the leader. This will eventually also affect the follower's impression of the leader's contribution to the joint relationship and the subsequent perception of how this contribution should be reciprocated.

Although the leader categorization process is usually thought to be automatic, and therefore largely unconscious and implicit, cognitive theory (Bechtel & Abrahamsen, 2002) would suggest that leader categorization is also entrenched in controlled, that is, conscious and explicit, information processing. In that sense, ILTs govern individuals' judgement of others in both ways, automatic and controlled. Thus, regardless of whether the information is processed automatically or in a more controlled way, ILTs are a lens through which leaders and their behaviours are evaluated as either contributing to the relationship or not.

The more a leader displays what followers believe to be the characteristics of a good leader (i.e., fit their ILTs), the more favourably followers respond to the leadership and the more they are willing to subordinate to it as part of an implicit "relationship agreement" (Eagly & Karau, 2002; Kenney et al., 1996; Lord & Hall, 2003; Lord & Maher, 1991; see overviews in Schyns & Meindl, 2005; Shamir et al., 2007). Further research on ILTs and on leader categorization uses the concept of prototype (mis)fit to explain, for instance, why some people are more likely to emerge as leaders, get promoted to (higher) leadership positions, and are viewed as legitimate leaders (Eagly & Karau, 2002; Engle & Lord, 1997; Heilman, Block, & Lucas, 1992; Ridgeway, 2001; cf. Conger & Kanungo, 1987). Reaction time experiments have substantiated this reasoning in that they show that people find it harder to activate respective leader schema and behavioural scripts when they perceive discrepancies between an actual leader and their leader prototype (Lord et al., 1984; Scott & Brown, 2006).

In short, we argue that the more the leader is seen to match the ILT— both in terms of characteristics and in terms of behaviour—the more the leader is seen to contribute to the LMX relationship. Or, put differently, we propose that ILTs are the lens through which leader behaviour is perceived and evaluated in terms of its contribution to the LMX relationship. This line of reasoning is supported by a recent study by Epitropaki and Martin (2005), who conducted two survey studies in which they found that a lower discrepancy between leader's actual behaviour and follower's ILT lead to higher ratings of LMX quality by followers.

However, followers are not alone in holding ILTs—leaders do too. This was noted by Lord and Maher (1991), who suggested that implicit theories serve not only as a basis to interpret the behaviour of the dyad partner, but also as a foundation for own behaviour. Leaders can thus be assumed to consciously or unconsciously rely on their ILTs to evaluate and generate own behaviour, and the closer leaders perceive their behaviour to be to their own ILTs, the higher they will perceive their own contribution to the LMX relationship.

By more firmly integrating insights from ILT research into LMX theory, we may thus extend our understanding of the currencies of exchange involved in LMX relationships, and ultimately increases our insights in the sources of LMX disagreement. When judging the followers' contribution to the LMX relationship, that is, the followers' currency of exchange, we suggest that a similar process takes place. However, the follower's contribution has to be judged along a different dimension. The leader categorization and ILT framework, although not directly identifying that dimension, does provide an extremely useful point of departure in this respect.

Followers' currency of exchange: Matching behaviour to Implicit Followership Theories

In their seminal work, Lord and Maher (1991) emphasized that leaders and followers alike rely on implicit theories to process social information and make social judgements. If the process of comparison between actual behaviour and implicit leadership theory exists for leaders, it thus seems only plausible to assume that there is an equivalent implicit theory for the follower. Indeed, to pay full heed to the dyadic conception of leader–follower relationship, we suggest that both dyadic members have implicit theories for followers as well, to which they compare the follower's behaviour, which we label Implicit Follower Theories (IFTs). Directly following from the previously outlined logic for ILTs, we propose that leaders and followers also hold IFTs that capture expectations about the follower role and about appropriate follower contributions to the LMX relationship. Accordingly, we further propose that both leaders and followers consciously and unconsciously assess followers' contribution to the LMX relationship using their IFTs as a benchmark, with more positive evaluations ensuring a greater match between IFT and perceived follower characteristics and behaviour. In short, whereas leaders' contribution to the LMX relationship is judged in reference to ILTs, followers' contribution is judged in reference to IFTs.

Interestingly, Engle and Lord (1997) partly addressed this very issue when they pointed out that the choice of a particular category or schema for the evaluation of the other member of a dyad is likely to differ between leaders and followers. They argue that, similar to followers' ILTs, leaders develop prototypes of effective followers, which they called Implicit Performance Theories, and then compare follower performance to this prototype (cf. Borman, 1987; Sanders, 1999; Wernimont, 1971). The result of this comparison process is the labelling of followers as either effectively or ineffectively contributing to relationship, much like the results of the leader categorization process. However, Engle and Lord conceptualized such theories that would provide a standard for judgement of followers as in a sense restricted to performance—that is, Implicit Performance Theories. In contrast, we propose that much like ILTs, the cognitive schemata related to conceptualizations of the follower role are not restricted to mere performance but include a more diverse set of attributes that would reflect on the overall quality of the relationship (e.g., being honest, enthusiastic, or trustworthy). Accordingly, although we recognize the important foundations that have been laid by Engle and Lord, we propose that IFTs are broader than Implicit Performance Theories and therefore better capture the range of behaviours and characteristics that followers may be expected to contribute to the LMX relationship.

Similar to our reasoning regarding leader match to ILTs, we expect that the effect of the perceptions of follower–IFT match differs for each member of the dyad. From the leader's perspective, a match between perceived follower behaviour and leader's IFTs will lead the leader to evaluate the LMX quality more favourably. From the follower's perspective, a match between own behaviour and IFT will lead to the perception of higher own contribution to the relationship. Mirroring the moderating role of leaders' perception of their own contributions in terms of ILT match, followers' perception of own contributions in terms of IFT match will moderate the relationship between perceived leader ILT match and perceptions of LMX quality, such that this (positive) relationship is stronger the more followers perceive themselves to match the role expectations as captured by their IFT.

A DYADIC MODEL OF LMX AGREEMENT

Our analysis up to this point provides the basic elements by which, we suggest, leaders and followers individually assess the quality of their LMX relationship. Summarizing this analysis and combining the insights into a dyadic model, we posit that (1) each party's perception of LMX quality is primarily determined by the perceived other party's contributions; (2) this positive relationship is moderated by the party's perceived own contributions; and (3) leaders' contributions to the relationship are judged through the lens of ILTs, whereas follower contributions are judged through the lens of IFTs. These relationships are captured in Figure 1.

Our proposed model is firmly grounded in research on LMX and ILTs, but it integrates and extends earlier research into a dyadic model that now allows us to identify sources of LMX (dis)agreement that were not evident in earlier treatment of these issues, namely: (1) differences between a leader and a follower in ILTs or IFTs, and (2) differences in perception of own and other's behaviour. In the following, we address these issues in more detail.

Sources of disagreement: Differences in ILTs and IFTs

Differences in ILTs and IFTs. We proposed that leaders and followers perceive their own and the other's behaviour through the lens of their personal ILTs and IFTs. Only when congruence between a leader's and a follower's implicit theories exists do both parties base their behaviour on the same guidelines and interpret each other's behaviour in the same way (cf. Engle & Lord, 1997). As a consequence, congruence between implicit theories fosters agreement about *what* should be contributed and thus increases the similarity in both partners' judgements about their mutual contributions. Conversely, the more leader and follower differ in their ILTs

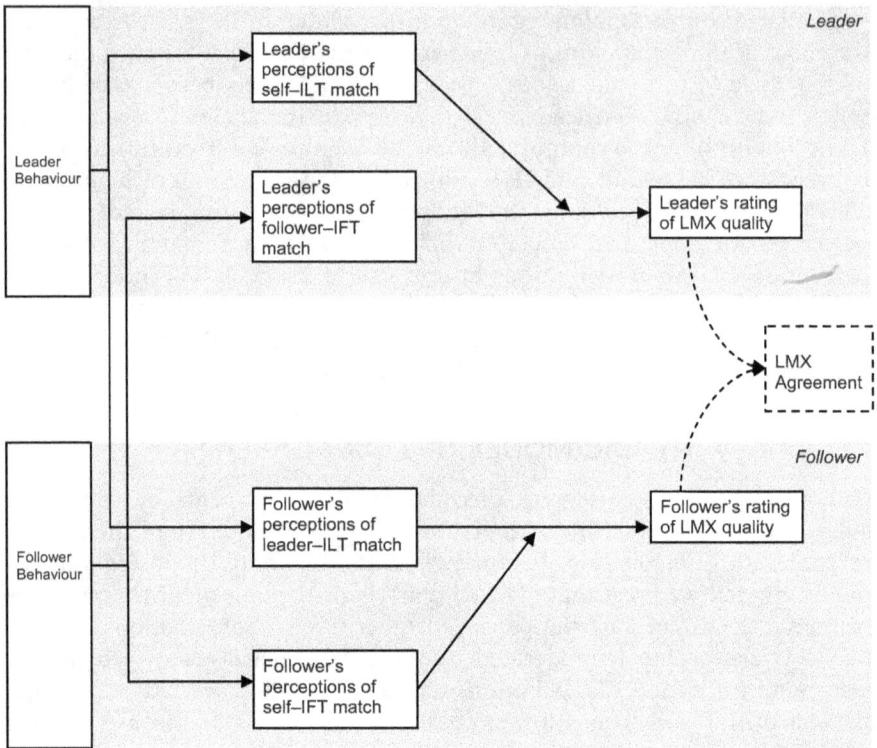

Figure 1. Dyadic model of LMX agreement.

and/or IFTs, the more the same behaviour will be perceived differently in terms of the extent to which it contributes to the LMX relationship, and the more potential there is for LMX disagreement. Perfect congruence of ILTs and IFTs between leaders and followers, however, seems unlikely (as standard deviations in the development of leader prototypicality measures, for instance, already suggest), because ILTs and IFTs are subject to (1) different experiences with both roles, (2) different contextual saliencies, and (3) different goals.

Regarding the differences in experiences with either role, van Quaquebeke and Brodbeck (2008) argued that implicit theories should generally be considered to be idiosyncratic, that is, they are not only formed as part of a collective socialization processes but also through unique individual experiences inside and outside of work life (cf. Keller, 1999; Lord & Maher, 1991)—with only a portion of such idiosyncratic implicit theories being socially shared, e.g., as part of national identities or cultural clusters (Brodbeck, Chhokar, & House, 2007; Gerstner & Day, 1994; House, Hanges, Javidan, Dorfman, & Gupta, 2004). Any similarity between leaders and followers in terms of socialization, such as having been raised in the same culture or having worked for the same company, increases the congruence of ILTs and IFTs, but perfect congruence of ILTs and IFTs is unlikely to occur in leadership dyads considering all possible socialization factors.

One evident source of different socializations is an individual's own experience in either role. Although this perspective has received little research attention in the tradition of ILTs and IFTs, there is substantial research in other domains that shows that prior experience with a task influences a person's mental model of subsequent tasks and according strategies for these. In other words, when a task is similar to a task one has completed before, people tend to rely on their previously gathered knowledge about such tasks and use this knowledge to guide them to a solution (Pirolli & Anderson, 1985; Reed, 1987; Ross, 1984, 1987). This effect even persists when a new task is not exactly similar to a previous task, as long as this new task activates similar mental models (Catrambone & Holyoak; 1989; Glick & Holyoak, 1980; Holyoak & Koh, 1987). In line with this research, we can expect that previous experiences with tasks attached to either the leader or the follower role will influence people's knowledge structures about these roles, that is, their implicit theories. To make it more concrete: Most people are likely to have been in some kind of followership position themselves. In these positions, some might have found a very rigorous and accurate working style to be the best strategy to obtain good performance ratings by their supervisors. Others, however, might have found that following the Pareto principle (i.e., the 80/20 rule) is the best strategy to obtain good performance ratings by their supervisors. For both, their experiences are likely to translate into their IFT concept; however, as their experiences differ, so will their IFTs. The same naturally should also hold true for experiences as a leader. Consequently, to the extent that the experiences two individuals have either as a follower or as a leader differ, there will also be differences in their ILTs and IFTs, that is, in the standards to which contributions to the relationship are compared.

With regard to experiences with the other's role, prior research on transference, for instance, shows that when people encounter a new leader who is similar to a previous leader, a mental representation of this previous leader is used to evaluate the new leader (Ritter & Lord, 2007). As leaders and their followers are likely to have experienced different leaders, it is thus likely that their exemplar-based ILTs differ. Hunt, Boal, and Sorenson (1990) argue along similar lines when suggesting that individual differences in ILTs may be a result of different childhood experiences. Specifically, they argue that different parents and parenting styles represent the core which people's later and more elaborate ILT conceptions are developed upon. In other words, parents provide anticipatory socialization about work, leadership, and communication and thus a blueprint for expectations about leader–follower interactions (Jablin & Krone, 1987). Hence, we can assume that the more a leader's and a follower's parents' parenting styles were different, the less congruent their ILTs will be in later life.

Similar factors that cause ILTs to differ will probably lead to differences in IFTs as well. Indeed, Lord and Maher (1991) suggest that leadership and followership are constructed as an inseparable pair. Therefore we can presume that, although extant research has mainly focused upon factors influencing ILTs, these factors will influence IFTs in much the same way. Any socialization regarding leadership thus always involves a socialization regarding respective followership and vice versa. In other words, personal ILTs and IFTs develop both at the same time, irrespective of the dyadic positions people are in. However, the specific content of these ILTs and IFTs will be individually determined by the experiences they acquire in these positions in their own roles as well as with their dyadic counterparts.

A second reason for differences in ILTs and IFTs apart from personal experiences can be found in the situational cues leaders and followers are subjected to. Research taking a connectionist approach to implicit theories (Lord, Brown, Harvey, & Hall, 2001) suggests that no single implicit theory applies to all situations, but that the influence of contextual factors such as task or group characteristics, organizational routines, or even just the content in the daily stream of emails, determine which specific aspects of one's implicit leadership and followership theory will be activated. Indeed, one and the same behaviour can be interpreted in quite different ways depending on the content of the activated category in the perceiver (Müller & Schyns, 2005). Considering a leader's and a follower's day at work, we can assume that they are subject to quite different contexts and routines. Indeed, although a leader might spend a lot of time in meetings to discuss strategies and the general development of the company, followers are likely to be occupied with getting their assignments done without thinking too far ahead. This implicit difference in temporal construal in daily activities affects in return the kind and scope of activities one regards as adequate for self and others in specific roles (Liberman, Trope, McCrea, & Sherman, 2007). In other words, leaders might think that, like themselves, followers should also have an eye on the implications of their doing for the future of the company, whereas followers would like to see that, like themselves, leaders start to get their "hands dirty" by actually being involved in and finishing projects. To sum this part up, different organizational contexts for leaders and followers will highlight different aspects in implicit theories which will affect how leaders and followers evaluate own as well as other's actions—ultimately, at the detriment of LMX agreement.

Related to these points, a third reason why a leader's and a follower's ILTs as well as IFTs are likely to differ can be assumed to be tied to the specific objectives that are seen as attached to roles (cf. connectionist conceptualizations of ILTs in Lord et al., 2001). Such differences can be found when people, for instance, depending on the context of leadership, construct a mental image of a leader who is most adequate for that specific context. Indeed, Lord and colleagues (1984) showed that people's concepts of leaders differ across different domains such as sports, politics, and business. Such differences in representation are not only informed by the different exemplars people perceive in these domains, but also by the objectives that are attached to each of these domains (Barsalou, 1985; van Quaquebeke, Graf, & Brodbeck, 2007). Although it can be argued that leaders and followers generally share the same context, and thus also the same objectives, that is only true on a higher level, that is, regarding domains. On a lower level, however, leaders and followers might not have an aligned understanding of the objectives that should be reached via leadership and the respective followership, that is, a leader might think that it is the objective of all employees to do anything in their power to ensure performance and drive up the stock price, whereas a follower might think that all employees should care for each other's well-being. Put differently, both leaders and followers probably have a tendency to conceptualize both roles anchored in own goals and needs. To the extent that these goals differ, a leader's and a follower's implicit theories are also likely to differ and thus their perceptions of contributions to the joint relationship (cf. Huang et al., 2008). Consequently, it is not the perception of the behaviour per se that differs between followers and leaders—for instance, both can perceive that the leader does a lot to drive up the stock price—but it is the difference in perceptions how such behaviour relates to one's goal definition (as part of one's implicit theory) that drives differences in perceived contributions (cf. Harris & Schaubroeck, 1988).

To recap, leaders' and followers' ILTs and IFTs will differ, (1) the more leaders and followers have had different experiences regarding both roles, (2) the more leaders and followers are subject to different contexts that provide different saliencies, and (3) the more leaders' and followers' goal definitions differ from each other. Consequently, one and the same behaviour is often judged against different standards by a leader and a follower.

Sources of disagreement: Differences in perception of own and other's behaviour

In addition to potential differences in ILTs and IFTs, leaders and followers have to establish an "exchange rate" between the different contributions. Such estimations about what constitutes a high value as opposed to a low value contribution are a different issue that influences the perceptions of

LMX quality in addition to differences in the content of ILTs and IFTs. Even if a leader's and a follower's ILTs and IFTs would be exactly similar, that is, leaders and follower agree *what* each party should contribute, leaders and followers can still differ in their perceptions concerning *how much* the other party contributes to the relationship and how much that is worth in own contributions. Here, disagreement is also likely as such assessments are subject to (1) self-serving biases, (2) biases in perceptions of others, as well as (3) biases due to privileged access to information (cf. Harris & Schaubroeck, 1988).

Generally, people's considerations regarding conversion rates result in an assessment that favours the self (Taylor & Brown, 1988). More specifically, most people hold unrealistically positive views of the self, for instance, by judging positive traits as more characteristic of themselves than negative traits (Alicke, 1985; Brown, 1986), by recalling information related to their own successes better than information related to failure (Silverman, 1964), and by overestimating their own task performance compared to their peers (Crary, 1966; John & Robins, 1994). These biases occur in various contexts such as athletic contests (Brawley, 1984), group discussions (Gilovich, Medvec, & Savitsky, 1999), problem-solving tasks (Burger & Rodman, 1983), and academic projects (Ross & Sicoly, 1979). Moreover, such self-serving biases become even more pronounced when people rate themselves on criteria that cannot be easily compared to objective standards, like sensitivity, discipline, sophistication (Dunning, Meyerowitz, & Holzberg, 1989), or morality (Allison, Messick, & Goethals, 1989). Further research on the endowment effect extends such insights in arguing that especially in the condition of an exchange of dissimilar resources (cf. currencies of exchange) people overestimate the value of their own resources as compared with those of the exchange partner and are therefore more conservative in contributing to the relationship (van Dijk & van Knippenberg, 2005).

However, susceptibility to such self-serving biases varies as a function of personality. Atwater and Yammarino (1997), for instance, provide an overview of personality factors that lead people to evaluate their own performance more accurately, such as internal locus of control, cognitive complexity, and self-awareness. In contrast, self-serving biases are especially prevalent in people who score high in narcissism (John & Robins, 1994). Interesting, research shows that narcissism is more prevalent among people in leadership positions (Deluga, 1997; Rosenthal & Pittinsky, 2006), which suggests that leaders may be more prone to overestimate their own contribution to the exchange relationship than followers. We may thus expect that such differences in personality between followers and leaders may influence the extent to which each of them falls prey to self-serving biases in their perceptions of contributions to the LMX relationship, and accordingly the extent to which there will be LMX disagreement.

Not only the perceptions of one's own contribution are subject to bias, the perceptions of others' contributions can be biased as well. Research has, for instance, repeatedly found that LMX quality is perceived more favourably when the other party is perceived as similar to oneself, for example, in demographic attributes (Duchon et al., 1986; Green, Anderson, & Shivers, 1996; Tsui, Egan, & O'Reilly, 1992, Tsui & O'Reilly, 1989) or in attitudes and education (Basu & Green, 2006). Although such general similarity-attraction effects (cf. Byrne, 1971) are less of an issue for LMX agreement, they do become an issue when the involved parties disagree on their perceptions of similarity, for instance, when one party is conscious of age similarity while the other is conscious of dissimilarity in attitudes (cf. Harrison, Price, & Bell, 1998; Hiller & Day, 2003; regarding the differentiation into surface-level similarity, such as demographics, and deep-level similarity, such as values). On which level people (care to) perceive similarity depends on whether they see the respective dimension as meaningful for normative fit, in other words, as meaningful for their identity construal (Oakes, Turner, & Haslam, 1991; Turner, 1987). A leader might perceive dissimilarity because the follower has not attended the same Ivy League university, whereas a follower can be inclined to perceive similarity because his or her leader attended a game of the soccer club of which the follower is a fan. As a consequence, when evaluating their joint relationship, the follower's rating of the leader's contribution to the relationship is likely to be more positively biased than the leader's perception of the follower's contribution to the relationship.

Another aspect affecting the perception of others can be found in the degree to which people are able to take each other's perspective. Although there are individual differences in the development of this skill, research has shown that there is a general tendency for people higher in the organizational hierarchy, to be less inclined to take a lower power individual's perspective (Galinsky, Magee, Inesi, & Gruenfeld, 2006). As perspective taking can be seen as indicative of having a feel for how much the other is contributing (or trying to) as well as how one's own contributions are perceived by the other, a lack of perspective taking can be related to a less exact and usually less favourable assessment of the other's contributions (similar to the effects of the self-serving bias discussed earlier). In other words, the power differential between leaders and followers makes differences in perspective taking especially likely and thus affects LMX disagreement via differences in perceptions of contributions.

A third factor, which feeds indirectly into biased perceptions of own and other's behaviour, is privileged access to information about behaviour— either due to cognitive or to physical access. First, when considering each person's contribution, it is typically easier to recall one's own contributions than someone else's, because such information is differently encoded and stored than information about other people's contributions

(Ross & Sicoly, 1979). The reasons for this are manifold: Own actions may distract from perceiving other people's actions; own actions are often rehearsed or repeated before being put into action and thus more deeply rooted in the cognitive apparatus (Carver, 1972); and own actions fit more likely into preexisting schema and are thus more likely to be retained (Bartlett, 1932; Bruner, 1961). Because the ease with which contributions come to mind is used as a proxy for actual contributions (Schwartz et al., 1991; Tversky & Kahneman, 1973), inflated views of own contributions are likely to occur. Second, some contributions to a relationship may take place outside of the awareness of the other party. A leader may, for instance, argue the case for a pay raise for the follower with the leader's own superior without the follower being aware of this, whereas the follower may work overtime to secure an important contract without the leader ever being aware of the extra effort invested by the follower. Simply put, one is aware of one's own actions but not necessary of those of the other party. As a consequence, biased perceptions of own and other's contributions may arise. Although it might be argued that leaders and followers are equally subject to this privileged access to information issue and thus equally affected in their LMX quality ratings, it is likely that leader–follower relationships are often characterized by an information asymmetry. Specifically, it is within the leader's role to supervise and as such know much about their subordinates' doing, whereas a follower is only likely to witness a leader's actions for the relationship in direct contact and less so when they are, for instance, happening in the board room. Leaders may thus in practice often have privileged access to information about their own behaviour to a greater extent than followers. Accordingly, as perceptions of potential contributions are based on all information one has about one's own and the other's behaviour that comes to mind, LMX quality perceptions are likely to differ between leaders and followers, with LMX disagreement as a consequence.

Summarizing this part, leaders and followers have different perceptions of how much each party contributes to the relationship based on (1) differences in biased perceptions of own and other's contributions, (2) differences in perspective taking, and (3) differences in access to own and other's behaviour. These factors relate to the extent to which leaders and followers think their standards for each role are met by the other as well as by themselves, and hence explain how disagreement can still persist in cases where these standards, that is, ILTs and IFTs, are the same.

TOWARDS A FULLER UNDERSTANDING OF LMX AGREEMENT

In the previous sections, we reconsidered antecedents of LMX quality ratings at an individual level and combined them into a dyadic model.

We outlined that each party's LMX quality rating is primarily dependent on the perceived other party's contributions moderated by perceived own contributions. We then went on to argue that both parties' behaviour should not be equated with contributions, but that both parties interpret their own and the other party's behaviour through the lens of Implicit Leadership and Followership Theories. The parties' currencies of exchange can therefore be argued to differ. This model eventually set the stage to explain that LMX disagreement can stem from (1) differences in both parties' implicit theories, and (2) differences in perceptions of own and other's behaviour. The first refers to *what* should be exchanged and thus governs *if* perceived behaviour translates into perceived contributions, and the second refers to people's estimations of *how much* is exchanged and thus governs the *magnitude* of perceived contributions. Based upon these propositions, it is clear that a match of ILTs and IFTs is an important precondition for LMX agreement, but also that biases in self and other perceptions can still interfere and thus render LMX disagreement likely. Both issues thus need to be addressed if LMX disagreement is to be overcome.

In general, we can assume that leaders and followers are largely unaware of their disagreement, because people have the tendency to suppose an implicit understanding. Discussing and making explicit what is implicit thus seems a good strategy to foster mutual agreement about contributions and, ultimately, also about the relationship quality. Indeed, we specifically predict reciprocal communication about mutual role expectations and values of contributions to have an effect on LMX agreement.

To begin with, the more both parties communicate about their mutual role expectations over time, the more each party should be able to understand *what* both are expected to contribute to the relationship. Additionally, the more both parties also specifically come to an understanding of the conversion rate (i.e., *how much* a follower's contribution is worth in leader contribution and vice versa), the better they should be able to balance their (perceived) contributions. Both acts of communication combined over time should thus enable both parties to fulfil a reciprocity norm (Cialdini, 1984; Uhl-Bien, 2003) that can be regarded as a precondition for reaching LMX agreement. As contexts can facilitate interaction (cf. Porter & McLaughlin, 2006), we suggest that in particular in contexts that allow for frequent and in-depth communication, leaders and followers will form more accurate perceptions of each other's contributions to the joint LMX relationship. This should be especially true for settings in which leaders and followers can additionally observe each other's behaviour, as these settings would allow for explicit communication and feedback about each person's behaviour before it is assessed as a potential contribution. In this respect, a study by Kacmar, Witt, Zivnuska, and Gully (2003) looks promising, because it shows that, at least for one side of the dyad, followers reporting frequent communication with the leader received more favourable job-performance ratings than did followers reporting infrequent communication. If expanded to both parties, these results can be brought in line with our prediction that communication allows for leaders and followers to exchange their mutual expectations better so that they can adjust their behaviour accordingly and ultimately reach LMX agreement (cf. "feedback" in Minsky, 2002). Although Sin et al. (2009) did not find a direct effect of communication frequency on the relationship between leaders' and followers' LMX ratings, they did find effects for dyadic tenure and intensity of dyadic interaction. In light of these findings, we argue that their data would hold the potential to find an effect of communication when it would, for instance, be interacted with relationship tenure or intensity of dyadic interaction. Indeed, we assume that the disjointed effects regarding tenure and a diversity of assessed communication processes (such as feedback, communication frequency, or interaction intensity) with regard to LMX agreement can be understood better when conceptualized in interaction with each other, that is, communication processes can be assumed to work best for aligning expectations (i.e., implicit theories) when they are enacted over longer periods of time. However, we are unaware of any study that attempted to find such more complex interaction patterns.

More specifically, we would be more confident that significant predictors of LMX agreement would be found if respective studies specifically assessed communication regarding mutual role expectations (i.e., ILTs and IFTs, a.k.a. *what* should be contributed) as well as communication explicating what each party does for the relationship that is not visible in regular face-to-face interactions (i.e., *how much* is contributed). Merely investigating the frequency of communication does not yield any insights in changes in leader's and follower's awareness of the other's implicit theories or in their awareness of how the other perceives the division of contributions to the relationship (cf. research which found that leaders and followers typically do not communicate about their mental models when interacting; Hollingshead, 1998; van Ginkel, Tindale, & van Knippenberg, in press). Therefore, we suggest that positive effects of frequency of communication on agreement will only be found in cases where the communication explicitly concerns ILTs and IFTs or the contributions made by both partners to the relationship.

In conclusion, we posit that differences in ILTs and IFTs as well as differences in the perception of own and other's behaviour cause LMX disagreement. Although some of those differences are personality based and thus less open for change, reciprocal communication about mutual role expectations as well as addressing issues related to information accessibility seem feasible strategies to overcome LMX disagreement.

Furthermore, but apart from the specific issue of LMX agreement, we would argue that our model also holds the potential to explain when and why consensus in follower perceptions of their leader is likely to occur—which is of equal concern in current reconsiderations of LMX theory (cf. Schyns & Day, 2010 this issue). Such research on consensus is interesting because it considers the variance in follower LMX perceptions as meaningful information and thus broadens the single-dyadic perspective to a multidyadic one (van Breukelen, Konst, & van der Vlist, 2002). Schyns (2006), for instance, integrated the notion of consensus with Heider's balance theory (1958) and showed that higher follower consensus in perceived leader contributions to the relationship relate to higher follower job satisfaction as well as higher commitment. However, although such studies are able to show that consensus is relevant, there is little explanation on the mechanisms whereby consensus can arise. In this respect, we would argue that expanding our presently single-dyadic model into a multidyadic one can elucidate the issue a little. We can, for instance, assume that perceptions of a leader's contributions vary between different followers. However, they vary not necessarily as a function of the leader that is perceived (i.e., such as LMX would posit that leaders behave differently towards different followers), but because different followers' standards, that is, their ILTs, might vary. It is thus only under the condition of ILT similarity among followers that followers apply the same benchmark and that they can be posited to interpret a leader's contributions to the relationship similarly. However, under conditions in which intrateam heterogeneity increases (such as in intercultural teams), it seems likely that the same leader's behaviour will be experienced differently by the individual team members. This difference in perceived contributions is then translated into different perceptions (i.e., nonconsensus) of LMX quality. According to our model, consensus in follower perceptions of their leader can thus be argued to vary as a function of followers' differences in ILTs.

SUGGESTIONS FOR FUTURE RESEARCH

LMX research commonly focuses on follower perceptions only. However, because LMX essentially reflects the relationship between leaders and followers, we believe that future research should concentrate on investigating LMX at the dyadic level (and pay appropriate heed to it in the assessment of LMX quality). Several authors issued calls for such a specification of level of analysis and for alignment of proposed theory and what is tested (Schriesheim et al., 1999; Schriesheim, Castro, Zhou, & Yammarino, 2001). Next to such fundamental considerations, an additional array of potential studies directly flows from the model presented in the present article, all of which have the potential to contribute to a more in-depth understanding of the dyadic nature of LMX relationships.

First of all, there is no measure to assess IFTs. To be able to test the model described in this article, research should start with the construction of such an IFT measure. Some research has already undertaken some steps towards measuring leaders' expectations for followers in leadership dyads (e.g., Engle & Lord, 1997; Wernimont, 1971), but we would recommend the construction of a new measure in several steps that parallel the construction of ILT measurements (cf. Lord et al., 1984; Offermann, Kennedy, & Wirtz, 1994). To do this, supervisors and subordinates should first indicate traits and behaviours that they consider to be typical of and make for a good follower (potential dimensions might span from central followership behaviours such as productivity, rule following, and loyalty to peripheral followership behaviours such as creativity, organizational citizenship behaviour, and critical thinking). Next, an independent group of leaders and followers should rate the prototypicality of these traits and behaviours for followers. Based on these ratings, the number of items should be reduced to form a scale of a reasonable length. Consecutive studies could reassess its factor structure over different work domains and cultures.

The development of an IFT measure already holds plenty of opportunities to compare followers' and leaders' IFTs with each other, but we recommend this topic is reserved for a separate line of research in which not only leaders' and followers' freely recalled ILTs and IFTs are compared to each other but also in which leaders' and followers' indications on existing ILT measures and the new IFT measures are compared. A valuable extension would further lie in research that would address possible antecedents of leader and follower (dis)agreement on ILTs and IFTs in either cross-sectional research (such as when comparing high reciprocal feedback leadership dyads with low ones, possibly interacted with dyadic tenure) or longitudinally (such as when comparing if and under which specific conditions leaders' and followers' ILT understanding as well their IFT understanding converge).

A different line of research could yet again employ standard ILT and IFT instruments and simply measure to what degree leaders and followers perceive each other to match the respective implicit theories. The resulting match scores could then be related to LMX quality perceptions much as we have outlined in Figure 1—essentially providing a test of the relationships proposed in our model. Moreover, when combined with the research questions above, one could assess whether LMX agreement is more likely to occur when the followers' and leaders' contents of ILTs and IFTs are congruent as opposed to when they are not.

Similarly, but related to general self-serving biases, one could assess precursors of self-serving biases such as narcissism, and investigate whether LMX agreement is affected by such tendencies. In dyads where the follower is fairly low in narcissism, we would, for instance, posit that LMX disagreement is more likely to occur when the respective leader is highly narcissistic than when the respective leader scores low in narcissism—simply because a narcissistic leader can be assumed to overestimate his or her own contribution.

Additionally, one could undertake experimental leadership dyad studies in which IFTs and ILTs are manipulated by, for instance, letting people read about great leaders or followers. Participants can then be asked to rate a confederate's behaviour (which either fits with the manipulated ILTs or IFTs or not) as a more or less valuable contribution to the relationship. According to our model, we would expect a fit effect, in that behaviour that is congruent (as opposed to incongruent) with the manipulation of the implicit theory will more likely be perceived as a contribution and ultimately translate into higher perceptions of relationship quality.

Finally, one could investigate the effects of mutual role expectation communication on LMX agreement. As briefly touched upon earlier, this could either be done cross-sectionally or in the lab, by, for instance, instructing one group of leadership dyads to explicitly discuss how they see a leader's and a follower's role concerning a specific task while depriving the other group of the chance to exchange such views (cf. van Ginkel & van Knippenberg, 2008). According to our model, we would predict to find that those leader–follower dyads that were able to communicate about their expectations beforehand are able to reciprocate each others' contributions better and thus ultimately rate the relationship better compared to those dyads that were not instructed to talk about their mutual role expectations.

BOUNDARIES TO THE MODEL

The presented model focuses mainly upon in-role behaviour as specified in ILTs and IFTs, and an obvious boundary lies in the fact that it does not account for every kind of extrarole behaviour. Extrarole behaviour that is accounted for in the present model is behaviour that is expected but not necessarily to that degree, e.g., being an even more visionary leader or being an extremely enthusiastic follower. Extrarole behaviour that is not accounted for is behaviour that totally falls out of the scope of ILTs or IFTs, e.g., when a leader pays a home visit to his or her follower who just became a parent, or when a follower arranges a birthday party for his or her leader. Such unexpected events are not catered for in the present model, but we would assume that the persons concerned rapidly process whether such behaviours are sufficiently congruent with their existing implicit theories regarding leaders and followers (cf. Lord et al., 2001), that is, ILTs and IFTs. Presumably, if they are, these behaviours will not only receive a positive valence but are also likely to be integrated in the respective ILT or IFT and will thus be part of the expectation for the next leader or follower.

Conversely, if such unexpected behaviour cannot be aligned with and extend existing knowledge structures, it is likely to be disapproved and potentially later used as a discriminant behaviour, that is, as part of an antiprototype.

A possible extension of our model, which goes beyond the scope of the current article, is to take a closer look at the consequences of agreement and disagreement at various levels of LMX quality. Essentially, we would predict that once it becomes clear to both parties that they disagree about the quality of their relationship, this will be a starting point for future discussion about their relationship and thus ultimately the development of their relationship. For cases of LMX agreement, however, the relationship dynamic is likely to be different and will depend on the level of LMX quality that is perceived and agreed upon. Although our model explains how such situations may arise, the consequences of LMX agreement at different levels of LMX quality for the relationship dynamics are not covered by it and thus seem interesting to explore in their own right. An obvious starting point would seem to be the possibility that agreement about low-quality LMX might motivate changes in the leader–follower relationship more than agreement about high-quality LMX.

IN CONCLUSION

To summarize, our model illustrates the complexity of the processes underlying leaders' and followers' assessments of their LMX relationship, and invites fuller integration of research on LMX and ILTs as well as extension of this research with the concept of IFTs. By thus outlining the many potential sources for LMX disagreement we hope to have opened the door towards open communication in research about the divergent LMX findings regarding leaders and followers, but also between leaders and followers themselves, so that they will engage in a dialogue to better understand each others' perspectives.

REFERENCES

Alicke, M. D. (1985). Global self-evaluation as determined by the desirability and controllability of trait adjectives. *Journal of Personality and Social Psychology, 49,* 1621–1630.

Allison, S. T., Messick, D. M., & Goethals, G. R. (1989). On being better but not smarter than others: The Muhammad Ali effect. *Social Cognition, 7,* 275–296.

Anseel, F., & Lievens, F. (2007). The long-term impact of the feedback environment on job satisfaction: A field study in a Belgian context. *Applied Psychology: An International Review, 56,* 254–266.

Atwater, L. E., & Yammarino, F. J. (1992). Does self-other agreement on leadership perceptions moderate the validity of leadership and performance predictions? *Personnel Psychology, 45,* 141–164.

Atwater, L. E., & Yammarino, F. J. (1997). Self-other rating agreement: A review and a model. *Research in Personnel and Human Resources Management, 15,* 121–174.

Barsalou, L. W. (1985). Ideals, central tendency, and frequency of instantiation as determinants of graded structure in categories. *Journal of Experimental Psychology: Learning, Memory, and Cognition, 11,* 629–654.

Bartlett, F. C. (1932). *Remembering.* Cambridge: Cambridge University Press.

Bass, B., & Yammarino, F. J. (1991). Congruence of self and other's leadership ratings of naval officers for understanding successful performance. *Applied Psychology: An International Review, 40,* 437–454.

Basu, R., & Green, S. G. (1997). Leader–member exchange and transformational leadership: An empirical examination of innovative behaviors in leader–member dyads. *Journal of Applied Social Psychology, 27,* 477–499.

Bechtel, W., & Abrahamsen, A. (2002). *Connectionism and the mind: Parallel processing, dynamics, and evolution in networks.* Cambridge, MA: Basil Blackwell.

Bernerth, J. B., Armenakis, A. A., Feild, H. S., Giles, W. F., & Walker, H. J. (2007). Leader–member social exchange (LMSX): Development and validation of a scale. *Journal of Organizational Behavior, 28,* 979–1003.

Blau, P. (1964). *Exchange and power in social life.* New York: Wiley.

Borman, W. C. (1987). Personal constructs, performance schemata, and "folk theories" of subordinate effectiveness: Exploration in an Army Officer sample. *Organizational Behavior and Human Decision Processes, 40,* 307–322.

Brawley, L. R. (1984). Unintentional egocentric biases in attributions. *Journal of Sport Psychology, 6,* 264–278.

Brodbeck, F. C., Chhokar, J., & House, R. (2007). Culture and leadership in 25 societies: Integration, conclusions, and future directions. In J. Chhokar, F. C. Brodbeck, & R. House (Eds.), *Managerial cultures of the world: A GLOBE report of in-depth studies of the cultures of 25 countries* (pp. 1025–1102). Mahwah, NJ: Lawrence Erlbaum Associates, Inc.

Brown, J. D. (1986). Evaluations of self and others: Self-enhancement biases in social judgments. *Social Cognition, 4,* 353–376.

Bruner, J. S. (1961). The act of discovery. *Harvard Educational Review, 31,* 21–32.

Burger, J. M., & Rodman, J. L. (1983). Attributions of responsibility for group tasks: The egocentric bias and the actor-observer difference. *Journal of Personality and Social Psychology, 45,* 1232–1242.

Burgess, R. L., & Huston, T. L. (1979). *Social exchanges in developing relationships.* New York: Academic Press.

Buunk, B. P., Doosje, B. J., Jans, L. G. J. M., & Hopstaken, L. E. M. (1993). Perceived reciprocity, social support, and stress at work: The role of exchange and communal orientation. *Journal of Personality and Social Psychology, 65,* 801–811.

Byrne, D. (1971). *The attraction paradigm.* New York: Academic Press.

Carver, R. P. (1972). A critical review of mathagenic behaviors and the effect of questions upon the retention of prose materials. *Journal of Reading Behavior, 4,* 93–119.

Catrambone, R., & Holyoak, K. J. (1989). Overcoming contextual limitations on problem-solving transfer. *Journal of Experimental Psychology: Learning, Memory, and Cognition, 15,* 1147–1156.

Choi, Y., & Mai-Dalton, R. R. (1999). The model of followers' responses to self-sacrificial leadership: An empirical approach. *Leadership Quarterly, 10,* 397–421.

Cialdini, R. B. (1984). *Influence: How and why people agree to things.* New York: William Morrow.

Cogliser, C. C., Schriesheim, C. A., Scandura, T. A., & Gardner, W. L. (2009). Balancing leader and follower perceptions of leader–member exchange: Relationships with performance and work attitudes. *Leadership Quarterly, 20,* 452–465.

Conger, J. A., & Kanungo, R. (1987). Toward a behavioral theory of charismatic leadership in organizational settings. *Academy of Management Review, 12,* 637–647.

Coyle-Shapiro, J., & Kessler, I. (2002). Exploring reciprocity through the lens of the psychological contract: Employee and employer perspectives. *European Journal of Work and Organizational Psychology, 11,* 69–86.

Crary, W. G. (1966). Reactions to incongruent self-experiences. *Journal of Consulting Psychology, 30,* 246–252.

Dansereau, F., Graen, G., & Haga, W. J. (1975). A vertical dyad linkage approach to leadership within formal organizations: A longitudinal investigation of the role-making process. *Organizational Behavior and Human Performance, 13,* 46–78.

Dansereau, F., Alutto, J. A., Nachman, S. A., Al-kelabi, S. A., Yammarino, F. J., Newman, J., et al. (1995). Individualized leadership: A new multiple-level approach. *Leadership Quarterly, 6,* 413–450.

Day, D. V., & Crain, E. C. (1992). The role of affect and ability in initial exchange quality perceptions. *Group and Organization Management, 23,* 189–216.

De Cremer, D., & van Knippenberg, D. (2004). Leader self-sacrifice and leadership effectiveness: The moderating role of leader self-confidence. *Organizational Behavior and Human Decision Processes, 95,* 140–155.

Deluga, R. J. (1997). Relationship among American presidential charismatic leadership, narcissism, and rated performance. *Leadership Quarterly, 8,* 49–65.

Dienesch, R. M., & Liden, R. C. (1986). Leader–member exchange model of leadership: A critique and further development. *Academy of Management Review, 11,* 618–634.

Dockery, T. M., & Steiner, D. D. (1990). The role of the initial interaction in leader–member exchange. *Group and Organization Studies, 15,* 395–413.

Duchon, D., Green, S. G., & Taber, T. D. (1986). Vertical dyad linkage: A longitudinal assessment of antecedents, measures and consequences. *Journal of Applied Psychology, 71,* 56–60.

Dunning, D., Meyerowitz, J. A., & Holzberg, A. D. (1989). Ambiguity and self-evaluation: The role of idiosyncratic trait definitions in self-serving assessments of ability. *Journal of Personality and Social Psychology, 57,* 1082–1090.

Eagly, A. H., & Karau, S. J. (2002). Role congruity theory of prejudice toward female leaders. *Psychological Review, 109,* 573–598.

Engle, E. M., & Lord, R. G. (1997). Implicit theories, self-schemas, and leader–member exchange. *Academy of Management Journal, 40,* 988–1010.

Epitropaki, O., & Martin, R. (2005). From ideal to real: A longitudinal study of the role of implicit leadership theories on leader–member exchanges and employee outcomes. *Journal of Applied Psychology, 90,* 659–676.

Erdogan, B., Liden, R. C., & Kraimer, M. L. (2006). Justice and leader–member exchange: The moderating role of organization culture. *Academy of Management Journal, 49,* 395–406.

Galinsky, A. D., Magee, J. C., Inesi, M. E., & Gruenfeld, D. H. (2006). Power and perspectives not taken. *Psychological Science, 17,* 1068–1074.

Gerstner, C. R., & Day, D. V. (1997). Meta-analytic review of leader–member exchange theory: Correlates and construct issues. *Journal of Applied Psychology, 82,* 827–844.

Gioia, D. A., Thomas, J. B., Clark, S. M., & Chittipeddi, K. (1994). Symbolism and strategic change in academia: The dynamics of sensemaking and influence. *Organization Science, 5,* 363–383.

Gilovich, T., Medvec, V. H., & Savitsky, K. (2000). The spotlight effect in social judgment: An egocentric bias in estimates of the salience of one's own actions and appearance. *Journal of Personality and Social Psychology, 78,* 211–222.

Glick, M. L., & Holyoak, K. J. (1980). Analogical problem solving. *Cognitive Psychology, 12,* 306–355.

Gouldner, A. W. (1960). The norm of reciprocity: A preliminary statement. *American Sociological Review, 25*, 161–179.

Graen, G. B. (Ed.). (2003). *Dealing with diversity, LMX leadership: The series* (Vol. 1). Greenwich, CT: Information Age Publishing.

Graen, G. B., & Cashman, J. F. (1975). A role-making model of leadership in formal organizations: A developmental approach. In J. G. Hunt & L. L. Larson (Eds.), *Leadership frontiers* (pp. 143–165). Kent, OH: Kent State University Press.

Graen, G. B., Novak, M. A., & Sommerkamp, P. (1982). The effects of leader–member exchange and job design on productivity and satisfaction: Testing a dual attachment model. *Organizational Behavior and Human Performance, 30*, 109–131.

Graen, G. B., & Scandura, T. A. (1987). Toward a psychology of dyadic organizing. *Research in Organizational Behavior, 9*, 175–208.

Graen, G. B., & Schiemann, W. (1978). Leader–member agreement: A vertical dyad linkage approach. *Journal of Applied Psychology, 63*, 206–212.

Graen, G. B., & Uhl-Bien, M. (1995). Relationship-based approach to leadership: Development of leader–member exchange (LMX) theory of leadership over 25 years: Applying a multi-level multi-domain perspective. *Leadership Quarterly, 6*, 219–247.

Green, S. G., Anderson, S. E., & Shivers, S. L. (1996). Demographic and organizational influences on leader–member exchange and related work attitudes. *Organizational Behavior and Human Decision Processes, 66*, 203–214.

Harris, M. M., & Schaubroeck, J. (1988). A meta-analysis of self-supervisor, self-peer, and peer-supervisor ratings. *Personnel Psychology, 41*, 43–62.

Harrison, D. A., Price, K. H., & Bell, M. P. (1998). Beyond relational demography: Time and the effects of surface- and deep-level diversity on work group cohesion. *Academy of Management Journal, 41*, 96–107.

Heider, F. (1958). *The psychology of interpersonal relations*. New York: Wiley.

Heilman, M. E., Block, C. J., & Lucas, J. A., (1992). Presumed incompetent? Stigmatization and affirmative action efforts. *Journal of Applied Psychology, 77*, 536–544.

Hiller, N. J., & Day, D. V. (2003). LMX and teamwork: The challenges and opportunities of diversity. In G. B. Graen (Ed.), *Dealing with diversity, LMX leadership: The series* (Vol. 1, pp. 29–57). Greenwich, CT: Information Age Publishing.

Hollingshead, A. B. (1998). Distributed knowledge and transactive processes in decision-making groups. In D. H. Gruenfeld (Ed.), *Research on managing groups and teams* (pp. 103–123). Stanford, CT: JAI Press.

Holyoak, K. J., & Koh, K. (1987). Surface and structural similarity in analogical transfer. *Memory and Cognition, 15*, 332–340.

House, R. J., Hanges, P. J., Javidan, M., Dorfman, P., & Gupta, V. (2004). *Culture, leadership, and organizations: The GLOBE study of 62 societies*. Thousand Oaks, CA: Sage.

Huang, X., Wright, R. P., Chiu, W. C. K., & Wang, C. (2008). Relational schemas as sources of evaluation and misevaluation of leader–member exchanges: Some initial evidence. *Leadership Quarterly, 19*, 266–282.

Hunt, J. G., Boal, K. B., & Sorenson, R. L. (1990). Top management leadership: Inside the black box. *Leadership Quarterly, 1*, 41–65.

Ilies, R., Nahrgang, J. D., & Morgeson, F. P. (2007). Leader–member exchange and citizenship behaviors: A meta-analysis. *Journal of Applied Psychology, 92*, 269–277.

Jablin, F. M., & Krone, K. J. (1987). Organizational assimilation. In C. Berger & S. H. Chaffee (Eds.), *Handbook of communication science* (pp. 711–746). Newbury Park, CA: Sage.

John, O. P., & Robins, R. W. (1994). Accuracy and bias in self-perception: Individual differences in self-enhancement and the role of narcissism. *Journal of Personality and Social Psychology, 66*, 206–219.

Kacmar, K. M., Witt, L. A., Zivnuska, S., & Gully, S. M. (2003). The interactive effect of leader–member exchange and communication frequency on performance ratings. *Journal of Applied Psychology, 88,* 764–772.

Keller, T. (1999). Images of the familiar: Individual differences and implicit leadership theories. *Leadership Quarterly, 10,* 589–607.

Kenney, R. A., Schwartz-Kenney, B. M., Blascovich, J. (1996). Implicit leadership theories: Defining leaders described as worthy of influence. *Personality and Social Psychology Bulletin, 22,* 1128–1143.

Kim, K. I., & Organ, D. W. (1982). Determinants of leader-subordinate exchange relationships. *Group and Organization Studies, 7,* 77–89.

Lagace, R. R. (1990). Leader–member exchange: Antecedents and consequences of the cadre and hired hand. *Journal of Personal Selling and Sales Management, 10,* 11–19.

Liberman, N., Trope, Y., McCrea, S., & Sherman, S. J. (2007). The effect of level of construal on the temporal distance of activity engagement. *Journal of Experimental Social Psychology, 43,* 143–149.

Liden, R. C., & Graen, G. (1980). Generalizability of the vertical dyad linkage model of leadership. *Academy of Management Journal, 23,* 451–465.

Liden, R. C., & Maslyn, J. M. (1998). Multidimensionality of leader–member exchange: An empirical assessment through scale development. *Journal of Management, 24,* 43–72.

Liden, R. C., Wayne, S. J., & Stilwell, D. (1993). A longitudinal study on the early development of leader–member exchanges. *Journal of Applied Psychology, 78,* 662–674.

Lord, R. G. (1985). An information processing approach to social perceptions, leadership perceptions and behavioral measurement in organizational settings. In B. M. Staw & L. L. Cummings (Eds.), *Research in organizational behavior* (Vol. 7, pp. 85–128). Greenwich, CT: JAI Press.

Lord, R. G., & Brown, D. J. (2004). *Leadership processes and follower identity.* Mahwah, NJ: Lawrence Erlbaum Associates, Inc.

Lord, R. G., Brown, D. J., Harvey, J. L., & Hall, R. J. (2001). Contextual constraints on prototype generation and their multilevel consequences for leadership perceptions. *Leadership Quarterly, 12,* 311–338.

Lord, R. G., Foti, R. J., & de Vader, C. L. (1984). A test of leadership categorization theory: Internal structure, information processing, and leadership perceptions. *Organizational Behavior and Human Performance, 34,* 343–378.

Lord, R. G., & Hall, R. J. (2003). Identity, leadership categorization, and leadership schema. In D. van Knippenberg & M. A. Hogg (Eds.), *Leadership and power* (pp. 48–64). London: Sage.

Lord, R. G., & Maher, K. J. (1991). *Leadership and information processing: Linking perceptions and performance.* Boston: Unwin Hyman.

Maslyn, J. M., & Uhl-Bien, M. (2001). Leader–member exchange and its dimensions: Effects of self-effort and other's effort on relationship quality. *Journal of Applied Psychology, 86,* 697–708.

Mayfield, J., & Mayfield, M. (1998). Increasing worker outcomes by improving leader follower relations. *Journal of Leadership Studies, 5,* 72–81.

Meindl, J. R. (1995). The romance of leadership as a follower-centric theory: A social constructionist approach. *Leadership Quarterly, 6,* 329–342.

Minsky, B. D. (2002). *LMX dyad agreement: Construct definition and the role of supervisor or subordinate similarity and communication in understanding LMX.* Unpublished doctoral dissertation, Louisiana State University, Louisiana.

Müller, A., & Schyns, B. (2005). The perception of leadership—leadership as a perception: An exploration using the Repertory Grid-Technique. In B. Schyns & J. R. Meindl (Eds.), *Implicit leadership theories: Essays and explorations* (pp. 81–101). Greenwich, CT: Information Age Publishing.

Nye, J. L. (2002). The eye of the follower: Information processing effects on attribution regarding leaders of small groups. *Small Group Research, 33*, 337–360.

Oakes, P. J., Turner, J. C., & Haslam, A. S. (1991). Perceiving people as group members: The role of fit in the salience of social categorizations. *British Journal of Social Psychology, 30*, 125–144.

Offermann, L. R., Kennedy, J. K., Jr., & Wirtz, P. W. (1994). Implicit leadership theories: Content, structure and generalizability. *Leadership Quarterly, 5*, 43–58.

Paglis, L. L., & Green, S. G. (2002). Both sides now: Supervisor and subordinate perspectives on relationship quality. *Journal of Applied Social Psychology, 32*, 250–276.

Pirolli, P. L., & Anderson, J. R. (1985). The role of learning from examples in the acquisition of recursive programming skills. *Canadian Journal of Psychology, 39*, 240–272.

Porter, L. W., & McLaughlin, G. B. (2006). Leadership and organizational context: Like the weather? *Leadership Quarterly, 17*, 559–576.

Reed, S. K. (1987). A structure-mapping model for word problems. *Journal of Experimental Psychology: Learning, Memory, and Cognition, 13*, 124–139.

Ridgeway, C. L. (2001). Gender, status, and leadership. *Journal of Social Issues, 57*, 637–655.

Ritter, B. A., & Lord, R. G. (2007). The impact of previous leaders on the evaluation of new leaders: An alternative to prototype. *Journal of Applied Psychology, 92*, 1683–1695.

Rosenthal, S. A., & Pittinsky, T. L. (2006). Narcissistic leadership. *Leadership Quarterly, 17*, 617–633.

Ross, B. (1984). Remindings and their effects in learning a cognitive skill. *Cognitive Psychology, 16*, 371–416.

Ross, B. (1987). This is like that: The use of earlier problems and the separation of similarity effects. *Journal of Experimental Psychology: Learning, Memory, and Cognition, 13*, 629–639.

Ross, M., & Sicoly, E. (1979). Egocentric biases in availability and attribution. *Journal of Personality and Social Psychology, 37*, 322–336.

Sanders, M. M. (1999). Leader, follower, team player, thief: An exploration of managers' performer categories. *Journal of Business and Psychology, 14*, 199–215.

Scandura, T. A., & Graen, G. B. (1984). Moderating effects of initial leader–member exchange status on the effects of a leadership intervention. *Journal of Applied Psychology, 69*, 428–436.

Schriesheim, C. A., Castro, S. L., & Cogliser, C. C. (1999). Leader–member exchange (LMX) research: A comprehensive review of theory, measurement, and data-analytic practices. *Leadership Quarterly, 10*, 63–113.

Schriesheim, C. A., Castro, S. L., Zhou, X., & Yammarino, F. J. (2001). The folly of theorizing "A" but testing "B": A selective level-of-analysis review of the field and a detailed leader–member exchange illustration. *The Leadership Quarterly, 12*, 515–551.

Schriesheim, C. A., & Gardiner, C. C. (1992). *An exploration of the discriminant validity of the leader–member exchange scale (LMX 7) commonly used in organizational research.* Paper presented at the meeting of the Southern Management Association, New Orleans, LA.

Schwarz, N., Bless, H., Strack, F., Klumpp, G., Rittenauer-Schatka, H., & Simons, A. (1991). Ease of retrieval as information: Another look at the availability heuristic. *Journal of Personality and Social Psychology, 61*, 195–202.

Schyns, B. (2006). Are group consensus in leader-member exchange (lmx) and shared work values related to organizational outcomes? *Small Group Research, 37*, 20–35.

Schyns, B., & Day, D. V. (2010). Critique and review of leader-member exchange theory: Issues of agreement, consensus, and excellence. *European Journal of Work and Organizational Psychology, 19*(1), 1–29.

Schyns, B., & Meindl, J. R. (Eds.). (2005). *Implicit leadership theories: Essays and explorations.* Greenwich, CT: Information Age Publishing.

Schyns, B., Paul, T., Mohr, G., & Blank, H. (2005). Comparing antecedents and consequences of leader–member exchange in a German working context to findings in the US. *European Journal of Work and Organizational Psychology, 14*, 1–22.

Scott, K. A., & Brown, D. J. (2006). Female first, leader second? Gender bias in the encoding of leadership behavior. *Organizational Behavior and Human Decision Processes, 101*, 230–242.

Shamir, B., Pillai, R., Bligh, M. C., & Uhl-Bien, M. (Eds.). (2007). *Follower-centered perspectives on leadership.* Greenwich, CT: Information Age Publishing.

Silverman, I. (1964). Self-esteem and differential responsiveness to success and failure. *Journal of Abnormal and Social Psychology, 69*, 115–119.

Sin, H. P., Nahrgang, J. D., & Moregeson, F. P. (2009). Understanding why they don't see eye-to-eye: An examination of leader–member exchange (LMX) agreement. *Journal of Applied Psychology, 94*, 1048–1057.

Taylor, S. E., & Brown, J. D. (1988). Illusion and well-being: A social psychological perspective on mental health. *Psychological Bulletin, 103*, 193–210.

Tekleab, A. G., & Taylor, M. S. (2003). Aren't there two parties in an employment relationship? Antecedents and consequences of organization-employee agreement on contract obligations and violations. *Journal of Organizational Behavior, 24*, 585–608.

Tsui, A. S., Egan, T. D., & O'Reilly, C. A. (1992). Being different: Relational demography and organizational attachment. *Administrative Science Quarterly, 37*, 549–579.

Tsui, A. S., & O'Reilly, C. A. (1989). Beyond simple demographic effects: The importance of relational demography in superior-sub-ordinate dyads. *Academy of Management Journal, 32*, 402–423.

Turner, J. (1987). *Rediscovering the social group: A self-categorization theory.* Oxford, UK: Blackwell.

Tversky, A., & Kahneman, D. (1974). Judgment under uncertainty: Heuristics and biases. *Science, 185*, 1124–1131.

Uhl-Bien, M. (2003). Relationship development as a key ingredient for leadership development. In S. E. Murphy & R. E. Riggio (Eds.), *The future of leadership development* (pp. 129–147). Mahwah, NJ: Lawrence Erlbaum Associates, Inc.

Uhl-Bien, M., & Maslyn, J. M. (2003). Reciprocity in manager-subordinate relationships: Components, configurations, and outcomes. *Journal of Management, 29*, 511–532.

Van Breukelen, W., Konst, D., & van der Vlist, R. (2002). Effects of LMX and differential treatment on work unit commitment. *Psychological Reports, 91*, 220–230.

Van Breukelen, W., Schyns, B., & LeBlanc, P. (2006). Leader–member exchange theory and research: Accomplishments and future challenges. *Leadership, 2*, 295–316.

Van Dijk, E., & van Knippenberg, D. (2005). Wanna trade? Product knowledge and the perceived differences between the gains and losses of trade. *European Journal of Social Psychology, 35*, 23–34.

Van Ginkel, W. P., Tindale, R. S., & van Knippenberg, D. (in press). Team reflexivity, development of shared task representations, and the use of distributed information in group decision making. *Group Dynamics.*

Van Ginkel, W. P., & van Knippenberg, D. (2008). Group information elaboration and group decision making: The role of shared task representations. *Organizational Behavior and Human Decision Processes, 105*, 82–97.

Van Quaquebeke, N., & Brodbeck, F. C. (2008). Entwicklung und erste Validierung zweier Instrumente zur Erfassung von Führungskräfte-Kategorisierung im deutschsprachigen Raum [Development and first validation of two scales to measure leader categorization in German-speaking countries]. *Zeitschrift für Arbeits- und Organisationspsychologie, 52*, 70–80.

Van Quaquebeke, N., Graf, M. M., & Brodbeck, F. C. (2007). *What do leaders have to live up to? Contrasting the effects of typical versus ideal leader prototypes for the process of leader categorization.* Paper presented at the 13th European Congress of Work and Organizational Psychology, Stockholm, Sweden.

Vecchio, R. P. (1995). The impact of referral sources on employee attitudes: Evidence from a national sample. *Journal of Management, 21,* 953–965.

Vecchio, R. P., & Norris, W. (1996). Predicting employee turnover from performance, satisfaction, and leader–member exchange. *Journal of Business and Psychology, 11,* 113–125.

Walster, E., Walster, G. W., & Berscheid, E. (1978). *Equity: Theory and research.* Boston: Allyn & Bacon.

Weick, K. E. (1995). *Sensemaking in organizations.* Thousand Oaks, CA: Sage.

Wernimont, P. F. (1971). What supervisors and subordinates expect of each other. *Personnel Journal, 50,* 204–208.

Wexley, K. N., Alexander, R. A., Greenawalt, J. P., & Couch, M. A. (1980). Attitudinal congruence and similarity as related to interpersonal evaluations in manager-subordinate dyads. *Academy of Management Journal, 23,* 320–330.

Yammarino, F. J., & Dansereau, F. (2002). Individualized leadership. *Journal of Leadership and Organizational Studies, 9,* 1–11.

EUROPEAN JOURNAL OF WORK AND
ORGANIZATIONAL PSYCHOLOGY
2010, 19 (3), 364–387

Ψ Psychology Press
Taylor & Francis Group

Transformational leadership and commitment: A multilevel analysis of group-level influences and mediating processes

Sabine Korek

University of Leipzig, Leipzig, Germany

Jörg Felfe

University of Siegen, Siegen, Germany

Ute Zaepernick-Rothe

Technical University of Braunschweig, Braunschweig, Germany

Researchers in the field of leadership have shown an increasing interest in examining the additional effect of consensus, which reflects on the variability of leadership perceptions in a team on outcomes. Based on theoretical assumptions with regard to social group processes and group-related mechanisms of transformational leadership it is hypothesized in this study that besides group-level transformational leadership, the consensus among group members will positively predict affective and normative commitment. In contrast, no relationship with continuance commitment was expected. Further we proposed that the influence of group-level transformational leadership is mediated by perceptions of meaningful tasks, whereas consensus is mediated by positive organizational climate. Multisource data were collected from 21 CEOs of small pharmacies and their subordinates. Subordinates ($N = 105$) rated their supervisors' transformational leadership, as well as their individual perceptions of task content, organizational climate, and organizational commitment, and CEOs rated their scope of influence. As expected, group-level transformational leadership and consensus were positively related to affective commitment. Further multilevel analyses revealed that meaningful task content mediated the influence of leadership on affective commitment. Positive organizational climate slightly mediated the relationship between consensus and affective commitment. Practical implications are discussed with

Correspondence should be addressed to Sabine Korek, Institute of Psychology II, Work and Organizational Psychology, University of Leipzig, Seeburgstraße 14–20, 04103 Leipzig, Germany. E-mail: korek@uni-leipzig.de

http://www.psypress.com/ejwop   DOI: 10.1080/13594320902996336

regard to commitment management by promoting meaningful work and strengthening consensus and climate.

Keywords: Consensus; Climate, Multilevel analyses; Organizational commitment; Task content; Transformational leadership.

The positive link between transformational leadership and organizational commitment has been shown in numerous studies (Meyer, Stanley, Herscovitch, & Topolnytsky, 2002). Most of these studies have been conducted on the base of analyses on the individual level. However, leadership can also be viewed as a group phenomenon (Mumford, Dansereau, & Yammarino, 2000; Yammarino, Dionne, Chun, & Dansereau, 2005), whereby a leader exerts a common influence on all of his subordinates with more or less equal relationships to the group members. Hence, group members should agree more or less on their leadership perceptions. Group-oriented leadership behaviour and within-group processes such as social contagion or interactions further strengthen the similarity of the perceptions of a leader within a group (Gavin & Hofmann, 2002). Accordingly the present study takes a follower-centred view and aims at conceptualizing transformational leadership as a group-level phenomenon. Besides the absolute level of transformational leadership in a group, the dispersion or variability of perceptions in a group contains valuable information. Prior research has shown consensus to be an incremental predictor when it comes to understanding leadership and its outcomes (Cole & Bedeian, 2007; Schyns, 2006).

It is the aim of the present study to investigate the link between group-level transformational leadership and commitment, and the additional impact of the consensus within a group referring to transformational leadership perceptions. We chose organizational commitment as our dependent variable, because it predicts a stable, long-term relationship between employees and employers. Committed employees will show higher levels of engagement, extra effort, and lower fluctuation in crisis situations (Cooper-Hakim & Viswesvaran, 2005; Meyer et al., 2002). We extend existing research by taking into account all three components of organizational commitment as proposed by Meyer and Allen (1997). They denote differential patterns of the psychological links between employees and their organization. Previous research has only investigated relationships with affective commitment (Avolio, Zhu, Koh, & Bhatia, 2004; Felfe & Heinitz, 2010 this issue). Moreover, the underlying mechanisms in terms of mediating processes that explain the effect of group-level variables have not been examined fully yet.

Therefore, we propose two different mediating processes that link group-level transformational leadership and consensus to organizational commitment: We expect perceptions of a meaningful task to account for the impact of group-level transformational leadership on commitment, whereas consensus should be mitigated by perceptions of a positive organizational climate. These potentially mediating processes have been widely neglected, because it may be questionable if middle-hierarchy-leaders in large organizations have considerable opportunities to influence or change working conditions. Therefore they only may have the chance to influence followers' perceptions and evaluations of working conditions (Purvanova, Bono, & Dzieweczynski, 2006). However, in small businesses, leaders are in the position of general managers and have more if not even full control (human resource management, technical equipment, scheduling and assigning tasks, etc.). In order to validate this assumption and not relying solely on followers' perceptions, we included leaders' scope of influence as a proxy for leaders' situational control and influence.

GROUP-LEVEL TRANSFORMATIONAL LEADERSHIP AND COMMITMENT

According to Bass (1999), transformational leadership behaviour is characterized by four strategies: idealized influence, inspirational motivation, intellectual stimulation, and individualized consideration. In general, transformational leadership is seen as moving beyond transactions in order to improve followers' performance and satisfaction by influencing their needs and values. Extending the dyadic perspective, in an organizational setting, a leader usually interacts with a group of followers. Next to different dyadic relationships between a leader and each of his followers, which is a core issue of the LMX approach (Graen & Uhl-Bien, 1995), leadership is also a group phenomenon. A leader addresses many of his/her actions towards the whole group by setting group goals, fostering team spirit, and developing a specific climate (Shamir, Zakay, Breinin, & Popper, 1998). It is one of the central tenets of transformational leadership to establish a collective identity, collective self-efficacy, and group cohesion (Bass, 1985; Shamir, House, & Arthur, 1993). Feinberg, Ostroff, and Burke (2005) even noted that building consensus is one of the main tasks of transformational leadership. Yukl (1999) suggested some additional group or organizational processes of transformational leadership, such as coordination of intergroup activities or utilization of personnel and resources. With regard to these group-directed behaviours, all group members are exposed to the same leadership behaviour. Therefore the perceptions within a group with regard to these group-directed activities should be rather similar. Several within-group processes such as social interactions or contagion strengthen the homogeneity of perceptions of leadership behaviour. This similarity is an inevitable prerequisite to conceptualize transformational leadership on the group level. This group level is reflected by the average level of transformational leadership within a group. It can serve as a proxy for transformational leadership climate if a substantial amount of perceptual agreement can be established (Bliese, 2000; Chan, 1998; James et al., 2008).

Organizational commitment was defined by Mathieu and Zajac (1990) as "a bond or linking of the individual to the organization" (p. 171). As mentioned earlier, we refer to the three-component model introduced by Meyer and Allen (1997), which consists of affective, normative, and continuance commitment. Affective organizational commitment (OCA) denotes the emotional attachment with the current organization, built on common values, identification, and fulfilment of needs. Affective committed employees stay, because they want to. Many studies have shown positive relationships between transformational leadership and affective commitment (Dvir, Kass, & Shamir, 2004; Felfe, 2006; Felfe, Yan, & Six, 2008; Meyer et al., 2002). Group-level transformational leadership should foster emotional attachment, call on feelings of identification and belonging, as well as emphasize the common mission and collective efficacy. Even individuals with lower perceptions of transformational leadership can benefit from a high level of transformational leadership in their group, because their affective commitment will be "lifted" by the overall good leadership climate. Otherwise, a group with low transformational leadership can bring down the affective commitment of an individual subordinate who perceives his/her leader as being transformational. As such, we expect the following:

Hypothesis 1a: Group-level transformational leadership is positively related to affective commitment.

The second component, normative commitment (OCN), refers to an ethical and value-based moral obligation to stay in the organization. Normative committed employees stay, because they think they ought to. They feel a kind of obligation towards others in the organization, for example their co-workers in the team, the supervisor, or customers and clients. Meyer et al. (2002) report a positive correlation with transformational leadership, which is lower than that for affective commitment. Group-level transformational leadership influences values and social identity that enhance beliefs such as loyalty and the sense of duty. Shamir et al. (1993) proposed that followers' morale development is fostered by internalization of their transformational leaders' morale and values. Bass (1985) suggested that followers' self-interests are transcended for the sake of the group and emphasized the collectivistic aspect of morale development. Again we argue that individuals with lower perceptions of transformational leadership can benefit from a high level of transformational leadership in their group, because their normative commitment will be "lifted" by the overall leadership climate. Accordingly, we expect:

Hypothesis 1b: Group-level transformational leadership is positively related to normative commitment.

Continuance commitment (OCC) finally is defined as the perception of the costs associated with leaving the organization and the investments and sacrifices one has made to reach one's position. Also the awareness of other available job alternatives is taken into account. Employees with high continuance commitment stay, because they have to. With regard to transformational leadership, many studies have reported slightly negative or zero relationships with OCC (Bycio, Hackett, & Allen, 1995; De Vries, Roe, & Taillieu, 1999). Some authors argue with the dual conceptualization of the continuance component: The perception of alternatives is affected by higher order economical constraints or the personal situation (e.g., education; Bycio et al., 1995). The perceptions of job alternatives outside the current organization may differ between persons, and should be unrelated to any leadership behaviour, including group-level transformational leadership. Furthermore, OCC denotes a cognitive-oriented attitude, whereas group-level transformational leadership calls on personal needs, beliefs, and values. Therefore, we expect no meaningful relationship between group-level transformational leadership and OCC.

CONSENSUS OF TRANSFORMATIONAL LEADERSHIP AND COMMITMENT

In addition to the average of all group members' perceptions (group level), the variability of these perceptions can also add valuable information to predict outcome variables (Gonzalez-Roma, Peiro, & Tordera, 2002; Lindell & Brandt, 2000; Schneider, Salvaggio, & Subirats, 2002). Besides the absolute level of transformational leadership, consensus captures the extent to which all team members perceive their leaders' behaviour in a similar way. As stated earlier, perceptions of a leader within a group should cluster for several reasons (Ehrhart, 2004; Gavin & Hofmann, 2002; Griffin & Mathieu, 1997). First, a leader often exerts consistent behaviours towards the whole group. DeGroot, Kiker, and Cross (2000) reasoned that the effects of leadership are stronger, if leaders use a homogeneous style to relate to their subordinates. Klein and House (1995), for instance, noted that a leader's homogenous relationships with all team members reinforces the sense of a common mission and may result in higher group outcomes. Second, intragroup processes (social interactions, contagion, or conformity) strengthen the similarity of perceptions. Lower consensus however may result from heterogeneous needs, values, and expectations among group members. Different treatment and different qualities of relationships between leader and group members (e.g., high ingroup–outgroup differentiation) may also lead to low consensus. Empirical work on the effects of consensus in leadership perception suggests that consensus on perceptions of leadership style within a work team can serve as an important resource for work outcomes (e.g., Sanders & Schyns, 2006; Schyns, 2006). To explain why consensus is important and how different perceptions of leadership style within a work team can affect work outcomes, Sanders and Schyns (2006) applied Heider's (1958) balance theory. This theory suggests that two team members, whose relationships with their leader differ, get along badly. A solution to this problem can be that both members adjust their perceptions, resulting in a high amount of agreement between them. This agreement on the leadership style can, in turn, lead to higher feelings of team cohesion, identification, and indicate a well-functioning social group with a shared reality. Some empirical work shows the positive impact of consensual perceptions on several outcomes: Sanders and Schyns (2006) found high consensus of transformational leadership to predict solidarity behaviour towards the supervisor. Further, Feinberg et al. (2005) found consensus of leadership behaviour to be related to leader effectiveness. Cole and Bedeian (2007) reported consensus on transformational leadership to be a cross-level moderator of work commitment. But how is consensus on transformational leadership related to the components of organizational commitment? Coming back to affective commitment, consensus reflecting a shared social environment, common beliefs, and values fosters attachment to and identification with the group (Tajfel & Turner, 1986). Social exchanges in a well-functioning group as indicated by consensus are a social resource and enhance the sense of belonging and affiliation (Meyer & Allen, 1997). Sharing key components of transformational leadership such as a compelling vision might strengthen pride to be a member of this leaders' group. So we expect:

Hypothesis 2a: Consensus on transformational leadership is positively related to affective commitment.

Normative commitment deals with the internalization of norms and morale values. This internalization should be fostered, if all group members share the same leadership environment regarding morale standards and values expressed by the leader. Furthermore, values such as duty or loyalty towards the organization, co-workers or the leader are internalized easier, if they are shared by many group members. We expect the following:

Hypothesis 2b: Consensus on transformational leadership will be positively related to normative commitment.

For OCC we expect no meaningful relationship to transformational leadership and the related consensus. For some persons consensus may lead to higher OCC because they experience that this social resource could get lost when quitting the job. However, high consensus should not strengthen but even decrease the view that low alternatives are an important reason to stay in an organization. Both tendencies might neutralize each other.

MEANINGFUL TASK CONTENT AS A MEDIATOR BETWEEN GROUP-LEVEL TRANSFORMATIONAL LEADERSHIP AND ORGANIZATIONAL COMMITMENT

So far we have developed hypotheses about the influence of group-level transformational leadership and consensus on different components of organizational commitment. However the question remains by which mechanisms these relationships may be explained. Bass (1999) stated that "much more explanation is needed about the workings of transformational leadership" (p. 24). Efforts have already been made to explore processes that may explain the positive effect of transformational leadership on organizational commitment. Empowerment (Avolio et al., 2004), self-concordance (Bono & Judge, 2003), direct sympathy and liking (Brown & Keeping, 2005), higher team cohesion (Pillai & Williams, 2004), and collective self-efficacy (Walumbwa, Peng, Lawler, & Kan, 2004) have been identified as mediators in recent studies. Extending this research stream and building on the differentiation between group-level transformational leadership and consensus, we propose two different mediators: meaningful task content and positive organizational climate.

It is argued that the effect of group-level transformational leadership should be mediated by meaningful task content. The underlying rationale is that one of the main tasks of a CEO is to structure, schedule, and assign work tasks. In designing these tasks with a meaningful content, it is possible for a leader to display transformational leadership behaviour. In opposite simple-structured, repetitive tasks without meaning may substitute leadership activities because no challenging problems have to be solved, and no extra effort or development of new skills is necessary. Effective strategies of transformational leadership involve the creation of meaningful work and challenging tasks, the strengthening of the decision latitude, the encouragement of increased job control, and the promotion of empowerment (Avolio et al., 2004; Bass, 1999). Specific activities within the scope of transformational leadership dimensions should influence the meaning of a task. A leader who is intellectually stimulating followers by encouraging to solve problems or perform tasks in a different or new way should increase followers' autonomy and competency (Bass & Avolio, 1997). However, these efforts may fail if simple or repetitive tasks do not allow autonomy, or do not require the development of problem-solving skills or new approaches to accomplish goals. Moreover, individual consideration by mentoring and coaching should enhance followers' abilities, knowledge, and responsibility. Again, these abilities are unnecessary if a task is too simple and restricted to make use of the skills. Communicating an inspiring vision and emphasizing followers' impact for goal attainment may elevate the followers' convictions that their tasks are meaningful and significant. The assignment of meaningful tasks forces followers to think of strategies to solve problems or new approaches and to show extra effort. Recent work by Piccolo and Colquitt (2006) and Purvanova et al. (2006) further support this rationale. All these studies found that transformational leadership predicted the way followers viewed their jobs in terms of core job characteristics (Hackman & Oldham, 1976). Arnold, Turner, Barling, Kelloway, and McKee (2007) demonstrated that followers' perception of meaning (finding a purpose in work that exceeds extrinsic work outcomes) was contingent upon the transformational leadership behaviour of their supervisors. As a consequence, followers with meaningful work should reciprocate with extra effort, loyalty, and commitment (Kanter, 1983; Spreitzer, 1995; Wayne, Liden, & Sparrowe, 2000; Wiley, 1999). Meaningful work and knowledge about the significance of the task, as well as knowledge about one's personal contribution to organizational goals, should lead to enhanced feelings of belonging, and strengthen the emotional "bond" between the individual and her/his organization. If followers perceive their tasks as interesting and meaningful, they should be proud to belong to the organization and therefore develop more affective commitment. A similar influence can be expected for normative commitment because followers may feel obliged to "pay back the credit". Many studies and meta-analyses have shown work characteristics to be meaningful antecedents of commitment. Mathieu and Zajac (1990) reported a positive correlation between job scope in terms of Hackman and Oldham's (1976) job characteristics model and commitment. In their meta-analysis, Meyer et al. (2002) found a strong relationship between intrinsic satisfaction and OCA, and a smaller but substantial relationship to OCN. Based on these arguments and empirical findings, we propose:

Hypothesis 3: Meaningful task content mediates the link between group-level transformational leadership and affective commitment (3a) and between group-level transformational leadership and normative commitment (3b).

While developing Hypotheses 3a and b, we implicitly assume that meaningful task content is influenced by transformational leadership.

A further essential precondition for a leader to assign meaningful tasks to his subordinates is the leader's scope of influence (making autonomous and independent human resource management decisions, e.g., the chance to recruit or release employees, to change or reorganize work flow and task assignment, to provide extra training, and to promote or pay extra bonuses). We expect that in addition to transformational leadership, leaders' scope of influence will predict followers' perception of meaningful tasks. Though we assume a CEO to have considerable control of scheduling work flow, there may be some differences due to economical, organizational, legal, or staff constraints. The size of the business or the education level of the employees may influence the specification of work tasks. Furthermore, the developmental stage (start-up vs. consolidated business) may impact task discretion.

Hypothesis 3c: Leaders' scope of influence positively predicts followers' perception of meaningful tasks.

POSITIVE ORGANIZATIONAL CLIMATE AS A MEDIATOR BETWEEN CONSENSUS AND COMMITMENT

For the consensus we propose that positive organizational climate serves as a mediator. Consensus of transformational leadership within a group is based on many social processes including interactions and exchange. These interactions may be more effective in establishing commitment if relationships among co-workers and supervisors are positive and pleasant. Some prior research has focused on climate constructs as mediators between transformational leadership and personal/organizational outcome variables (e.g., Barling, Loughlin, & Kelloway, 2002; Nemanich & Keller, 2007). Organizational climate refers to estimations of the overall quality of relationships and communication in an organization. It includes perceptions of transparent decision making, policies, organizational support and justice, and the quality of relationships (Luria, 2008; Rentsch, 1990). According to the cognitive schema approach, climate can be viewed as individuals' cognitive representations of their environment (Anderson & West, 1998). As such, consensus should be strongly related to organizational climate, because the consensus denotes group members' perceptions of the quality of their shared social environment (Cole & Bedeian, 2007). High consensus groups are characterized by reliable interpretations of the environment and stable, predictable relationships between group members. Hence, interaction quality and intergroup relations as denoted by a positive organizational climate should be perceived as comfortable and pleasant. A positive organizational climate should, in turn, contribute to organizational commitment. It should strengthen affective commitment, because emotional attachment and identification should be fostered by good relationships in the group. We also expect positive effects on normative commitment due to a stronger sense of loyalty towards a well-functioning group with overall good relationships.

Hypothesis 4:   A positive organizational climate mediates the link between consensus of transformational leadership and affective commitment (4a) and between consensus of transformational leadership and normative commitment (4b).

METHOD

Sample and data collection

Our multisource data were collected from 21 CEOs of small German businesses (pharmacies) and 105 of their subordinates. The participants were volunteers and the results were reported to them, as well as to their CEO (survey-feedback method). All respondents completed the survey anonymously and were assured by the investigators that their responses would remain confidential. In our sample of subordinates, 97% were female, which reflects the high proportion of women in this profession. To guarantee anonymity, age and organizational tenure were collected as categorical variables (under 21, between 21 and 30, and so forth). Thirty-four per cent of the subordinates were aged between 21 and 30 years, 23% ranged between 31 and 40 years, 18% were between 41 and 50 years, and 23% were older than 50 years of age. Ten per cent of the participants had been working in their current organization for less than 6 months, 4% for less than 1 year, 26% for between 1 and 4 years, 20% for 5–10 years, and 40% for more than 10 years. Nineteen per cent held a university degree, and 25% had a bachelor degree. The 21 leaders had 7.24 subordinates ($SD = 3.49$) and had been business owners for 14.00 years ($SD = 8.92$). Other demographical data were not collected.

Measures

Organizational commitment was measured with Meyer and Allen's (1997) multidimensional instrument, which was adapted for use in Germany (Felfe, Schmook, & Six, 2006). The scale ranged from 1 ("not true at all") to 5 ("completely true"). The internal consistencies (Cronbach's alpha) for affective commitment equalled .88, for continuance commitment, .73 (Item 5 removed), and for normative commitment, .83. Item examples are:

"I'mproud to be part of this organization" (OCA), "Too much of my life would be disrupted if I decided I wanted to leave my organization now" (OCC), and "Even if it was to my advantage, I do not feel it would be right to leave my organization now" (OCN).

To measure group-level transformational leadership, a translated and modified version (Felfe, 2006) of the MLQ5X Short by Bass and Avolio (1995) was administered. It contained five subscales (IIA, IIB, IS, IC, and IM). Following Felfe's (2006) proposal, we added four items to assess special and outstanding leader behaviour associated with perceiving the leader as a charismatic role model. We combined all transformational leadership items to a composite scale of transformational leadership, as has been done in the past by other researchers (Barling et al., 2002; Bono & Judge, 2003; Purvanova et al., 2006; Shin & Zhou, 2003). This was justified by relatively high intercorrelations between the subscales. The internal consistency (Cronbach's alpha) equalled .96.

As we were interested in group-level transformational leadership, individual scores were averaged within each business. As mentioned earlier, a certain amount of perceptual agreement is necessary to justify aggregation to the group level. We therefore examined intraclass correlations and Rwg (Bliese, 2000; James, Demaree, & Wolf, 1993). Bliese (2000) suggests ICC(1) > .05 and Rwg > .70 as conventional criteria for aggregation. For the composite group-level transformational leadership measure, we obtained an ICC(1) of .40, and an Rwg of .77, justifying aggregation to the group level.

Consensus of transformational leadership was operationalized by calculating the standard deviation for each business. Low standard deviations refer to high consensus. For better interpretation, these values were then multiplied by -1, so that high values reflect high consensus.

To measure meaningful task content, a short subscale (three items) taken from an instrument which assesses different facets of the working context was used (Felfe & Liepmann, 2004). Participants were asked the extent to which the following work features were fulfilled: "interesting and diversified tasks", "identification with tasks", "autonomous and independent work". The answering format ranged from 1 ("not true at all") to 5 ("completely true"). Cronbach's alpha was .80. We obtained an ICC(1) of .10 and a Rwg(j) of .41.

Task content was therefore treated as a variable on the individual level, because aggregation was not justified. However, this is consistent with the way it is usually treated in the literature (Hackman & Oldham, 1980). Although we assume that group-level transformational leadership within one organization will affect all subordinates' perceptions of their tasks, we still expect individual differences, due to the fact that the subordinates all perform different jobs (e.g., interacting with costumers vs. ordering and pigeon-holing goods). These objectively differing task contents should be reflected in employees' differing perceptions.

The measure of positive organizational climate (Felfe & Liepmann, 2004) consisted of three items that reflect friendly relationships with co-workers and a general positive climate in the organization. Participants were again asked about the extent to which the following conditions were fulfilled: "good relationship with colleagues", "good relationship with supervisors", and "overall good climate". Again, a response scale with five categories was used, ranging from 1 ("not at all true") to 5 ("completely true"). The internal consistency (Cronbach's alpha) was .83. We did obtain values for climate that justified aggregation, ICC(1) = .43, Rwg = .83. Consistent with the climate literature (James et al., 2008; Luria, 2008), climate was aggregated to the group level.

Leaders' scope of influence was measured with 12 items which were developed for this purpose by the second author. To improve the quality of this measure, we excluded items with either low item-total correlations or low factor loadings. Additionally, items with very high means were excluded to prevent a restriction of variance (ceiling effect). The final scale contained seven items. Sample items are: "As the leader/supervisor I can design the workflow in my area of autonomy", "As the leader/supervisor I can decide which task is assigned to each subordinate in my department", "In my area of responsibility I can decide many things by myself", or "As the leader/ supervisor I can schedule and organize work in my department as I think best". The leaders answered the items with a format from 1 ("not true at all") to 5 ("completely true"). Cronbach's alpha equalled .76.

Preliminary analyses

Prior to examining the hypothesized links between study variables, we assessed the measurement properties of our dependent variables. Due to the hierarchical data structure (subordinates nested in businesses) and our hypotheses about group-level influences, multilevel methods (Raudenbush & Bryk, 2002) were deemed to be the appropriate approach to test our hypotheses. To investigate whether this kind of analysis was appropriate for our data, we calculated the F-ratios and ICC(1) for the dependent variables. For affective commitment we calculated a significant F-ratio, $F(18) = 2.21$, $p < .01$, and an ICC(1) of .20. Twenty per cent of the variance in affective commitment was found to be between groups and could therefore be explained by group-level variables. For continuance commitment, we calculated an F-ratio of 3.07, $df = 18$, $p < .001$, and an ICC(1) of .30. These values indicate a sufficient amount of group-level variance to analyse with HLM. The F-ratio for normative commitment, on the other hand, did not reach significance, $F(18) = 1.42$, ns, and the ICC(1) was .06. There was no variance in normative commitment that could be explained by group-level variables. However, as the aim of our study was to investigate the influence of group-level transformational leadership and consensus on all three components of commitment, analyses for normative commitment were not possible due to the lack of group-level variance. Analyses for affective and continuance organizational commitment were performed with HLM. Means, standard deviations, and correlations between all study variables are shown in Table 1.

RESULTS

Group-level transformational leadership and consensus

We stated that group-level transformational leadership (Hypotheses 1a and 1b) and consensus (Hypotheses 2a and 2b) will be positively related to affective and normative commitment. We expected no relationship with continuance commitment. For affective and continuance commitment we calculated two models with HLM: The first model contained group-level transformational leadership, and in the second model the consensus was added. The results for affective and continuance organizational commitment are shown in Table 2. Analyses for normative organizational commitment were not calculated due to the nonsignificant group-level properties.

Inspection of Table 2 reveals that group-level transformational leadership is positively related to affective commitment, $\gamma = .33$, $p < .05$. Additionally, consensus was also a significant predictor, $\gamma = .91$, $p < .05$. We could confirm the hypotheses (1a and 2a) for affective commitment. The results in Table 2 reveal a different pattern for continuance commitment: Neither the group level, $\gamma = .02$, ns, nor the consensus, $\gamma = -.74$, ns, were significant. As expected, we did not find any substantial relationship.

Mediator analyses

In Hypotheses 3a and 3b we proposed that the effect of group-level transformational leadership on affective and normative commitment would be mediated by meaningful task content. Likewise, we proposed in Hypotheses 4a and 4b, that the influence of consensus on affective and normative commitment would be mediated by positive organizational climate. To test the mediating effect of the intervening variables we followed the procedures proposed by Baron and Kenny (1986) and Krull and MacKinnon (2001). Mediation is evidenced if the following conditions are met: (1) a significant relationship between predictor and mediator, (2) a significant relationship between predictor and outcome variable, and (3) a

TABLE 1
Descriptive statistics and correlations

Variable	Level	M	SD	1	2	3	4	5	6	7	8	9	10
1. Age	Individual	3.26	1.21	—									
2. Organizational tenure	Individual	3.75	1.31	.42***	—								
3. Transformational leadership	Group	3.97	0.54	.18	.15	—							
4. Consensus of transformational leadership	Group	−0.50	0.31	−.01	.05	.49*	—						
5. Task content	Individual	3.81	0.83	.13*	−.00	.45***	.30*	(.80)					
6. Climate	Group	4.47	0.51	.14°	.14	.68**	.63**	.18*	(.46)				
7. Affective commitment	Individual	4.39	0.77	.32***	.19°	.45***	.40**	.58***	.33***	(.88)			
8. Continuance commitment	Individual	4.02	0.93	.44***	.18*	.05	−.13	.23*	.05	.42***	(.73)		
9. Normative commitment	Individual	3.63	0.99	.34**	.14°	.16	.05	.41***	.11	.54***	.48***	(.83)	
10. Leaders' scope of influence	Group	4.79	0.32	−.16	−.03	.10	−.03	.24*	.08	.01	−.35*	−.08	(.76)

Individual level: $N = 105$; group level: $N = 21$. Cronbach's alpha is displayed on the diagonal. Correlations individual and group variables were calculated as univariate cross-level effects with HLM. $°p < .10$, $*p < .05$, $**p < .01$, $***p < .00$, two tailed.

significant relationship between mediator and outcome variable in the full model, together with a declining effect for the predictor. The mediating effects were tested for significance using the online calculator on http://people.ku.edu/~preacher/sobel/sobel.htm.

Mediator analyses were calculated only for affective commitment, normative commitment was neglected here due to the lack of group-level properties. Tables 3 and 4 show the results for both mediation models. Group-level transformational leadership, consensus, and climate were treated as group-level predictors. Task content was introduced on the individual level.

Condition 1 which is a significant relationship between group-level transformational leadership and task content was met (see right-hand side of Table 3). The γ coefficient was .37, $p < .05$. Group-level transformational

TABLE 2
Multilevel results for the prediction of organizational commitment (affective and continuance) by group level and consensus of transformational leadership

Step	Transformational leadership	γ	SE	df
Affective organizational commitment				
1	Group	.33*	.15	19
2	Consensus	.91*	.41	18
Continuance organizational commitment				
1	Group	.02	.22	19
2	Consensus	−.74	.65	18

*$p < .05$, two tailed.

TABLE 3
Mediation of the transformational leadership–affective commitment link by meaningful task content

		Dependent variable					
		Affective organizational commitment			Mediator (Task content)		
Step	Independent variable	γ	SE	df	γ	SE	df
1	Transformational leadership	.33*	.15	19			
2	Transformational leadership				.37*	.13	19
3	Transformational leadership	.15	.14	19			
	Task content	.51***	.08	102			

Task content resides on individual level and transformational leadership resides on group level. *$p < .05$, ***$p < .001$, two tailed.

TABLE 4
Mediation of the consensus–affective commitment link by positive organizational climat

		Dependent variable					
		Affective organizational commitment			Mediator (Climate)		
Step	Independent variable	γ	SE	df	γ	SE	df
1	Consensus	1.00**	.30	19			
2	Consensus				.63**	.29	19
3	Consensus	.29	.33	18			
	Climate	.43**	.13	18			

Consensus and climate reside on group level. **$p < .01$, two tailed.

leadership was also a significant predictor for affective organizational commitment, $\gamma = .33$, $p < .05$. Thus, Condition 2 was fulfilled. When task content was introduced into the full model, the slope for group-level transformational leadership declined, $\gamma = .15$, ns, whereas task content was significant, $\gamma = .51$, $p < .001$. The Sobel test revealed a significant mediation effect, $t = 2.57$, $p < .05$, and Hypothesis 3a was confirmed.

In Hypothesis 3c we proposed that besides transformational leadership, leaders' scope of influence will be a predictor for task content too. We calculated an additional model with transformational leadership and leaders' scope of influence as predictors on group level. Transformational leadership was a significant predictor for task content, $\gamma = .36$, $p < .05$. Leaders' scope of influence was significant too, $\gamma = .56$, $p < .05$. Hypothesis 3c could be confirmed.

Hypotheses 4a and 4 b proposed positive organizational climate as a mediator of the relationship between consensus and affective and normative commitment. Again, we did not include normative commitment due to nonsignificant group-level variance. The results for affective commitment are shown in Table 4. Consensus was a significant predictor for positive organizational climate, $\gamma = .81$, $p < .01$, as well as for affective commitment, $\gamma = 1.00$, $p < .01$. Conditions 1 and 2 were met. When both variables were included in the full model to predict affective commitment, the coefficient for consensus dropped to .29 (ns), whereas organizational climate was significant, $\gamma = .43$, $p < .01$. The Sobel test revealed a significant result on the 10% level, $t = 1.82$, $p < .10$. Due to small sample size on Level 2 we argue that it is justified to cautiously interpret results on the 10% level as meaningful in order to compensate limited power. Therefore, we can state that Hypothesis 4a was approximately confirmed.

DISCUSSION

In this study, we have addressed multilevel issues and mediating effects in our examination of the relationship between transformational leadership and organizational commitment. We were able to confirm findings from previous studies by replicating the positive link between these variables. The structure of the following discussion parallels the two different study objectives by first focusing on the results that refer to the influences of group-level transformational leadership and consensus on commitment and then turning to the mediation analyses.

Group-level transformational leadership and consensus were moderately correlated in our study, indicating that both constructs are related but different too. This finding is in line with the climate literature (Feinberg et al., 2005; Lindell & Brandt, 2000). The first objective was to detangle the effects of both constructs and to test the additional effect of consensus on the three components of commitment, hypothesizing positive links to affective and normative commitment and no relationship to continuance commitment. Unfortunately, we did not find any group-level properties in the measure for normative commitment and so could not test our hypotheses concerning this component. Clearly, further research is needed here.

As expected group-level transformational leadership was a positive predictor for affective commitment, replicating previous findings. Consensus as a group-level construct proved to be a positive resource for affective commitment above and beyond the absolute level of transformational leadership. This result adds to the relatively new stream of literature indicating that besides information on the perceived level of leadership behaviour in a group, the variability of those perceptions can also add valuable information when it comes to predicting organizational outcome variables. The flipside of this finding suggests that even consensus on the fact that the CEO is low on transformational leadership can strengthen affective commitment in an organization. The social context and group cohesion might be a social resource for employees. A test of this consensus effect would have required conceptualizing consensus as a moderator, which was not appropriate due to the small number of groups in our sample. Future research should investigate whether consensus can buffer the reduced effectiveness of low transformational leadership.

Surprisingly, we did not find any group-level properties in normative commitment. Due to our small sample and the rather exploratory character of this study, one should therefore not conclude, that they do not exist. Likewise, the conclusion that transformational leadership is not important for building normative commitment is also not justified on the basis of our data.

For continuance commitment, we found no relationship with group level or consensus of transformational leadership; this result is also in line with our expectations and previous research. Interestingly, we found significant group-level differences in continuance commitment, but could not explain them by our leadership constructs. Nevertheless, meaningful task content was a relevant predictor for continuance commitment. This result may be explained by the dual character of this component, which involves both the evaluation of high potential sacrifices, as well as low alternatives for turnover. Completing meaningful tasks may be seen as a benefit in the current job that should not be sacrificed by quitting. Further research should investigate whether other group-level variables such as human resource practices or pay can affect employees' continuance commitment. Again, the results of our study should be interpreted with caution due to the small sample size and the rather homogeneous sample.

As a second objective, we could confirm the assumption that the positive link between affective commitment and group-level transformational leadership and consensus were mediated by two different variables. We found that meaningful task content accounted for the relationship between group-level transformational leadership and affective commitment. Our line of reasoning for the mediating effect was built on Bass' (1999) proposal that transformational leadership should affect followers by creating meaningful work. This can take place in two different ways: First, a transformational leader can objectively change working procedures, improving work and task content by upgrading job characteristics such as autonomy, task variety, or feedback. Second, transformational leadership can influence the perceptions of his subordinates, changing their evaluation or attitude by providing deeper sense, meaning, or understanding, even when the work is actually quite low in job characteristics, or even when no objective changes have been made. In an early work, for instance, Griffin (1981) demonstrated that managers could elevate their followers' perceptions of the core job characteristics solely by means of persuasive communication, even though no tangible changes to their actual jobs were made. The former refers to real work design processes, whereas the latter refers to elevating the perception of subordinates.

Besides group-level transformational leadership, leaders' scope of influence was a predictor for meaningful task content in our study as well. As expected the CEOs in our sample reported high levels of scope of influence. Nevertheless, this result points to the fact that a certain degree of autonomy for CEOs in decision-making seems to be an important attendant circumstance for effective transformational leadership. However, the assessment of leaders' scope of influence and its positive relationship with meaningful task content may hint at the fact that followers' perceptions of meaningful work were affected by leaders' activities and not only by altering their attitudes and views.

Although these results should still be interpreted with caution because of the cross-sectional assessment of these variables, they support recent empirical findings (Piccolo & Colquitt, 2006; Purvanova et al., 2006). Meaningful and challenging work is an important motivator and predicts several beneficial work outcomes (Hackman & Oldham, 1976; Loher, Noe, Moeller, & Fitzgerald, 1985). Longitudinal designs are, of course, required in order to clarify the issue of causality.

Positive organizational climate was found to be a second mediating process to explain the relationship between consensus and affective commitment. Although the mediating effect missed the conventional significance criterion of 5%, we can conclude, with caution, that good and reliable relationships in an organization can be a resource for affective commitment. This result enables leaders to influence followers' commitment in a second way by fostering consensus, which is one of the features of transformational leadership. Luria (2008) notes that climate is influenced by horizontal social group interactions, e.g., by relationships with co-workers. So the behaviour of all group members to improve consensus and organizational climate plays a second important role in strengthening affective commitment.

The results and conclusions of our study should be interpreted in light of some limitations. The database of our study is rather small, and all findings need to be confirmed in bigger samples. The data from our study are cross-sectional and causal interpretations are speculative. Reversed causation—e.g., highly committed subordinates or enriched jobs foster the perception of transformational leadership—cannot be ruled out. The same source–same method bias in dependent and independent variables may have led to effect size inflation. All data were collected via surveys and the measurement of leadership by subordinates is particularly prone to perceptual distortions (Biernat, 2003; Dvir & Shamir, 2003). Participants may have difficulties in clearly separating leader behaviour and consequences. As a result, both concepts may have been inappropriately merged. Nevertheless we were especially interested in subordinates' perception of transformational leadership. Another possible explanation for positive linkages between transformational leadership and our outcome variables may be the undetected effect of a nonmodelled third variable (e.g., positive affectivity). In future research, it would consequently be fruitful to objectively control for job characteristics or even the effects of job design activities by supervisors. In our study, we solely relied on perceptions of meaningful task content. Due to our sample characteristics (97% female, same businesses), we cannot generalize our results per se. Further research is needed to prove our findings on larger samples from different professional and cultural backgrounds. In particular, the nonsignificant group-level properties in normative commitment should not be interpreted here, and we recommend testing the corresponding hypotheses in other samples.

PRACTICAL IMPLICATIONS AND CONCLUSION

Leaders are the most prominent aspect in a workplace environment and shape followers' perceptions of many work-related information. Leaders can use this extraordinary impact to improve followers' work-related attitudes and feelings. CEOs of small businesses with full control of work scheduling and task assignment should do this in a way that enables followers to perform meaningful, motivating work with appropriate autonomy. In large companies, on the other hand, a leader's influence on workflow and task assignment is rather limited. Nevertheless, leaders can engage in "management of meaning" or organizational sense making to provide followers with a deeper understanding of how important and meaningful their tasks are. This, in turn, strengthens organizational commitment. A second fruitful approach can be to give lower and middle hierarchy leaders, in particular, greater autonomy and degrees of freedom. These enriched leadership positions should enable leaders to show many behaviours of the transformational leadership pattern, such as individual consideration or intellectual stimulation. Likewise, leaders in any organization or hierarchy should facilitate a positive organizational climate by providing opportunities for contact and support or other social activities—on and off the job. At this point, the role of team members in promoting consensus and positive organizational climate should be emphasized, by their own fair and respectful behaviour towards their co-workers they can promote consensus and a positive climate, which have been shown to strengthen affective commitment as well.

Studies conducted by Barling, Kelloway, and Weber (1996) or Frese, Beimel, and Schönborn (2003) show that the training of transformational leadership is worthwhile. The results of this work suggest that training should consist not only of learning how to convincingly communicate a vision, or how to motivate the reaching for common goals; they should also include knowledge of work design and the importance of social relations and support at work. Activities that help establish consensus—such as treating all followers respectfully and not showing preference—are also helpful in promoting organizational commitment.

REFERENCES

Anderson, N., & West, M. (1998). Measuring climate for work group innovation: Development and validation of the team climate inventory. *Journal of Organizational Behavior, 19*, 235–258.

Arnold, K. A., Turner, N., Barling, J., Kelloway, E. K., & McKee, M. C. (2007). Transformational leadership and psychological well-being: The mediating role of meaningful work. *Journal of Occupational Health Psychology, 12*, 193–203.

Avolio, B. J., Zhu, W., Koh, W., & Bhatia, P. (2004). Transformational leadership and organizational commitment: Mediating role of psychological empowerment and moderating role of structural distance. *Journal of Organizational Behaviour, 25*, 951–968.

Barling, J., Kelloway, E. K., & Weber, T. (1996). Effects of transformational leadership training on attitudinal and financial outcomes: A field experiment. *Journal of Applied Psychology, 81*, 827–832.

Barling, J., Loughlin, C., & Kelloway, E. K. (2002). Development and test of a model linking transformational leadership and occupational safety. *Journal of Applied Psychology, 87*, 484–496.

Baron, R. M., & Kenny, D. A. (1986). The moderator mediator variable distinction in social psychological research: Conceptual, strategic, and statistical considerations. *Journal of Personality and Social Psychology, 51*, 1173–1182.

Bass, B. M. (1985). *Leadership and performance beyond expectations.* New York: Free Press.

Bass, B. M. (1999). Two decades of research and development in transformational leadership. *European Journal of Work and Organizational Psychology, 8*, 9–32.

Bass, B. M., & Avolio, B. J. (1995). *MLQ: Multifactor Leadership Questionnaire.* Redwood City, CA: Mind Garden.

Bass, B. M., & Avolio, B. J. (1997). *Full range of leadership: Manual for the Multifactor Leadership Questionnaire.* Palo Alto, CA: Mind Garden.

Biernat, M. (2003). Toward a broader view of social stereotyping. *The American Psychologist, 58*(12), 1019–1027.

Bliese, P. D. (2000). Within-group agreement, non-independence, and reliability. Implications for data aggregation and analysis. In K. Klein & S. W. J. Kozlowski (Eds.), *Multilevel theory, research and method in organizations* (pp. 349–381). San Francisco: Jossey-Bass.

Bono, J. E., & Judge, T. A. (2003). Self-concordance at work: Toward understanding the motivational effects of transformational leaders. *Academy of Management Journal, 46*, 554–571.

Brown, D., & Keeping, L. M. (2005). Elaborating the construct of transformational leadership: The role of affect. *Leadership Quarterly, 16*, 245–272.

Bycio, P., Hackett, R. D., & Allen, J. S. (1995). Further assessments of Bass's (1985) conceptualization of transactional and transformational leadership. *Journal of Applied Psychology, 80*, 468–478.

Chan, D. (1998). Functional relations among constructs in the same content domain at different levels of analysis: A typology of composition models. *Journal of Applied Psychology, 83*, 234–246.

Cole, M. S., & Bedeian, A. G. (2007). Leadership consensus as a cross-level contextual moderator of the emotional exhaustion-work commitment relationship. *Leadership Quarterly, 18*, 447–462.

Cooper-Hakim, A., & Viswesvaran, C. (2005). The construct of work commitment: Testing an integrative framework. *Psychological Bulletin, 131*, 241–259.

DeGroot, T., Kiker, D. S., & Cross, T. C. (2000). A meta-analysis to review organizational outcomes related to charismatic leadership. *Canadian Journal of Administrative Science, 17*, 356–371.

De Vries, R. E., Roe, R. A., & Taillieu, T. C. B. (1999). On charisma and need for leadership. *European Journal of Work and Organizational Psychology, 8*, 109–133.

Dvir, T., Kass, N., & Shamir, B. (2004). The emotional bond: Vision and organizational commitment among high–tech employees. *Journal of Organizational Change Management, 17*, 126–143.

Dvir, T., & Shamir, B. (2003). Follower developmental characteristics as predicting transformational leadership: A longitudinal field study. *Leadership Quarterly, 14*, 327–344.

Ehrhart, M. G. (2004). Leadership and procedural justice climate as antecedents of unit-level organizational citizenship behavior. *Personnel Psychology, 57*, 61–94.

Feinberg, B. J., Ostroff, C., & Burke, W. W. (2005). The role of within-group agreement in understanding transformational leadership. *Journal of Occupational and Organizational Psychology, 78*, 471–488.

Felfe, J. (2006). Validierung einer deutschen Version des "Multifactor Leadership Questionnaire" (MLQ 5 X Short) von Bass und Avolio (1995) [Validation of a German version of the "Multifactor Leadership Questionnaire" by Bass and Avolio (1995)]. *Zeitschrift für Arbeits- und Organisationspsychologie, 50*, 61–78.

Felfe, J., & Heinitz, K. (2010). The impact of consensus and agreement of leadership perceptions on commitment, organizational citizenship behaviour and customer satisfaction. *European Journal of Work and Organizational Psychology, 19*, 279–303.

Felfe, J., & Liepmann, D. (2004). *Skalendokumentation zur Organisationsdiagnostik.* [Technical report for organizational diagnostics]. Unpublished report, Berlin and Halle.

Felfe, J., Schmook, R., & Six, B. (2006). Die Bedeutung kultureller Wertorientierungen für das Commitment gegenüber der Organisation, dem Vorgesetzten, der Arbeitsgruppe und der eigenen Karriere [The relevance of cultural value orientations to organizational, supervisor, team, and career commitment]. *Zeitschrift für Personalpsychologie, 5*, 94–107.

Felfe, J., Yan, W., & Six, B. (2008). The impact of individual collectivism on commitment and its influence on OCB, turnover, and strain in three countries. *International Journal of Cross-Cultural Management, 8*, 211–237.

Frese, M., Beimel, S., & Schönborn, S. (2003). Action training for charismatic leadership: Two evaluations of studies of a commercial training module on inspirational communication of a vision. *Personnel Psychology, 56*, 671–697.

Gavin, M. B., & Hofmann, D. A. (2002). Using hierarchical linear modeling to investigate the moderating influence of leadership climate. *Leadership Quarterly, 13*, 15–33.

Gonzalez-Roma, V., Peiro, J. M., & Tordera, N. (2002). An examination of the antecedents and moderator influences of climate strength. *Journal of Applied Psychology, 87*, 465–473.

Graen, G. B., & Uhl-Bien, M. (1995). Relationship-based approach to leadership: Development of leader-member exchange (LMX) theory of leadership over 25 years: Applying a multi-level multi-domain perspective. *Leadership Quarterly, 6*, 219–247.

Griffin, M. A., & Mathieu, J. E. (1997). Modeling organizational processes across hierarchical levels. *Journal of Organizational Behavior, 18*, 731–744.

Griffin, R. W. (1981). Supervisory behaviour as a source of perceived task scope. *Journal of Occupational Psychology, 54*, 175–182.

Hackman, J. R., & Oldham, G. R. (1976). Motivation through the design of work: Test of a theory. *Organizational Behavior and Human Performance, 16*, 250–279.

Hackman, J. R., & Oldham, G. R. (1980). *Work redesign.* London: Addison-Wesley.

Heider, F. (1958). *The psychology of interpersonal relations.* New York: Wiley.

James, L. R., Choi, C. C., Ko, C.-H. E., McNeil, P. K., Minton, M. K., Wright, M. A., & Kim, K. I. (2008). Organizational and psychological climate: A review of theory and research. *European Journal of Work and Organizational Psychology, 17*, 5–32.

James, L. R., Demaree, R. G., & Wolf, G. (1993). Rwg: An assessment of within-group inter-rater agreement. *Journal of Applied Psychology, 78*, 306–309.

Kanter, R. M. (1983). *The change masters.* New York: Simon & Schuster.

Klein, K. J., & House, R. J. (1995). On fire: Charismatic leadership and levels of analysis. *The Leadership Quarterly, 6*, 183–198.

Krull, J. L., & MacKinnon, D. P. (2001). Multilevel modeling of individual and group level mediated effects. *Multivariate Behavioral Research, 36*, 249–277.

Lindell, M. K., & Brandt, C. J. (2000). Climate quality and climate consensus as mediators of the relationship between organizational antecedents and outcomes. *Journal of Applied Psychology, 85*, 331–348.

Loher, B. T., Noe, R. A., Moeller, N. L., & Fitzgerald, M. P. (1985). A meta-analysis of the relation of job characteristics to job satisfaction. *Journal of Applied Psychology, 70*, 280–289.

Luria, G. (2008). Climate strength—How leaders form consensus. *Leadership Quarterly, 19*, 42–53.

Mathieu, J. E., & Zajac, D. M. (1990). A review and meta-analysis of the antecedents, correlates, and consequences of organizational commitment. *Psychological Bulletin, 108*, 171–194.

Meyer, J. P., & Allen, N. J. (1997). *Commitment in the workplace: Theory, research and application.* Thousand Oaks, CA: Sage.

Meyer, J. P., Stanley, D. J., Herscovitch, L., & Topolnytsky, L. (2002). Affective, continuance, and normative commitment to the organization: A meta analysis of antecedents, correlates and consequences. *Journal of Vocational Behavior, 61*, 20–52.

Mumford, M. D., Dansereau, F., & Yammarino, F. J. (2000). Followers, motivations, and levels of analysis: The case of individualized leadership. *Leadership Quarterly, 11*, 313–340.

Nemanich, L. A., & Keller, R. T. (2007). Transformational leadership in an acquisition: A field study of employees. *Leadership Quarterly, 18*(1), 49–68.

Piccolo, R., & Colquitt, J. (2006). Transformational leadership and job behaviors: The mediating role of core job characteristics. *Academy of Management Journal. 49*, 327–340.

Pillai, R., & Williams, E. A. (2004). Transformational leadership, self-efficacy, group cohesiveness, commitment, and performance. *Journal of Organizational Change Management, 17*, 144–159.

Purvanova, R. K., Bono, J. E., & Dzieweczynski, J. (2006). Transformational leadership, job characteristics, and organizational citizenship performance. *Human Performance, 19*, 1–22.

Raudenbush, S. W., & Bryk, A. S. (2002). *Hierarchical linear models: Applications and data analysis methods* (2nd ed.). Thousand Oaks, CA: Sage.

Rentsch, J. R. (1990). Climate and culture: Interaction and qualitative differences in organizational meanings. *Journal of Applied Psychology, 75*, 668–681.

Sanders, K., & Schyns, B. (2006). Leadership and solidarity behaviour: Consensus in perception of employees within teams. *Personnel Review, 35*, 538–556.

Schneider, B., Salvaggio, A. N., & Subirats, M. (2002). Climate strength: A new direction for climate research. *Journal of Applied Psychology, 87*, 220–229.

Schyns, B. (2006). Are group consensus in LMX and shared work values related to organisational outcomes? *Small Group Research, 37*, 20–35.

Shamir, B., House, R. J., & Arthur, M. B. (1993). The motivational effects of charismatic leadership: A self-concept based theory. *Organization Science, 4*, 577–594.

Shamir, B., Zakay, E., Breinin, E., & Popper, M. (1998). Correlates of charismatic leader behavior in military units: Subordinates' attitudes, unit characteristics, and superiors' appraisals of leader performance. *Academy of Management Journal, 41*, 387–409.

Shin, S., & Zhou, J. (2003). Transformational leadership, conservation, and creativity: Evidence from Korea. *Academy of Management Journal, 46*, 703–714.

Spreitzer, G. M. (1995). Psychological empowerment in the workplace: Dimensions, measurement and validation. *Academy of Management Journal, 38*, 1442–1465.

Tajfel, H., & Turner, J. C. (1986). The social identity theory of intergroup behaviour. In S. Worchel & W. G. Austin (Eds.), *Psychology of intergroup relations* (pp. 7–24). Monterey, CA: Brooks/Cole.

Walumbwa, F. O., Peng, W., Lawler, J., & Kan, S. (2004). The role of collective efficacy in the relations between transformational leadership and work outcomes. *Journal of Occupational and Organizational Psychology, 77*, 515–530.

Wayne, S., Liden, R., & Sparrowe, R. (2000). An examination of the mediating role of psychological empowerment on the relations between the job, interpersonal relationships, work outcomes. *Journal of Applied Psychology, 85*, 407–416.

Wiley, D. M. (1999). *Impact of locus of control and empowerment on organizational commitment.* Doctoral dissertation, United States International University, Nairobi, Kenya.

Yammarino, F. J., Dionne, S. D., Chun, J. U., & Dansereau, F. (2005). Leadership and levels of analysis: A state-of-the-science review. *Leadership Quarterly, 16*, 879–919.

Yukl, G. (1999). An evaluation of conceptual weaknesses in transformational and charismatic leadership theories. *Leadership Quarterly, 10*, 285–305.

EUROPEAN JOURNAL OF WORK AND
ORGANIZATIONAL PSYCHOLOGY
2010, 19 (3), 388–406

Ψ Psychology Press
Taylor & Francis Group

Understanding the relationship between span of control and subordinate consensus in leader–member exchange

Birgit Schyns
University of Portsmouth, Portsmouth, UK

John M. Maslyn
Belmont University, Nashville, TN, USA

Jürgen Weibler
Fern Universität Hagen, Hagen, Germany

Leader–member exchange (LMX) refers to the relationship quality a leader shares with members of his or her work group, typically described as differentiation in quality within the group. Numerous empirical studies demonstrate that the quality of this relationship is positively related to followers' attitudes and organizational outcomes. It has been proposed that the quality of possible relationships between the leader and the led will be affected by the number of employees directly reporting to the leader, with empirical findings showing a slight negative relationship between span of control and LMX. Little is known, however, about how span of control influences variability in the quality of leader–member exchange within the context of work groups. Therefore, following a recognized assumption to strive for as many as possible leadership relations on a high LMX level, we examine how individual- and group-level (consensus in) LMX can be based on different dimensions of the LMX relationship. We suggest how LMX consensus and a high LMX level can be established even in large spans of control.

Keywords: Leadership; Span of control.

Correspondence should be addressed to Birgit Schyns, Portsmouth Business School, Human Resource and Marketing Management, University of Portsmouth, Portland Street, Portsmouth PO1 3DE, UK. E-mail: Birgit.Schyns@port.ac.uk

http://www.psypress.com/ejwop   DOI: 10.1080/13594320903146485

Leader–member exchange (LMX) refers to the relationship quality a leader shares with individual members of his or her work group. From the outset of research in this area it has been shown that leaders differentiate their relationships and their behaviour towards subordinates within their work groups (Graen & Cashman, 1975; Liden & Graen, 1980). That is, in the course of their interactions, leaders develop qualitatively different relationships with followers suggesting little consensus among those subordinates regarding LMX quality. Such differentiation among followers by leaders is central to LMX theory (Liden, Sparrowe, & Wayne, 1997). The issue of differentiation is particularly relevant because many individual studies and indeed meta-analyses (e.g., Gerstner & Day, 1997; Ilies, Nahrgang, & Morgeson, 2007) confirm that leader-member exchange quality is positively related to followers' positive attitudes and organizational outcomes, implying that only high-level exchanges would be preferable.

Initially proposed as a dyadic-level theory to capture the leader–member relationship, LMX has been discussed and examined from multiple levels of analysis. Most frequently, an individual level of analysis, where the quality of the exchange has been assessed from one dyad member's perspective, has been used (Schriesheim, Castro, Zhou, & Yammarino, 2001). At the dyad level, researchers have focused on and examined the essence of exchanges or reciprocity between dyad members, including discussions of multiple dimensions of LMX (e.g., Dienesch & Liden, 1986; Uhl-Bien & Maslyn, 2003) as well as agreement between leader and follower (Gerstner & Day, 1997). Further, LMX has been viewed as a relative phenomenon (individuals-within-groups level), where variability in the relationship quality within groups serves as the relevant approach to understanding the impact of different quality relationships (e.g., Cogliser & Schriesheim, 2000; Schyns, van Veldhoven, & Wood, 2009). Finally, more recent examinations (e.g., Boies & Howell, 2006; Cogliser, Schriesheim, Scandura, & Gardner, 2009; Liden, Erdogan, Wayne, & Sparrowe, 2006) have considered the importance of the group level, using differentiation itself as a key variable.

Despite the extant literature showing the great extent of differentiation by leaders, it is often suggested that leaders should strive for high-quality exchange relationships across their entire work group (Graen & Uhl-Bien, 1995; Maslyn & Uhl-Bien, 2005). Consequently, a high absolute average of LMX ratings on the follower side (high level of LMX quality), accompanied by a low variability of ratings of followers reporting to the same leader (high consensus) and a high level of shared perceptions (leaders and members rating their relationship the same) about the LMX quality between leader and follower regarding the same dyadic relationship (high agreement) should be a manager's goal, a combination called LMX excellence by Schyns and Day (2010). Ultimately, however, it has also been suggested in the LMX literature (e.g., Dansereau, Graen, & Haga, 1975;

Liden et al., 1997) that although managers should attempt such broad high-quality relationship development, it is extremely difficult to accomplish, especially in large work groups.

For example, Dansereau et al. (1975) argue that leaders possess limited resources of time and energy, which automatically limits the number of possible high-quality relationships they can develop and maintain. Similarly, there is support in the LMX literature for the proposition that increased span of control fosters greater differentiation (Green, Anderson, & Shivers 1996; Schriesheim et al., 2000; Schyns, Paul, Mohr, & Blank, 2005). Other studies, however, have failed to support and even disagree with this assertion (Cogliser & Schriesheim, 2000; Kinicki & Vecchio, 1994), leaving the question more equivocal than certain. As high LMX quality is shown to be a positive asset for organizations and because current organization structuring tends to increase the span of control through downsizing, decentralization, and empowerment, it is worthwhile to look deeper into this contradicting research.

The organizational terminology "span of control" describes the number of employees who are formally and directly subordinated to a superior and are reporting to her/him. Though thinking about the optimal span of control and the impact of span of control has been a foundational issue in organization theory since the classical study of Graicunas appeared (1937), LMX research has not considered span of leadership beyond the core tenets of the exchange of limited resources to key individuals in the work group. In this article, we define span of control in a practical rather than theoretical fashion: A large span of control is defined as the number of followers led by a leader that make "close" (high-quality) relationships difficult to pursue across all members. The actual number of followers that render a work group large may vary depending on, for example, the structure of a work group (e.g., team vs. individual direct reports; task interdependence).

The aim of this article is examine the impact of the manager's span of control on individual- and group-level LMX (consensus) as a means of understanding the circumstances that could affect LMX within work groups. Rather than centre on LMX as a composite of multiple dimensions or currencies of exchange, we offer propositions that focus on the influence of span of control on different dimensions of LMX (Dienesch & Liden, 1986; Liden & Maslyn, 1998). One of our key assumptions is that increased leader distance (Antonakis & Atwater, 2002; Shamir, 1995) created by a large span of control influences LMX dimensions differently. We concentrate here on the individual-level effect (quality of LMX relationship as seen by one follower) and the group-level effect (consensus regarding LMX quality in a group of followers reporting to the same leader). With this baseline, we discuss a number of implications regarding consensus among group members in high-quality LMX relationships.

DIMENSIONS OF LMX

Different types of currencies of exchange, discussed in depth in the multidimensional approach to LMX (Dienesch & Liden, 1986; Liden & Maslyn, 1998), are central to our understanding of the LMX–span relationship. In early conceptualizations of LMX theory, the exchanges made between members were considered to be essentially work-related and consistent with the traditional roles of manager and subordinate (Graen & Scandura, 1987; Graen & Uhl-Bien, 1995). For example, followers might contribute a high level of effort towards the job, whereas leaders might reciprocate by providing favourable task assignments. As research in LMX theory progressed, however, various researchers (e.g., Dienesch & Liden, 1986; Liden et al., 1997) argued that LMX was not based solely on the job-related elements emphasized in earlier work but may also include socially related currencies. Specifically, Dienesch and Liden (1986) and Liden and Maslyn (1998) proposed multiple dimensions of LMX that included both material and nonmaterial currencies of exchange. These dimensions were labelled Contribution (e.g., performing work beyond what is specified in the job description), Affect (e.g., friendship and liking), Loyalty (e.g., loyalty and mutual obligation), and Professional Respect (e.g., respect for professional capabilities). Other LMX research has produced measures of these constructs and demonstrated validity of these dimensions (Liden & Maslyn, 1998; Schriesheim, Neider, Scandura, & Tepper, 1992).

The multidimensional approach to LMX has received growing attention in the literature and scholars have started utilizing the LMX-MDM (LMX multidimensional measure; Liden & Maslyn, 1998) to assess LMX in their research. Maslyn and Uhl-Bien (2001) provided an early glimpse into the value of a multidimensional approach in finding unique effects among the dimensions in an examination of effort towards relationship development. Use of the component dimensions of the LMX-MDM (contribution, affect, loyalty, and professional respect) as either independent antecedents or outcomes, however, is still limited with the vast majority of research using the LMX-MDM combining the dimensions to form a broader measure of LMX (see, for recent exceptions, Ansari, Hung, & Aafaqi, 2007; Schyns & Paul, 2005).

Investigating LMX in large spans of control opens up the question as to whether or not these different currencies of exchange are manifested in different ways in larger work groups. As prior research has concentrated on the relationship between span of control and a composite measure of LMX (Green et al., 1996; Schriesheim et al., 2000; Schyns et al., 2005), we know virtually nothing about the role of dimensions with regard to span of control. However, because the different dimensions require different reinforcement, helping leaders to understand the role of dimensions in

LMX relationships seems a fruitful way to support LMX relationships also in large spans of control.

In the following, we will first set out our general theoretical background relating to the role of dimensions of LMX in large spans of control and then derive how individual-level LMX is shaped by those dimensions in large spans of control. Subsequently, we will transfer these considerations to the group level.

INDIVIDUAL LEVEL: THE INFLUENCE OF SPAN OF CONTROL ON DIFFERENT LMX CURRENCIES OF EXCHANGE

We propose that not all currencies of exchange are equal in the amount of effort needed by leaders to develop or maintain a high-quality relationship. LMX relationships develop through testing processes and the exchange of valued currencies of exchange (Graen & Uhl-Bien, 1995; Liden et al., 1997). Given a large span of control, managers have resource constraints that can lead to a differential exchange among their followers. A primary resource examined in the literature is time available from managers to interact with and provide other resources to subordinates. Dansereau et al. (1975) noted that the size of the work group directly impacted the time managers can spend with their subordinates. Judge and Ferris (1993) similarly suggested that the larger the span of control the less actual manager–follower contact occurs. Still other researchers (e.g., Cogliser & Schriesheim, 2000; Goodstadt & Kipnis, 1970; Green et al., 1996) proposed or found support for this contention. Time effects, however, have not been any more consistent regarding LMX than have studies of span of control. In a study by Kinicki and Vecchio (1994) time constraints were actually positively related to LMX quality, whereas Cogliser and Schriesheim (2000) found no relationship, leaving open the question of possible differences in bases of relationship quality associated with a manager's time. An examination of the differential process for the development and maintenance of exchanges based on different currencies of exchange offers an alternative view to a rigid resource constraint approach. Rather than the actual time spend with followers, we argue that the different results found for the impact of span of control on LMX are due to the different effects of span of control on the different LMX dimensions. We thus explore the question whether leader distance is responsible for the effect of span of control on LMX relationships.

According to Napier and Ferris (1993), organizational distance is comprised of physical distance, structural distance, and functional distance. The leadership distance literature (e.g., Antonakis & Atwater, 2002; Napier & Ferris, 1993; Shamir, 1995; Weibler, 2004) defines leader distance as consisting of status and power distance, physical distance, and infrequent contact with followers. The latter two are especially characteristic for large spans of control. Antonakis and Atwater's (2002) review and extension of the leader distance literature holds that leaders and followers may operate at different distances from one another. High-quality LMX relationships have been conceptualized as falling in the category of "close" relationships, with quality diminishing as distance increases, but Antonakis and Atwater's position challenges the universality of this notion by suggesting that followers can identify with leaders whether social distance is large or small. This identification implies that followers can ascribe or, as noted by Shamir (1995), attribute characteristics to leaders even when distant, whereas in closer relationships they base their judgement on actual leader behaviour rather than attribution.

Therefore, the question arises as to whether and which LMX dimensions are more or less likely to occur in the case of small or large leader distance. Research and theory concerning psychological distance and level of construal (Liberman, Trope, & Stephan, 2007) facilitates the answer to this question.

"According to CLT [construal level theory], individuals use concrete, low-level construals to represent near events and abstract, high-level construal to represent distant events. Low-level construals are relatively unstructured, contextualized representations that include subordinate and incidental features of events. High-level construals, in contrast, are schematic, decontextualized representations that extract the gist from available information." (Trope, Liberman, & Wakslak, 2007, p. 83)

Psychological distance is characterized by temporal, spatial, and social distance as well as hypotheticality (referring to decisions under uncertain outcomes; Trope et al., 2007). Leader distance can be set into relation to this construct in so far as both comprise spatial and social distance. We therefore assume that some of the predictions Trope et al. (2007) make with regard to psychological distance are valid for leader distance as well. According to Trope et al., psychological distance leads to a higher level of abstraction in representations of events. Transferring this assumption to leader distance, we argue that in cases of higher leader distance or large spans of control, more abstract representations of the leader–member relationship will be more relevant. To apply this thought to the different dimensions of LMX we need to look closer at the dimensions of LMX suggested by Dienesch and Liden (1986) and Liden and Maslyn (1998) in order to determine their level of abstraction.

The dimension "affect" comprises items referring to liking and direct work experience, thus is not abstract. Liden and Maslyn (1998) specifically note that a characteristic of this dimension involves frequent interaction because the members enjoy each others' company. "Contribution" is characterized by the "perception of the amount, direction and quality of work-oriented" (Dienesch & Liden, 1986, p. 624) contributions of the follower, again something that is related to direct experience and does not imply leader distance. That means that the currencies being exchanged when relationships are based on contribution and affect need to be replenished frequently. As with closer forms of manager–follower relationships, we consider that contribution and affect are based less on attribution and more on direct interaction between managers and followers. The reason for this assumption is that the dimensions of contribution and affect are more specific in their scope and impact on followers, characterized by an interdependence that Uhl-Bien, Graen, and Scandura (2000) note is typical of high-quality, "close" LMX relationships. Specifically, contribution's definition as a "perception of the current level of work-oriented activity each member puts forth toward the mutual goals (explicit or implicit) of the dyad" (Liden & Maslyn, p. 50) implies more frequent short-term exchanges. Similarly, the affect dimension of LMX includes "personally rewarding components and outcomes (e.g., a friendship)" (p. 50) suggestive of frequent exchanges and investments on the part of dyad members.

We suggest that the LMX dimensions of loyalty and professional respect can and do exist from a "distance". That is, followers can obtain these currencies based on their beliefs and expectations of the leader without experiencing them directly, but instead through vicarious means such as the reputation of their manager. "Professional respect", for example, refers to the follower's appreciation of the leader's professional abilities. It is a rather abstract construct as it is not comprised of specificities of what this respect is exactly built on or what it refers to. For professional respect, work on the importance of expectations of competence (e.g., Liden, Wayne, & Stilwell, 1993) and the importance of expert power (Antonakis & Atwater, 2002) support this contention. Having an admirable reputation as an expert provides potential present and future value to followers, even if it is accessed only occasionally. Further, the maintenance of this expertise requires little extra work on the part of managers beyond normal day-to-day interactions with followers in general or with others in the organization because reputation is by definition a social phenomenon. As such, once developed, professional respect is likely to continue as a valid currency without placing either continued demands on the manager, or increased demands across multiple followers.

In the same way, loyalty to each other, or the expression of public support or the expectation that the manager will remain faithful in that support from situation to situation (Liden & Maslyn, 1998), does not require constant reinforcement by managers but only the absence of disloyalty. The items of the LMX-MDM bear out that the value of loyalty is found in a future expectation—two of the three items of the loyalty subscale include statements such as "My supervisor would come to my defence if . . ." and "My supervisor would defend me to others in this organization if . . .". Because of this expectation, loyalty can exist at a distance or be considered valuable by subordinates without a manager ever demonstrating loyalty directly or frequently. Further, in terms of construal theory, loyalty is a hypothetical dimension ("My supervisor would come to my defence if I were 'attacked' by others"), implying a higher construal level.

Consequently, we propose that contribution and affect are more characteristic in close leader–member relationships with high-quality of LMX relationships, thus, in large spans of control resulting in fewer subordinates with high-quality relationships. Loyalty and professional respect on the other hand are currencies that do not demand frequent exchange but instead are characteristics that can be achieved even in the case of psychological or leader distance. On the basis of these arguments, we propose the following:

> *Proposition 1a:* In large spans of control, there will be a negative relationship between span of control and contribution and affect.
> *Proposition 1b:* In large spans of control, a greater number of quality LMX relationships will be based on the dimensions of loyalty and professional respect than on contribution and affect.

GROUP LEVEL: THE INFLUENCE OF SPAN OF CONTROL ON CONSENSUS REGARDING DIFFERENT LMX CURRENCIES OF EXCHANGE

Much of the research on LMX has focused on the outcomes of a good relationship quality between leader and his or her subordinates, often differentiating between an ingroup of trusted members and an outgroup of members with whom a purely contractual relationship is upheld (Graen & Uhl-Bien, 1995). In the context of the larger work group, differentiation research has shown that consensus among followers of the same leader is an important predictor of organizational outcomes. Research indicates that perceived differences in LMX quality within groups affects the judgements of co-workers' use of ingratiation (Maslyn & Uhl-Bien, 2005), negatively influences job satisfaction and well-being (Hooper & Martin, 2008); similarity in LMX is positively related to co-worker exchange (Wikaningrum, 2007) and that the variability of one dimension of LMX (contribution; cf. Liden & Maslyn, 1998) is negatively related to satisfaction and commitment (Schyns, 2006). These studies underscore that it is beneficial for leaders to uphold positive relationships with *all* members of their work groups. Henderson, Wayne, Shore, Bommer, and Tetrick (2008) extended this line of enquiry to examine differentiation from both the individual-within-group and group levels and found that LMX at both levels significantly predicted judgements of psychological contract fulfilment. They noted that variability in LMX quality at the group level was dysfunctional but interestingly also noted that differentiation could be functional under certain circumstances, for example, when differentiation is based on individual contribution and, thus, accepted by other followers (see also van Breukelen & Weselius, 2007).

Besides empirical work showing negative effects of lack of consensus in LMX quality, simple differential treatment of followers by their leaders has been proposed to have implications for justice or perceived fairness. Empirical research is inconclusive at this stage: Van Breukelen, Konst, and van der Vlist (2002) as well as Sias and Jablin (1995) look into the effect of differential leader treatment on LMX relations. Van Breukelen et al. found no direct effect of differential treatment, but they found an interaction effect of differential treatment and LMX quality on commitment. Sias and Jablin, on the other hand, found a direct effect of differential treatment on communication between co-workers. In a theoretical contribution, Scandura (1999) suggests that justice and LMX are closely related and that justice is associated with the differentiation between in- and outgroup. In an empirical study, Pillai, Scandura, and Williams (1999) showed that distributive justice mediated the relationship between LMX and job satisfaction in US, Australian, Columbian, and Middle Eastern samples. Ansari et al. (2007) extended this research, using commitment and turnover intention as outcomes. They found that procedural justice mediated the relationship between the respect dimension of LMX and commitment in a Malaysian sample. Consequently, not only should the expected good results associated with high-quality LMX relationships motivate leaders to uphold as many positive relationships as possible, but a justice or fairness perspective make treating followers similarly appear vital ethically. Consequently, both research on LMX differentiation and its results as well as LMX differentiation and justice have led some LMX scholars to recommend to leaders to avoid differentiation (e.g., Uhl-Bien et al., 2000).

In essence, two broad levels of consensus can be differentiated: Followers of the same leader can agree in their rating regarding the relationship with their leader on a high or a low level of LMX quality. Extreme variability or a lack of consensus, on the other hand, would lead to a mid-level LMX average. In accordance with the positive outcomes of high-quality LMX relationships, on the one hand, and consensus, on the other hand, in this article, we are most interested in the consensus among followers of the same leader with regard to their individual (dyadic relationship between one leader and one follower) relationship quality *on a high level of LMX quality*. That is, high consensus with an average high LMX quality at the same time. However, as we have argued earlier, depending on the number of followers reporting to one leader, establishing a good relationship quality with all followers and, thus, achieving high consensus on high-quality LMX might be next to impossible in large spans of control. Again, examining the different dimensions of LMX can be useful to differentiate which type of consensus is achievable and which is not achievable because consensus in LMX must be built from the bottom up (Graen, 2009).

We argued previously that different dimensions of LMX can be related to different levels of closeness/distance, namely, that high LMX between leaders and followers with a large leader distance will be characterized by loyalty and respect rather than affect and contribution. In large spans of control, not all followers can be close to the supervisor, meaning that consensus regarding LMX quality is unlikely to be built on dimensions that need closeness, such as affect and contribution. However, loyalty and respect can flourish in the case of leader distance as well, making it more likely that if consensus develops at all in large spans of control, it will be shaped by loyalty and respect.

Proposition 2:   In large spans of control, followers are more likely to have a high consensus concerning the LMX dimensions of loyalty and professional respect and a low consensus concerning the LXM dimensions of affect and contribution.

SUMMARY AND DISCUSSION

As Johns (2006) argues, the influence of context on organizational behaviour "is often unrecognized or underappreciated" (p. 389). With this article, we bring organization structure and practice in the form of span of control to a discussion of leadership as it is a potential key factor for organizational context in which leader–member relationships are placed (see also Porter & McLaughlin, 2006).

Although there is some consideration within LMX theory regarding contextual factors, our analysis takes the discussion into a rather new direction. Instead of only demonstrating that certain effects (e.g., satisfaction) go along with different sizes of span of control (e.g., narrow), or that larger spans of control are necessarily associated with lower average LMX quality, as prior research has done, our contribution has argued that analysing the different dimensions of LMX quality more closely leads to an insight into the working of LMX in large groups. As such, we look at dimensions of LMX as a means to collectively examine both bottom-up influences on consensus (Graen, 2009) with top-down or contextual realities in organizations. One the one hand, the idea that relationships can be built on different dimensions can explain the contradictory results of prior studies that were based on composite LMX measures. On the other hand, it can support leaders in coping with large spans of control more effectively. That is, we identify means by which managers may build greater high-quality LMX consensus within their work groups even under conditions of larger spans of control. Our focus was on individual-level as well as group-level LMX (consensus) as a function of different dimensions of LMX, an approach consistent with researchers who suggested or found that LMX operates at multiple levels of analysis simultaneously (Henderson et al., 2008).

We postulated that different currencies of exchange between managers and their subordinates will have different effects on LMX quality consensus, depending on how necessary personal interaction or psychological closeness might be for the different currencies involved in the exchange process. We suggested that the "affect" and "contribution" currencies needed to be exchanged more frequently and more directly, thus making low leader distance necessary. Loyalty and professional respect, on the other hand, rely more on attribution processes and can, therefore, be developed and sustained in large groups. Integrating leader distance into LMX is a new way of looking at the different dimensions of LMX. Although so far, the question leading to the development of dimensions was mainly how leader–member relationships can be described (Berneth, Armenakis, Feild, Giles, & Walker, 2007; Liden & Maslyn, 1998), we explained how the different dimensions contribute to positive leader–member relationships in specific context (small vs. large span of control).

Practical implications and future research

Based on our discussion, some practical implications can be articulated. Regarding the broader or more narrowly based impact of different currencies of exchange, leaders can be trained to show and communicate more consciously the professional respect and loyalty dimensions in their exchanges with subordinates instead of relying as heavily on the contribution and affect dimensions. Again, a high level of professional respect and loyalty can be accomplished from a "distance" by communicating critical incidents where examples of professional capabilities and loyalty were present. This approach can create the expectation that these are characteristic of the leader more generally. Before such an approach is recommended and applied, however, more research is necessary as to the different outcomes that are likely to accompany each unique dimension. For example, Liden and Maslyn (1998) found that contribution is highly related to organizational commitment, whereas loyalty is highly related to leader-rated performance. Future research needs to investigate in how far these relationships are stable in different spans of control.

In terms of large spans of control and the creation of LMX beyond professional respect and loyalty, an ongoing discussion has emerged as to how leaders can more effectively differentiate among followers (Maslyn & Uhl-Bien, 2005). This more instrumental approach to relationship development suggests that in cases where factors such as span of control present constraints on managers' time spent with individual subordinates (large leader distance), manager's efforts should be invested in fewer targeted subordinates as opposed to most or all subordinates (Liden et al., 2006). For example, Liden et al. (1997) proposed that under such circumstances managers would be advised to establish higher quality relationships with those followers that possess greater network centrality. Harmon and van Dyne (2008) also suggest prescriptive role making with a recommendation that managers target top performers within work groups for the development of high-quality relationships. Consequently by targeting such employees, leaders could strive to substitute for their own lack of possibility to establish LMX relationships on the basis of affect and contribution. However, this discussion implies that the decision to target certain employees is made on an explicit level. Looking into research that shows that, for example, value similarity is positively related to the development of a high-quality exchange relationship (e.g., Ashkanasy & O'Connor, 1997) may imply that the differentiation in LMX relationships is made unconsciously. That would mean that, before using the approach of targeting followers instrumentally, leaders need to be made aware of their choices and the implications of these choices.

The development of high-quality LMX relationships with targeted followers are then likely to be the key contributors in creating co-worker exchange (CWX; Sherony & Green, 2002). CWX is conceptualized as a dyadic process between respective team members along similar dimensions as used by LMX. Drawing from balance theory (Heider, 1958), Sherony and Green (2002) showed that there was a tendency within individuals to balance exchange qualities between triads (leader–member and member–member relationships). This indicates that a good CWX quality would lead to a good LMX quality even considering "close" LMX dimensions such as affect and contribution. Sherony and Green suggested that a few positive LMX relationships with certain co-workers could have a contagion effect on the whole team. Thus, leaders who are able to establish and maintain high-quality LMX relationships with significant co-workers will provoke direct positive effects on exchange relationships between co-workers.

The possibility of influencing targeted co-workers, however, depends on the group structure. Leadership research has just begun exploring this topic (e.g., Balkundi & Kilduff, 2006; Graen & Graen, 2006; Mayo, Meindl, & Pastor, 2003; Uhl-Bien, 2006). For example, Balkundi and Kilduff (2006) outline a network approach to leadership, emphasizing the need to include different relationships into the leadership process. When introducing the notion of target co-workers, one has to take into account that relying on others enhances the dependency on them and leads—in this case and at least indirectly—to a shared leadership approach (see, for instance, Pearce & Conger, 2003) where efficiency of a work group is dependent on the productive co-acting of different formal and informal leaders. Therefore, organizational support for LMX relationship should concentrate either on the optimal match between a leader and the situation or on shaping selected substitutes or context factors that support superiors to lead larger groups effectively.

If we broaden our view regarding in terms of networks of leadership and look into organizational "chains of command", we recognize that leaders are mostly followers themselves. This means that as with their own followers, they are members of their respective leaders' in- or outgroup (Graen, Cashman, Ginsburg, & Schiemann, 1977). Weibler (1994, 2004), for instance, empirically demonstrated that the next higher leader influences the ease with which a leader–member relationship is managed. Thus, we can assume that the possibilities as well the effectiveness of more positive LMX relationships based on different dimensions will be influenced by a powerful and resourceful next higher leader. If leaders do not share a good relationship quality with their own leader, they may have fewer resources available to establish many high-quality LMX relationships with followers. For example, if followers perceive that the next higher leader does not respect their leader professionally, this may lead to lower follower respect as well.

Researchers should also consider factors potentially affecting leader distance and LMX quality, such as the use of a team structure and variance in relationship tenure. Leaders who interact and communicate with followers regularly on a one-to-one basis (direct reports, e.g., sales and distribution), those that have only one team versus several teams, or those whose subordinates are located in different regions (e.g., research and development), are likely to have different experiences regarding LMX and span of control. For example, contagion effects may be limited in noncollocated work groups. Within different teams, different levels of leader distance can emerge, influencing the dimension of LMX quality relevant to that group.

Possibly, this notion is also dependent on follower characteristics that might be conducive to high levels of consensus regarding LMX. One example comprises followers' implicit leadership theories as prior research has shown that implicit leadership theories are related to the perception of leadership (e.g., Schyns, Felfe, & Blank, 2007). Assuming that the same is true for LMX, it could be argued that when followers agree in their implicit leadership theories, they will also agree more in terms of their perception of LMX quality and the related dimensions. However, in a large span of control, achieving consensus among followers may be difficult simply due to the fact that there will be many different views. For example, in a large group, some followers may be more or less likely to accept professional respect as part of a good LMX relationship.

Other follower-oriented research might consider the role of followers' needs in their perception of LMX quality. For example, Schyns, Kroon, and Moors (2008) found that follower needs are related to their perception of LMX quality. They argue that follower needs are relevant for leaders as they can only establish good relationships with their followers if they are aware of their followers' needs. Again, in a large span of control, aligning followers' needs can be more difficult than in a small span of control. This is in line with diversity research, which suggests that in order to cooperate and agree on issues, similarity in terms of values and needs (deep-level diversity as opposed to surface-level diversity based on demographic dissimilarity) among members of the same group is crucial. Transferring this prior research into consensus and span of control, we would expect that with a larger span of control, the advantage of leading teams—in contrast to isolated followers—is only and undoubtedly conducive to high-level, high-consensus LMX when followers are similar in their implicit leadership theories and in their needs, and thus show deep-level similarity.

In this article, we have concentrated on the effects a large span of control has on individual- and group-level LMX (consensus) and how the suggested negative effects can be overcome by emphasizing different dimensions of the LMX relationship. However, we did not consider the effects of a large span of control on the agreement between leader and follower on their mutual relationship. Prior research has shown that, although we would expect a high agreement between leader and member when rating their mutual relationship, this is not the case (Gerstner & Day, 1997). According to Liberman et al. (2007), power can imply social distance, meaning that leaders see themselves as separate from their followers. They argue that power leads to more abstract perceptions. With respect to LMX relationships, we could thus assume that especially in large spans of control that have been associated with larger structurally induced distance and larger power distance (Napier & Ferris, 1993), supervisors will tend to view relationship in a more abstract way than followers. Consequently, leaders may perceive more respect and loyalty rather than affect and contribution, whereas this may be different for followers. Given that Gibson, Cooper, and Conger (2009) argue and find that perceptual distance between a leader and his/her team negatively affects team performance, this is an important area for future research.

Our focus in this article was on span of control as an indicator of leader distance. Looking into the literature around leader distance, span of control is only one indicator of leader distance. An interesting route to pursue in future research would be to look into the personality of the leader and how it can convey psychological distance leading to similar constrains regarding the dimensions of LMX that define good relationship qualities as indicated here for span of control. The example of attachment styles may illustrate this point:

Attachment styles are differentiated into avoidant, anxious, and secure (Ainsworth, Blehar, Waters, & Wall, 1978; Hazan & Shaver, 1987). Essentially, individuals with an avoidant attachment style do not look for relationships but rather try to avoid establishing relationships, preferring to work alone (Hazan & Shaver, 1990). In the workplace, managers with this style are likely to be inattentive, manipulative, and provide little interpersonal support to subordinates (Keller & Cacioppe, 2001), characteristics that could be used to describe distance. Therefore, managers with this attachment style would not be expected to be willing or able to develop many high-quality relationships. In contrast, individuals who show an anxious attachment style are concerned about relationships to fulfil their need for attachment (Hazan & Shaver, 1990). Keller and Cacioppe (2001) suggest that leaders with this attachment style may be attentive to followers as a means of creating dependence by followers on the leader, though still not trusting in their competence. This one-sided relationship runs counter to a high-quality LMX relationship where there is mutual dependence and a high level of trust between members of the dyad (Graen & Uhl-Bien, 1995).

Finally, leaders with a secure attachment style feel comfortable about interdependence with others and have been shown to recognize and balance the needs of the parties to the relationship (Hazan & Shaver, 1987). Leadership research has linked a secure attachment style to relational competence (Manning, 2003), and to transformational leadership behaviour such as individualized consideration and intellectual stimulation (Popper & Mayseless, 2003; Popper Mayseless, & Castelnovo, 2000). Keller and Cacioppe (2001) note that secure-type leaders "may positively approach their leadership role and express more certainty of their ability to perform well in that role" (p. 72). These characteristics are consistent with high-quality LMX relationships (Graen & Uhl-Bien, 1995). Thus, with respect to leader distance, we can assume that only a secure attachment style allows the closeness that the LMX dimensions affect and contribution need to be developed and maintained even when other factors might suggest a greater distance between leader and follower.

CONCLUSION

In conclusion, this overview identified how focusing on different dimensions of LMX can explain the effects of span of control on individual- and group-level LMX, and also provides guidance for organizations that wish to expand the number of high-quality relationships within their expanding work groups. Although some recent research has identified certain conditions under which differentiation may be beneficial (e.g., Liden et al., 2006; van Breukelen & Weselius, 2007), overall we believe that an understanding of how to maximize LMX quality within groups is important for researchers and managers alike.

REFERENCES

Ainsworth, M. D. S., Blehar, M., Waters, E., & Walls, S. (1978). *Patterns of attachment.* Hillsdale, NJ: Lawrence Erlbaum Associates, Inc.

Ansari, M. A., Hung, D. K. H., & Aafaqi, R. (2007). Leader-member exchange and attitudinal outcomes: Role of procedural justice climate. *Leadership and Organization Development Journal, 28,* 690–709.

Antonakis, J., & Atwater, L. (2002). Leaders distance: A review and a proposed theory. *Leadership Quarterly, 13,* 673–704.

Ashkanasy, N. M., & O'Connor, C. (1997). Value congruence in leader-member exchange. *Journal of Social Psychology, 137,* 647–662.

Balkundi, P., & Kilduff, M. (2006). The ties that lead: A social network approach to leadership. *Leadership Quarterly, 17,* 419–439.

Berneth, J. B., Armenakis, A. A., Feild, H. S., Giles, W. F., & Walker, H. J. (2007). Leader-member social exchange (LMSX): Development and validation of a scale. *Journal of Organizational Behavior, 28,* 979–1003.

Boies, K., & Howell, J. M. (2006). Leader-member exchange in teams: An examination of the interaction between relationship differentiation and mean LMX in explaining team-level outcomes. *Leadership Quarterly, 17,* 246–257.

Cogliser, C. C., & Schriesheim, C. A. (2000). Exploring work unit context and leader-member exchange: A multi-level perspective. *Journal of Organizational Behavior, 21,* 487–511.

Cogliser, C. C., Schriesheim, C. A., Scandura, T. A., & Gardner, W. L. (2009). Balancing leader and follower perceptions of leader-member exchange: Relationships with performance and work attitudes. *Leadership Quarterly, 20,* 452–465.

Dansereau, F., Graen, G., & Haga, W. (1975). A vertical dyad linkage approach to leadership within formal organizations: A longitudinal investigation of the role making process. *Organizational Behavior and Human Performance, 13,* 46–78.

Dienesch, R. M., & Liden, R. C. (1986). Leader-member exchange model of leadership: A critique and further development. *Academy of Management Review, 11,* 618–634.

Gerstner, C. R., & Day, D. V. (1997). Meta-analytic review of leader-member exchange theory: Correlates and construct issues. *Journal of Applied Psychology, 82,* 827–844.

Gibson, C. B., Cooper, C. D., & Conger, J. A. (2009). Do you see what we see? The complex effects of perceptual distance between leaders and teams. *Journal of Applied Psychology, 94,* 62–76.

Goodstadt, B., & Kipnis, D. (1970). Situational influences on the use of power. *Journal of Applied Psychology, 54,* 201–207.

Graen, G., Cashman, J. F., Ginsburg, S., & Schiemann, W. (1977). Effects of linking-pin quality on the quality of working life of lower participants. *Administrative Science Quarterly, 22,* 491–504.

Graen, G., & Graen, J. A. (Eds.). (2006). *Sharing network leadership, Vol. 4.* Greenwich, CT: Information Age Publishing.

Graen, G. B. (2009). *LMX beyond the dyad: Concepts and operations.* Panel discussion at the annual meeting of the Society for Industrial and Organizational Psychology, New Orleans, LA.

Graen, G. B., & Cashman, J. F. (1975). A role-making model of leadership in formal organizations: A developmental approach. In J. G. Hunt & L. L. Larson (Eds.), *Leadership frontiers* (pp. 143–165). Kent, OH: Kent State University.

Graen, G. B., & Scandura, T. A. (1987). Toward a psychology of dyadic organizing. *Research in Organizational Behavior, 9,* 175–208.

Graen, G. B., & Uhl-Bien, M. (1995). Development of leader-member exchange (LMX) theory of leadership over 25 years: Applying a multi-level multi-domain perspective. *Leadership Quarterly, 6,* 219–247.

Graicunas, V. A. (1937). Relationship in organization. In L. Gulick & L. Urwick (Eds.), *Papers on the science of administration* (pp. 181–187). New York: Institute of Public Administration.

Green, S. G., Anderson, S. E., & Shivers, S. L. (1996). Demographic and organizational influences on leader-member exchange and related work attitudes. *Organizational Behavior and Human Decision Processes, 66,* 203–214.

Harmon, S. J., & van Dyne, L. (2008). *Targeted role-making: A new perspective on LMX with implications for group level performance.* Paper presented at the annual meeting of the Society for Industrial and Organizational Psychology, San Francisco, CA.

Hazan, C., & Shaver, P. R. (1987). Romantic love conceptualized as an attachment process. *Journal of Personality and Social Psychology, 52,* 511–524.

Hazan, C., & Shaver, P. R. (1990). Love and work: An attachment-theoretical perspective. *Journal of Personality and Social Psychology, 59,* 270–280.

Heider, F. (1958). *The psychology of interpersonal relations.* New York: Wiley.

Henderson, D. J., Wayne, S. J., Shore, L. M., Bommer, W. H., & Tetrick, L. E. (2008). Leader-member exchange, differentiation, and psychological contract fulfilment: A multi-level examination. *Journal of Applied Psychology, 93,* 1208–1219.

Hooper, D. T., & Martin, R. (2008). Beyond personal leader-member exchange (LMX) quality: The effects of perceived LMX variability on employee reactions. *Leadership Quarterly, 19,* 20–30.

Ilies, R., Nahrgang, J. D., & Morgeson, F. P. (2007). Leader-member exchange and citizenship behaviors: A meta-analysis. *Journal of Applied Psychology, 92,* 269–277.

Johns, G. (2006). The essential impact of context on organizational behavior. *Academy of Management Review, 31,* 386–408.

Judge, T. A., & Ferris, G. R. (1993). Social context of performance evaluation decisions. *Academy of Management Journal, 36,* 80–105.

Keller, T., & Cacioppe, R. (2001). Leader-follower attachments: Understanding parental images at work. *Leadership and Organizational Development Journal, 22,* 70–75.

Kinicki, A. J., & Vecchio, R. P. (1994). Influences on the quality of supervisor-subordinate relations: The role of time-pressure, organizational commitment, and locus of control. *Journal of Organizational Behavior, 15*(1), 75–82.

Liberman, N., Trope, Y., & Stephan, E. (2007). Psychological distance. In A. W. Kruglanski (Ed.), *Social psychology* (pp. 353–381). New York: Guilford Press.

Liden, R. C., Erdogan, B., Wayne, S. J., & Sparrowe, R. T. (2006). Leader-member exchange, differentiation, and task interdependence: Implications for individual and group performance. *Journal of Organizational Behavior, 27,* 723–746.

Liden, R. C., & Graen, G. B. (1980). Generalizability of the vertical dyad linkage model of leadership. *Academy of Management Journal, 23*, 451–465.

Liden, R. C., & Maslyn, J. M. (1998). Multidimensionality of leader-member exchange: An empirical assessment through scale development. *Journal of Management, 24*, 43–72.

Liden, R. C., Sparrowe, R. T., & Wayne, S. J. (1997). Leader-member exchange theory: The past and potential for the future. In G. R. Ferris (Ed.), *Research in personnel and human resources management* (Vol. 15, pp. 47–119). Greenwich, CT: JAI Press.

Liden, R. C., Wayne, S. J., & Stilwell, D. (1993). A longitudinal study on the early development of leader-member exchanges. *Journal of Applied Psychology, 78*(4), 662–674.

Manning, T. (2003). Leadership across cultures: Attachment style influences. *Journal of Leadership and Organizational Studies, 9*, 20–30.

Maslyn, J. M., & Uhl-Bien, M. (2001). Leader-member exchange and its dimensions: Effects of self-effort and other's effort on relationship quality. *Journal of Applied Psychology, 86*, 697–708.

Maslyn, J. M., & Uhl-Bien, M. (2005). LMX differentiation: Key concepts and related empirical findings. In G. B. Graen & J. Graen (Eds.), *LMX leadership: Vol. 3. Global organizing designs* (pp. 73–98). Greenwich, CT: Information Age Publishing.

Mayo, M., Meindl, J. R., & Pastor, J. C. (2003). Shared leadership in work teams: A social network approach. In C. L. Pearce & J. A. Conger (Eds.), *Shared leadership: Reframing the hows and whys of leadership* (pp. 1–18). Thousand Oaks, CA: Sage.

Napier, B. J., & Ferris, G. R. (1993). Distance in organizations. *Human Resource Management Review, 3*, 321–357.

Pearce, C. L., & Conger, J. A. (Eds.). (2003). *Shared leadership: Reframing the hows and whys of leadership*. Thousand Oaks, CA: Sage.

Pillai, R., Scandura, T. A., & Williams, E. A. (1999). Leadership and organizational justice: Similarities and differences across cultures. *Journal of International Business Studies, 30*, 763–779.

Popper, M., & Mayseless, O. (2003). Back to basics: Applying a parent perspective to transformational leadership. *Leadership Quarterly, 14*, 41–65.

Popper, M., Mayseless, O., & Castelnovo, O. (2000). Transformational leadership and attachment. *Leadership Quarterly, 11*, 267–289.

Porter, L. W., & McLaughlin, G. B. (2006). Leadership and organizational context: Like the weather? *Leadership Quarterly, 17*, 559–576.

Scandura, T. A. (1999). Rethinking leader-member exchange: An organizational justice perspective. *Leadership Quarterly, 10*, 25–40.

Schriesheim, C. A., Castro, S. L., & Yammarino, F. J. (2000). Investigating contingencies: An examination of the impact of span of supervision and upward controllingness on Leader-Member Exchange using traditional and multivariate within- and between-entities analysis. *Journal of Applied Psychology, 85*, 659–677.

Schriesheim, C. A., Castro, S. L., Zhou, X., & Yammarino, F. J. (2001). The folly of theorizing "A" but testing "B": A selective level-of-analysis review of the field and a detailed Leader-Member Exchange illustration. *Leadership Quarterly, 12*, 515–551.

Schriesheim, C. A., Neider, L. L., Scandura, T. A., & Tepper, B. J. (1992). Development and preliminary validation of a new scale (LMX-6) to measure Leader-Member Exchange in organizations. *Educational and Psychological Measurement, 52*, 135–147.

Schyns, B. (2006). Are group consensus in LMX and shared work values related to organizational outcomes? *Small Group Research, 37*, 20–35.

Schyns, B., & Day, D. V. (2010). Critique and review of leader–member exchange theory: Issues of agreement, consensus, and excellence. *European Journal of Work and Organizational Psychology, 19*(1), 1–29.

Schyns, B., Felfe, J., & Blank, H. (2007). Is charisma hyper-romanticism? Empirical evidence from new data and a meta-analysis. *Applied Psychology: An International Review, 56*, 505–527.

Schyns, B., Kroon, B., & Moors, G. (2008). Follower characteristics and the perception of Leader-Member Exchange. *Journal of Managerial Psychology, 23,* 772–788.

Schyns, B., & Paul, T. (2005). Dyadic leadership and organizational outcomes: Different results of different instruments? In G. B. Graen & J. A. Graen (Eds.), *LMX leadership: Vol. 3. Global organizing designs* (pp. 173–203). Greenwich, CT: Information Age Publishing.

Schyns, B., Paul, T., Mohr, G., & Blank, H. (2005). Comparing antecedents and consequences of leader-member exchange in a German working context to findings in the US. *European Journal of Work and Organizational Psychology, 14,* 1–22.

Schyns, B., van Veldhoven, M. J. P. M., & Wood, S. (2009). Organizational climate, relative psychological climate and job satisfaction: The example of supportive leadership climate. *Leadership and Organizational Development Journal, 30,* 649–663.

Shamir, B. (1995). Social distance and charisma: Theoretical notes and an exploratory study. *Leadership Quarterly, 6,* 19–47.

Sherony, K. M., & Green, S. G. (2002). Co-worker exchange: Relationships between co-workers, leader-member exchange, and work attitudes. *Journal of Applied Psychology, 87,* 542–548.

Sias, P. M., & Jablin, F. M. (1995). Differential superior-subordinate relations, perceptions of fairness, and co-worker communication. *Human Communication Research, 22,* 5–38.

Trope, Y., Liberman, N., & Wakslak, C. (2007). Construal levels and psychological distance: Effects of representation, prediction, evaluation, and behavior. *Journal of Consumer Psychology, 17,* 83–95.

Uhl-Bien, M. (2006). Relationship leadership theory: Exploring the social processes of leadership and organizing. *Leadership Quarterly, 17,* 654–676.

Uhl-Bien, M., Graen, G. B., & Scandura, T. (2000). Implications of leader-member exchange (LMX) for strategic human resource management systems: Relationships as social capital for competitive advantage. In G. Ferris (Ed.), *Research in personnel and human resource management* (Vol. 18, pp. 137–185). Greenwich, CT: JAI Press.

Uhl-Bien, M., & Maslyn, J. M. (2003). Reciprocity in manager-subordinate relationship: Components, configurations, and outcomes. *Journal of Management, 29,* 511–532.

Van Breukelen, J. W. M., & Wesselius, W. (2007). Differentiatie door coaches binnen amateursportteams: terecht of onterecht? *Gedrag en Organisatie, 20,* 427–444.

Van Breukelen, W., Konst, D., & van der Vlist, R. (2002). Effects of LMX and differential treatment on work unit commitment. *Psychological Reports, 91,* 220–230.

Weibler, J. (1994). *Führung durch den nächsthöheren Vorgesetzten* [*Leading by the next highest superior*]. Wiesbaden, Germany: Gabler.

Weibler, J. (2004). *Leading at a distance.* In G. R. Goethals, G. Sorenson, & J. M. Burns (Eds.), *The encyclopedia of leadership* (pp. 874–880). Thousand Oaks, CA: Sage.

Wikaningrum, T. (2007). Co-worker exchange, leader-member exchange, and work attitudes: A study of co-worker dyads. *Gadjah Mada International Journal of Business, 9,* 187–215.

Original manuscript received June 2008
Revised manuscript received June 2009
First published online June 2009

EUROPEAN JOURNAL OF WORK AND
ORGANIZATIONAL PSYCHOLOGY
2010, 19 (3), 407

Ψ Psychology Press
Taylor & Francis Group

Erratum

Please note that in Volume 19 Issue 1 of the *European Journal of Work and Organizational Psychology* (February 2010), in the paper by Birgit Schyns and David Day, entitled 'Critique and review of leader-member exchange theory: Issues of agreement, consensus, and excellence' (pp. 239–248), the wrong affiliation for David V. Day was printed. The correct affiliations are printed below:

Birgit Schyns
Portsmouth Business School, University of Portsmouth, Portsmouth, UK

David Day
University of Western Australia Business School, Crawley, WA, Australia

© 2010 Psychology Press, an imprint of the Taylor & Francis Group, an Informa business
http://www.psypress.com/ejwop   DOI: 10.1080/1359432X.2010.501688

Published by Psychology Press, in association with the International Association of Applied Psychology.

Subscription rates to Volume 19, 2010 (6 issues) are as follows:

To institutions (full subscription):	£519.00 (UK);	€687.00 (Europe);	$864.00 (Rest of World).
To institutions (online only):	£493.00 (UK);	€653.00 (Europe);	$820.00 (Rest of World).
To individuals:	£239.00 (UK);	€315.00 (Europe);	$396.00 (Rest of World).

Dollar rate applies to all subscribers outside Europe. Euro rates apply to all subscribers in Europe, except the UK and the Republic of Ireland where the pound sterling rate applies. All subscriptions are payable in advance and all rates include postage. Journals are sent by air to the USA, Canada, Mexico, India, Japan and Australasia. Subscriptions are entered on an annual basis, i.e., January to December. Payment may be made by sterling cheque, dollar cheque, euro cheque, international money order, National Giro or credit cards (Amex, Visa, and Mastercard).

An institutional subscription to the print edition also includes free access to the online edition for any number of concurrent users across a local area network. Subscriptions purchased at the personal (print only) rate are strictly for personal, non-commercial use only. The reselling of personal subscriptions is strictly prohibited. Personal subscriptions must be purchased with a personal cheque or credit card. Proof of personal status may be requested. For full information please visit the Journal's homepage.

Members of the European Association of Work and Organizational Psychology (EAWOP) receive the journal as part of their membership package. Membership enquiries for EAWOP should be sent to cgoffinet@ulg.ac.be, and further information about EAWOP can be obtained from http://www.eawop.org/. Members of the International Association of Applied Psychology (IAAP) qualify for a reduced subscription rate – please contact customer services (see address below) for details.

European Journal of Work and Organizational Psychology (**USPS 021134**) is published six times a year (in February, April, May, July, September, and November). by Psychology Press, 27 Church Road, Hove, BN3 2FA, UK. The 2010 US Institutional subscription price is $864.00. Airfreight and mailing in the USA by Agent named Air Business, C/O Worldnet Shipping USA Inc., 155-11 146th Avenue, Jamaica, New York, NY 11434, USA. Periodicals postage paid at Jamaica NY 11431. **US Postmaster:** Please send address changes to *the European Journal of Work and Organizational Psychology* (PEWO), Air Business Ltd, C/O Worldnet Shipping USA Inc., 155-11 146th Avenue, Jamaica, New York, NY 11434.

Subscription records are maintained at T&F Customer Services, Informa UK Ltd, Sheepen Place, Colchester, Essex, CO3 3LP, UK. E-mail: tf.enquiries@tfinforma.com. Please send change of address notices at least six weeks in advance, and include both old and new addresses.

Aims and scope

The mission of the *European Journal of Work and Organizational Psychology* is to promote and support the development of Work and Organizational Psychology by publishing high-quality scientific articles that improve our understanding of phenomena occurring in work and organizational settings. The journal publishes empirical, theoretical, methodological, and review articles that are relevant to real-world situations.

The journal has a world-wide authorship, readership and editorial board. Submissions from all around the world are invited.

The journal primarily publishes freely submitted contributions, but will occasionally also publish a themed issue, although all contributions are submitted to rigorous peer review. Papers and themed issues are published on a wide range of topics covered by the umbrella of work, organizational, industrial and occupational psychology.

Submission of manuscripts

Manuscripts are invited for submission. New manuscripts should be submitted through our ScholarOne Manuscripts online submission site at: **http://mc.manuscriptcentral.com/pewo**.

Submitted papers are subject to a double blind academic peer review process. Please ensure your submitted files include a blinded copy with all identifying information removed.

Your covering e-mail/letter must include full contact details (including e-mail), the title of the journal to which you are submitting, and the title of your article.

All manuscripts should be submitted in American Psychological Association (APA) format following the latest edition of *Publication Manual of the APA* (currently 6th edition).

Full instructions for authors are available on the journal website at: **www.psypress.com/ejwop**

Abstracting services

This Journal is covered by the following indexing/abstracting services: Current Contents/Social & Behavioral Sciences, Ergonomics Abstracts, European Reference Index for the Humanities (ERIH), PsycINFO, PubsHub, SCOPUS, Social Sciences Citation Index, Social Scisearch, Social Services Abstracts, Sociological Abstracts.

Copyright

Back issues

Taylor & Francis retains a 3-year back issue stock of journals. Older volumes are held by our official stockists: Periodicals Service Company, 11 Main Street, Germantown, NY 12526, USA to whom all orders and enquiries should be addressed. Tel: +1 518 537 4700; Fax: +1 518 537 5899; E-mail: psc@periodicals.com; URL: http://www.periodicals.com/tandf.html

Disclaimer

Typeset by KnowledgeWorks Global Limited, Chennai, India.

For Product Safety Concerns and Information please contact our EU
representative GPSR@taylorandfrancis.com
Taylor & Francis Verlag GmbH, Kaufingerstraße 24, 80331 München, Germany

www.ingramcontent.com/pod-product-compliance
Lightning Source LLC
Chambersburg PA
CBHW070757290326
41931CB00011BA/2044

9 781848 727281